THE WORLD OF JOHN CLEAVELAND

THE WORLD OF JOHN CLEAVELAND

FAMILY AND COMMUNITY IN EIGHTEENTH-CENTURY NEW ENGLAND

by

CHRISTOPHER M. JEDREY

W·W·NORTON & COMPANY
New York / London

Library of Congress Cataloging in Publication Data

Jedrey, Christopher M.
The world of John Cleaveland.

Bibliography: p.
Includes index.
1. Ipswich, Mass.—Rural conditions.   2. Ipswich,
Mass.—Genealogy.   3. Cleaveland, John,
1722–1799.   4. New England—Church history.
5. New England—Intellectual life—Case studies.
I. Title.
HN80.I67J42   1979   309.1'744'5   79-16410
ISBN 0-393-01270-0

Book designed by Jacques Chazaud
Typeset in Weiss and Garamond
Manufactured by the Maple-Vail Book Manufacturing Group

1 2 3 4 5 6 7 8 9 0

For Micheline

Contents

THE MALE ANCESTRY OF JOHN CLEAVELAND

MOSES
(1624?–1702)
Ipswich, Eng.; Woburn, Mass.

Moses II (1651–?) Woburn; Charlestown; Martha's Vineyard; Southold, L.I.

Aaron (1655–1716) Woburn

Samuel (1657–1736) Woburn; Chelmsford; Canterbury, Conn.

Edward (1664–1746) Woburn; N. Kingston, R.I.; Canterbury, Conn.; Pomfret

JOSIAH (1667–1709) Woburn; Chelmsford; Canterbury, Conn.

Isaac (1669–1714) Woburn; Charlestown; Canterbury, Conn.; Norwich

Enoch (1671–1729) Woburn; Charlestown; Sudbury; Framingham; Acton; Marlboro; Concord

Joseph (1692–1752) Canterbury

John (1696–1718) Canterbury

Jonathan (1698)

Henry (1699–1779) Canterbury; Mansfield

Jonathan (1701–1713)

Deliverance (1707–1787) Canterbury

JOSIAH II (1690–1750) Canterbury

Elisha (1717–?) Canterbury; Amenia, N.Y.; Landaff; Bath, N.H.; Pawlett, Vt.

JOHN (1722–1799) Canterbury; Boston, Mass.; Ipswich;

Ebenezer (1725–1805) Canterbury; Gloucester, Mass.

Aaron (1727–1785) Canterbury

Moses (1730–1741)

Josiah III (1713–1793) Canterbury

SOURCE: *The Genealogy of the Cleveland and Cleaveland Families* (Hartford, Conn.., 1899). 3 vols.

Acknowledgments

LIKE THE FARMERS in John Cleaveland's village, I am entering into my new estate heavily encumbered with obligations. I am particularly indebted to three nineteenth-century gentlemen—Nehemiah Cleaveland, the Reverend Elisha Lord Cleaveland, and the Reverend Oliver A. Taylor—who gathered and preserved the papers of John Cleaveland. I like to think I have in some measure fulfilled their ambition of writing a "memoir" of their grandfather. To the staff of the Essex Institute, especially Dorothy Potter and Irene Norton, I owe my access to the Cleaveland papers and other Chebacco materials. The staff of the New England Historic Genealogical Society—Ralph Crandall, Margaret Hazen, Mary Lean, Susan Patterson, and Gary Roberts—provided aid and comfort during a long year spent reconstituting Chebacco families.

My friends Jon Roberts and Rob Silverman gave critical readings to earlier versions of several chapters, for which I am grateful. Other friends—Fred Anderson, Chris Clark, and David Jaffee—were kind enough to read the whole manuscript at a later stage and offered a variety of useful suggestions. Steve Botein has read this work more times than either of us would care to recall and each time has had something illuminating to say. His criticism, always gentle

ACKNOWLEDGMENTS

and always penetrating, has been much appreciated. My thesis advisor, Bernard Bailyn, suggested the topic of this book, and his criticism and encouragement have helped me to make it work. Like most of his students, I was caught as a first-year graduate student by his infectious enthusiasm for history and have spent long years since then trying to meet the high standards set by his own work.

My greatest debt is to my wife, Micheline. She helped me research the origins of the Cleavelands in Woburn, Massachusetts, and Canterbury, Connecticut. We cataloged the Cleaveland papers, item by item, at the Essex Institute and then numbered the frames of my microfilm copy and coordinated those numbers with the catalog. She helped me to track down Cleaveland materials at Bowdoin, Dartmouth, Yale, and in the Connecticut Archives. And once, when the tedium of my work at the Essex County Courthouse was about to overwhelm me, she spent a week of vacation time abstracting land transactions. She also typed the drafts of the thesis. She supported me, in more ways than one, for six long years, while I sought a degree in a field with a most unpromising future. I have tendered to her what help I could, but there is a substantial balance in her favor still owing. I can only hope for many more years together with her in which to repay it.

C.M.J.

Lowell House
Harvard University
Cambridge, Massachusetts
January 1979

✦

Introduction

THE SOCIAL HISTORY of colonial America is most often written about the country folk, and its intellectual history about the urban elites. But the *mentalité* of the rural majority is no less important than that of the urban leadership. Studying in all its aspects the life of one village and its minister provides a unique perspective on the historical evolution of rural New England and on the social and intellectual context of the American Revolution in that region.

The Reverend John Cleaveland (1722–1799) was minister in Chebacco Parish (Ipswich, Massachusetts) during the second half of the eighteenth century. Born in eastern Connecticut, he came in 1746 to a village plunged into turmoil and confusion by the Great Awakening. An evangelical Calvinist out of Yale College, he began his life in Chebacco preaching to New Light dissidents and then gradually reunited the community under his care. He married a local woman and spent the rest of his long life as a farmer and a preacher in the little village on Massachusetts's North Shore. More than two hundred family letters, several short diaries and journals (including two kept by his wife), more than one hundred and fifty sermons, and some scattered accounts and financial records have survived from his long tenure; they provide a revealing picture of the life of a country pastor and his flock in the eighteenth-century. I have supplemented his papers with a reconstitution, so far as the records allow, of the lives of the villagers. I have used as a base list the 1771 valuation, which lists all the householders and provides a detailed enumeration of their personal property (houses, livestock, commercial properties) and improved land. These men and their families have been traced through every available record. This has entailed a search of vital records and genealogies for their births, marriages, migrations, and deaths, as well as land and probate records for the transfer of their property from generation to generation. These records enabled me to follow in this manner the families of the villagers, as well as that of the minister, from formation at marriage through their dissolution and the transfer of their property to the new families of the next generation. This social information indicates the norms of behavior, while the Cleaveland materials suggest the motives and aspirations behind that behavior. The relationship between the two kinds of sources is complementary and mutually reinforcing.

My research has made me aware of the stable, conservative character of rural New England before the Revolution. Recent historical writings on New England society have stressed the unsettling effects of population pressure against a limited supply of land. This resulted, it is argued, in a greater concentration of wealth and increased social conflict. I have found, however, that in the countryside wealth was distributed according to age more than any other factor. One's expectations in life were strongly shaped by the size of the patrimony and by one's right in it as an elder son, a younger son, or a daughter. Farm families, by giving surplus sons a trade or cheaper lands to the west and north, were able to maintain from generation to generation the economic integrity of the original holding in the village. These tough, adaptable family networks slowed the growth of population in the older communities and kept the distribution of wealth stable, as each family struggled individually to bring its numbers and resources into alignment.

Attitudes, no less than land, may be inherited. In a society with relatively few extracommunal sources of information, a proportionally larger part of one's world view is simply passed on from the previous generation. This includes various sorts of traditional beliefs, such as those expressed in local folklore, as well as more formal religious beliefs, as manifested in the ritualized narratives of religious experiences. The most important support for these beliefs outside of the family was the minister, who preached to his congregation two or three times a week, year in and year out. The villagers of rural New England thought of the great world beyond their borders in religious terms, expressive of an archaic geopolitical world view rooted in the England of Elizabeth's time and Foxe's *Book of Martyrs*. When Cleaveland wrote for the press as "Johannes in Eremo" during the revolutionary crisis, he did publicly what many ministers were doing in their own congregations, that is, expressing rural fears of a foreign and imperial presence that was seen as a threat to their way of life. Cleaveland interpreted the political crisis in light of the ancient understanding of New England's relationship to the deity, God's covenant with his "New English Israel," and so justified revolutionary resistance for the rural majority.

In the revolutionary crisis, as in the religious controversies that racked the village in the 1740s, Cleaveland helped the villagers to refashion and articulate long-established beliefs to meet the problems of the day. The war itself he used to further the career of his sons, and his later years were occupied with domestic responsibilities and ecclesiastical concerns. The rising generation would look elsewhere for leaders attuned to the problems of a new day.

THE WORLD OF JOHN CLEAVELAND

CHAPTER ONE

✤

Family History

IN SEPTEMBER 1741, John Cleaveland, a nineteen-year-old boy from Canterbury, Connecticut, entered Yale College. He had been raised as a farmer, like his father and his grandfather before him. In the century that had passed since the first Cleaveland came to New England, he was the first to leave the land. Young John's decision, while a break with family tradition, grew out of the Cleaveland family's experiences in rural New England.

I. Migration to New England

In 1642, Moses Cleaveland left his home in England for the New World. John Cleaveland knew something of the family's founding in New England.

My Great Grand-father's name was MOSES CLEAVELAND, and came from Ipswich, in Suffolk. He was young when he came to New England, and was an apprentice to a joyner, and came with His Master. He settled in Woburn, near Boston, married, and had seven Sons, besides Daughters, and his sons all left Children, and all in New-England, of the Name, are his Posterity, and all spell the Name as I do, tho' we are not certain that we spell it exactly as the same Family does in England. Because, as the said Moses was young when he left England and could not read and write if I am not misinformed.[1]

Moses Cleaveland came to the New World at about the same age that his great-grandson would enter Yale. He came, like Governor Winthrop, from Suffolk, a hotbed of Puritan sentiment. He was an unlettered carpenter's apprentice, but in America he became a farmer. It was probably some combination of adherence to Puritan principles and the desire to better himself that led young Moses to seek his future in New England.

The first New England record of John Cleaveland's emigrant ancestor was made in 1643, when the colonial government saw fit to admit Moses Cleaveland to the status of freeman. This suggests that he had joined the Woburn church, which had been gathered in August 1642. Captain Edward Johnson, Woburn's leading citizen and author of the *Wonder-Working Providence of Sions Saviour in New England,* felt that "the greater part" of the settlers had been "converted by the preaching of the word in New England." Whatever Moses Cleaveland's reasons for migration, within a year or so of his arrival he stood before his pastor and then before the whole congregation, as Johnson describes the process, to "declare the manner of his conversion" and the work of the Lord "in the inward parts of his soul, to bring him out of that natural darkness, which all men are by nature in and under, as also the measure of knowledg the Lord hath been pleased to indue him withal."[2]

The church Moses Cleaveland joined represented, in a particularly intense form, the widespread and profound lay resistance to clerical innovation that shaped the religious development of seventeenth-century Massachusetts. In 1642, two lay members ordained the first minister, fearing that ordination by neighboring ministers "might be an occasion of introducing a dependency of churches, etc., and so a presbytery."[3] In 1653, this same commitment to congregational independence led Woburn to oppose a new law that required licensing of preachers by four neighboring churches, because "it circumvents the liberty of Christian

Churches."[4] In 1663, the town officers refused to accept the King's Letter on Toleration, which was being sent from town to town, because it "tended to Popery."[5] The congregation's stern commitment to the religious principles of the earliest days in New England led them to oppose bitterly the Half-Way Covenant, a clerically sponsored attempt to extend church membership and discipline beyond only those people who could give an account of personal conversion. To the ministers who proposed it, this reform was necessary for the fulfillment of the church's responsibility to the community as a whole; to its opponents, it seemed no less than a betrayal of the principle of church purity, that is, the limitation of membership to those deemed likely to be saved.[6] The Woburn delegation was almost certainly among the dissenters at the Synod of 1662, where the new practice was approved. In 1670, Woburn's first citizen, Captain Edward Johnson, chaired a committee in the lower house of the General Court whose report bemoaned

declension from primitive foundation work, innovation in doctrine and worship, . . . an invasion of the rights, liberties and privileges of churches, an usurpation of a lordly and prelatical power over God's heritage . . . with a dangerous tendency to the utter devastation of these churches, turning the pleasant gardens of Christ into a wilderness.[7]

Opposition to clerical innovation took other forms as well. In the early 1660s, some men and women, mostly from Middlesex County, repudiated the principle of infant baptism, and with it the idea of church membership for any but adults who could declare their faith in public assembly. This was almost certainly a reaction against the recent clerical attempts to make the church more inclusive and less pure. The point was made more strongly by the Baptists' use of lay preachers, as if they had lost their faith in an educated ministry as well. Unlike most other dissident groups in Massachusetts Bay, the sect was comprised for the most part of attendants and communicants of churches in Charlestown, Boston, and Woburn—"God-fearing, hard-working, sober farmers, tailors, cobblers, and mechanics," neither intellectuals like Roger Williams, Anne Hutchinson, and Henry Dunster, nor rootless outcasts like the Quakers and Baptists who had earlier plagued the Commonwealth.[8]

Among the original members of this Baptist church was John Johnson, church member, proprietor, and son of Woburn's leading citizen. Between 1667 and 1679, twenty-six residents of Woburn were brought before the Middlesex County Court for Baptist offenses, like turning one's back during the baptism of infants, haranguing ministers and congregations on their errors, and holding separate meetings with others of similar belief. North Woburn, where the Cleavelands lived, contained the Wymans, the Pierces, the Wilsons, and the Pollys—four of Woburn's Baptist families. Aaron Cleaveland, Moses's second son, married Dorcas Wilson in 1675, the year her parents, brother, and sister-in-law were convicted for Baptist practices. Two years later Aaron too was convicted, along with his uncle George Polly. The Grand Jury presentments, surely an incomplete record, indicate the presence of Baptists in Boston, Charlestown, Woburn, Concord, Cambridge, Newbury, Malden, Reading, and Billerica. Some of the colonies' most venerable leaders, such as Governor John Leverett, and most substantial men, such as Captain Edward Hutchinson, opposed the Half-Way Covenant, and hence were inclined toward toleration for these Baptists who had sprung up in their midst.[9]

The principles of Baptism—congregational independence, adult membership, lay leadership—were increasingly compelling to the laymen fearful of the direction of religious change. The growth of an indigenous Baptist movement in New England, as well as of sympathy for them among the religious traditionalists of the colony, indicates the depth of lay commitment to the pure-church ideal.

II. A New Beginning

If Moses Cleaveland found his religious needs fulfilled by the Woburn church, the town seemed no less able to meet his worldly needs. The town of Woburn had its origin in a grant of land made to Charlestown by the General Court and was incorporated under its present name in 1642. Although Moses Cleaveland had been resident in the town as early as 1643, it was only when he married his master's daughter, Ann Winn, in September 1648, and when he received a share in the common lands the next spring that he assumed full adult status in the community. His first grant of land was of "thurty acres of land five of it is to be medow to be laid out in Bull Medow [,] the upland of which their hous lotts are to bee . . . laid out in the new field."[10]

Like most towns founded in the seventeenth century, Woburn readily gave land to new settlers from its seemingly inexhaustible holdings of undistributed lands. However, as the amount of available land shrank, it became important to determine who was entitled to a share of the remainder, who was a proprietor of the common lands. The question arose in a town meeting in February 1666, and the next year a list of the eighty proprietors was made, excluding some latecomers and younger sons. A decision was also made "that all the land that lyeth in common, both land and timber, shall be divided" among the proprietors. By 1680, most of Woburn's common land was gone, for the most part granted in the great divisions of 1667 and 1677.[11] The final distribution of the commonage, distributed according to "persons and esteats," tended to reinforce the inequalities of landed wealth among the townsmen.

Moses Cleaveland had done well. His initial grant of

twenty-five acres of upland and five of meadow placed him, according to Edward Johnson's account of the land-distribution process, among "the poorest."[12] But over the next thirty years, Moses received 166 more acres to support his family. On the even of the first great division he had 92 acres; at the end of the second, 196 acres. These holdings put him just slightly below the mean (198) and the median (197) of the eighty proprietors in 1677.[13] On a rate for the new meeting house in 1671, he was ranked thirty-second among 101 taxpayers. He was a church member and held minor offices, appropriate to his station, after attaining the age of thirty-five.[14] The penniless young artisan was now a respectable farmer of mature years and substantial acres. His energy and ambition for his family, which were to characterize his descendants as well, earned him ample rewards in the New World.

Yet the future of his seven sons was not assured. Moses's youth—he was only nineteen when he settled in the newly founded town and was not admitted to rights in the commons until six years later—put him in the position of a second-generation proprietor without the compensation of paternal accumulation of lands. Moses Cleaveland's share of the common land measures up well against other individual proprietors, but not against the accumulations of the sixteen family groups that comprised forty-six of the eighty proprietors. Their holdings ranged from the 281 acres held by James Tompson and his son to the 962 acres held by Captain Johnson and his three sons and the 975 acres held by the three Convers brothers, sons of the late deacon.[15]

The young men of the Cleaveland family, born in the 1650s and 1660s, came to maturity in the 1670s and 1680s, when the proprietorship was closed, most of the common lands were gone, and their father was a hale and hearty fifty years of age. Moses, like members of the first generation elsewhere, lived his three score and ten and better, dying in 1702 at the age of seventy-six.[16] The community felt the pressure of the young Cleavelands and their peers and made some limited accommodations for them. At a town meeting in February 1678, leave was granted to the "young men of the place" to build a gallery for themselves in the meeting house. More important, at that same meeting "was granted by the towne to these fourty and four young men the tract of land that wase left" after the last great division. Moses, Jr., and Aaron, eldest sons of Moses Cleaveland, were among the "fourty and four," and they received, like the rest, a flat grant of seven acres. The grant, while helpful, was obviously inadequate for their support.[17]

Moses, Sr., had made a great advance in the world, but he and his sons were apparently not satisfied merely to divide the newly acquired patrimony. With old Moses's support, most of his sons ventured out into the world to find land sufficient for themselves and their descendants. The three oldest sons, Moses, Jr., Aaron, and Samuel, first left to fight in King Philip's War. Aaron served only briefly in the war, returning to Woburn to become a freeman and, it would seem, Moses's principal heir. But Moses, Jr., moved to Charlestown, where he joined the church, and Samuel to Chelmsford, where he bought twenty-three acres of land. His younger brother Josiah, the grandfather of John, joined him there in about 1690.[18]

Moses, Jr., who became a fisherman, later moved to Edgartown on Martha's Vineyard and then to Southold on Long Island. The rest of the Cleavelands stayed with the land and stayed together. In the early 1690s, Josiah and Samuel moved to the Quinebaug Country, which later became part of Windham County in eastern Connecticut. In the fifteen years that followed, their brothers Isaac and Edward joined them there, along with two nephews, sons of Aaron. With income from the sale of their small holdings in eastern Massachusetts and probably with money from Moses, Sr., they bought land in the wilderness.

Northeastern Connecticut was the "frontier" of the late

seventeenth and early eighteenth centuries. King Philip's War and the uncertainties of the Dominion period had discouraged settlement there in the 1670s and 1680s.[19] The territory first opened up in the 1690s, and the third generation in the towns of eastern Masachusetts, like the young Cleavelands in Woburn, faced newly restricted prospects. The middle third of the seventeenth century had marked the closing of proprietorships—Haverhill in 1653, Dedham in 1656, Ipswich in 1660, Cambridge in 1664, Woburn in 1665, Barnstable in 1670—and the concomitant divisions of the common lands.[20]

The Cleavelands in Connecticut became founders of towns, an advantage their father had not had in Massachusetts. There they might hope to find land sufficient for several generations. They came to northeastern Connecticut with the first wave of settlers, before the explosive growth of the eighteenth century. Twenty Connecticut towns were settled between 1690 and 1720; the population, which grew only 18 percent from 1690 to 1700, expanded in increments of 50 percent in each of the next two decades.[21]

Settlement, however, raised the question of legal title to these lands. The first settlements in the Windham County area were orderly. A group from Roxbury founded Woodstock in 1686, and a group from Norwich founded Windham in 1691. But the Quinebaug Country, later the towns of Plainfield and Canterbury, was settled haphazardly by settlers from Massachusetts and Connecticut, all caught in the struggle for proprietorship between the Winthrop family and Major James Fitch of Norwich. A species of border warfare ensued between the Winthrop and Fitch tenants and supporters during much of the 1690s, each group defending the source of their land titles.[22]

In an early autobiographical sketch, John Cleaveland wrote, "respecting my discent,"

My father was the eldest son of Mr. Josiah Cleaveland (deceased) who settled at Canterbury about A.D. 1694. Whose family as I

8

have been informed was the second English family that settled in the town aforesaid.[23]

John's grandfather Josiah and his great-uncle Samuel came to the Quinebaug Country as tenants of the Winthrop family.[24] Some time afterward, the Cleavelands made their peace with Major Fitch, perhaps because Fitch was the more visible of the contenders, especially after he established his headquarters on the west side of the plantation in 1697, thus becoming a more dangerous enemy or a more effective protector; or perhaps it was because Fitch sold land more readily than the Winthrops, and that would, of course; better suit that land-hungry Cleavelands; or it may have been that they were alienated by the greed of the hated Gallup family, chief representatives of the Winthrops in the area.[25]

In 1699, Josiah, along with Major Fitch and another, purchased 300 acres from the Sachem Owaneco, titular overlord of the area, "in trust for the inhabitants of the plantation of Quinebaug . . . to promote plantation work."[26] In May of that year, twenty-two settlers, including Josiah and Samuel Cleaveland, petitioned the General Court for township status. Fitz-John Winthrop, now governor, approved the petition "provided it doth not prejudice any particular person's property" and named the new plantation Plainfield. In 1703, the west-side settlers, among them the Cleavelands, were separated from the east side and formed into the town of Canterbury. Major Fitch was the most prominent citizen of the new town, which numbered only ten families, and he found much of his local support there.[27]

Investigations in 1702 and 1706 could fully confirm neither Fitch's nor the Winthrops' claim. Fitz-John and Waitstill Winthrop were therefore ready to abandon their father's shadowy empire for legal grants of a thousand acres apiece elsewhere.[28] In return they confirmed the lands of Plainfield, both common and divided. But Canterbury, and the aging and irascible Major Fitch, remained in turmoil. A quarter-century of active and often contradictory land sales by Fitch and other speculators had vastly complicated the town's internal boundaries, and the various commissions called to settle the Fitch–Winthrop disputes left its western, eastern, and northern boundaries in controversy.[29] Some settlers were vigorously taxed by two towns, and others, such as Samuel Adams, who

bought first of Major Fitch; then of Captain Mason and Owaneco; third of Captain John Mason, so as to avoid all trouble, and lastly of Captain Bushnell; and in addition to all this, was harassed by suits with the Tracys,[30]

sought vainly for clear title.

In similar fashion, Josiah Cleaveland bought his first recorded piece of property first from Owaneco in December 1699, and then again from Caleb Bushnell, who had bought it from Fitch, in January 1700. But Josiah surged sturdily forward, emerging from the confusion with more than 500 acres. The Cleaveland-family strategy had succeeded. Instead of owning just a small farm in eastern Massachusetts, Josiah at forty could boast of an estate two and a half times larger than his father's had been. His accumulation of lands, however, was cut short by his premature death in 1709 at the age of forty-two.[31]

Josiah and Samuel Cleaveland had struggled with Owaneco, Major Fitch, the Winthrops, speculators like the Bushnells and the Tracys, and the colonial government in order to carve out and defend their substantial holdings. The sale of their bits of land in eastern Massachusetts, and probably also their father, had provided them with money to buy great tracts of unimproved land in the wilderness, which would appreciate in value if further settlement occurred. Josiah and Samuel had the requisite aggressiveness, sense of timing, and luck to make a notable success of this game. They faced the eighteenth century in the advantageous position of resident proprietors the value of whose holdings increased steadily as settlers flocked to Canterbury from the older and more thickly settled communities of New England.[32]

Between the founding of the town in 1703 and 1716, the number of householders increased from ten to sixty-three. On a rate taken in the latter year, Josiah Cleaveland's widow paid taxes on an estate of 100 pounds, well above the mean (55 pounds) and the median (48 pounds). She was the wealthiest Cleaveland and the sixth-wealthiest person in Canterbury. Her property, however, represented only a portion of Josiah's holdings, because two of his sons had recently reached their majority and had received a due share of the estate. If one also considers their combined taxable estate of 80 pounds when assessing the relative position of Josiah's family, then one finds the standing of Josiah's heirs among the village elite to be even more secure.[33]

Canterbury finally settled its external land disputes and in 1723 managed to secure and divide the common lands. There was a cluster of Cleavelands among Canterbury's proprietors, three among the "first settlers and planters" with a share and a half, two among the "proprietors under the patent" with a share, and two among the "latter settlers" with a half-share.[34]

III. Rural Prominence

The Cleavelands fulfilled other, less tangible needs at Canterbury as well. The three towns most important in the settling of Canterbury—Woburn, Dorchester, and Barnstable—had all been notable for their resistance to the Half-Way Covenant.[35] Moreover, the Woburn group—the Cleavelands, the Pierces, the Brooks, the Johnsons—all had had relatives among the Woburn Baptists of the 1660s and 1670s. The church that they founded at Canterbury in 1711 was rigidly orthodox and, despite the recently approved Presbyterian Saybrook Platform, recognized no ec-

clesiastical power above that of the congregation. The
church did accept the Half-Way Covenant, by then all but
universal in New England, but only in its strictest form.[36]
There was considerable sympathy in other parts of New England for what amounted to virtually universal baptism,
but Canterbury baptized only the children of members.[37]
The tendency toward congregational independence was confirmed in the late 1720s, when candidates for the Canterbury pulpit were asked to sign a statement explicitly reject-
ing the Saybrook Platform in favor of the older and more
congregational Cambridge Platform.[38]

Although the specific issue had changed from the Half-
Way Covenant to the Saybrook Platform, the broader question of lay participation in and control of the church remained. The Saybrook Platform, by creating a conciliar
structure of clergymen, greatly strengthened the minister's
hand in disputes with his congregation. Lay resistance was
strongest in eastern Connecticut, New London County and
what became Windham County, where the Woodstock
church, Canada Parish in the town of Windham, and the
Canterbury church refused to accept the new platform. In
addition, there were vigorous protests against it in Voluntown and in Mortlake Parish in Pomfret. Reverend John
Woodward of Norwich, secretary of the Saybrook Synod,
got initial approval from his church, but in 1714 the
church reversed its decision and dismissed him. Lisbon
Parish in Norwich, founded in 1723, never wavered in its
adherence to the Cambridge Platform. The New London
association of ministers, which included Plainfield, Pomfret, Canterbury, Killingly, and Voluntown, was quickly
formed, but the consociation of churches was long delayed,
presumably owing to this local opposition.[39]

The commitment of the Cleaveland family to this conservative church was impressive. Samuel, the eldest male in
the family, was one of the seven men who gathered the
Church in June 1711. Mary Bates Cleaveland, Josiah's

widow, her eldest son, Josiah, Jr., and his wife, Abigail, joined soon after. Of the four Cleaveland brothers who came to Canterbury, Josiah died and Isaac moved on before the church was formed. The other two, Samuel and Edward, joined in full communion, followed by all but one of their children who stayed in Canterbury, as well as their nephews Moses and Benjamin.[40] The worldly success they had met with in Canterbury did not shake their commitment to the tradition of lay control and doctrinal orthodoxy in which they had been nurtured.

The second generation of Cleavelands in Canterbury was equally active in secular pursuits, as they confronted the challenges and opportunities of life in a frontier community. Josiah Cleaveland, Jr., in particular, contemplated mixed prospects. As his son observed in a poetic eulogy, he was burdened at an early age with responsibility for a large family.

> . . . e're one twenty Years, he had pass'd thro',
> Into Eternity, his *Father* flew.——
> Now on his Hands, devolv'd the Care of all;
> The Widow, Fatherless, the Great, the Small,
> Now in the Family, he led the Van,
> In Things relating both to God and Man.[41]

However, his father's premature death, when Josiah, Jr., was only nineteen, also left him as eldest son with a double share of one of the more substantial estates in the community. Having realized his prospects at so early an age, he was able to marry, which he did less than a year after his father's death, when he was only twenty. In August 1710, he married Abigail Paine, who, like so many Cleaveland brides, belonged to a family whose standing in the community was superior to that of the Cleavelands. Her father, Elisha, had migrated from Barnstable about 1700 and purchased 2,000 acres from Major Fitch. He had become one of the leading citizens of Canterbury.[42] Abigail's dowry may have supported Josiah's extensive land dealings. Josiah, Jr., took part in at least twenty-five land transactions between 1718 and his death in 1750.

Although prosperous and ambitious, Josiah Cleaveland was not a land speculator. He soon set about trying to reconstruct and augment his father's estate in order to better provide for his own children. There were, in effect, twenty-seven shares of differing sizes in the estate of the first Josiah Cleaveland. Nine children survived to claim their portion of Josiah's legacy, eight to divide the dower, the widow's one-third share in the estate that reverted to the children upon the death of their mother. In each case Josiah, as the eldest son, was entitled to a double share. Eight children divided equally the share inherited by their brother John, who had died childless and unmarried in 1718. The shares were comprised of personal and real property with a higher proportion of land in the sons' shares and of movable goods in the daughters' shares. Between 1721 and 1733, Josiah, Jr., managed to accumulate the real estate in twenty of the twenty-seven shares. He reassembled, according to the available records, more than three-fifths of his father's landholdings.[43]

His few other purchases fit this pattern of consolidation. His first dealings were with a neighbor, Henry Smith. Smith agreed, in 1718, on a boundary line between his land and Josiah's and, in 1719, to the sale of one and a half acres that adjoined Josiah's farm. In 1723, he exchanged a hundred acres in Haddam, plus eighty pounds, for a farm of thirty-six acres in Canterbury, which he then exchanged for his brother Deliverance's share of the paternal estate. Twelve years later he bought thirty-five acres adjoining the Cleaveland farm for 110 pounds. His last purchase, made in 1737, was of three hundred acres of land in Canterbury.

The direction of his land transactions changed in the mid-1730s as he prepared to meet the needs of his growing children. On December 9, 1734, he granted to "my well beloved son" Josiah one-half of the family farm "as his full portion in my real estate." Young Josiah was then twenty-one, the second child and eldest son. He married the following October. In April 1739, Josiah transferred 240 of the 300 acres he had recently purchased to his second son, Elisha, then twenty-two years old and to be married in June of the following year. In the spring of 1739, he sold more of the family farm to his eldest son for 200 pounds and the remaining 60 acres of the 300 to Thomas Stanton of Groton for 105 pounds. He raised more cash that same spring by selling to one of his wife's brothers her share in her father's estate, much as his brothers-in-law had done for him in the 1720s. The raising of this money was spurred by the marriage of his daughter Abigail and his son John's decision to attend Yale. In 1743, with one son at Yale, another planning to enroll, and another daughter about to be married, he sold 90 acres "belonging to lands that I now live on" to his son Elisha.

The second Josiah Cleaveland was able to provide a better start in life for his children than any previous Cleaveland had done, but he did so according to the old family strategy. He gave his eldest son and namesake the bulk of the paternal estate that he had so carefully reassembled. He bought another farm in Canterbury for his second son. He then sold off the remainder of his lands, both to his older sons and to outsiders, in order to raise money for his daughters and his younger sons. With greater resources came raised expectations; Josiah Cleaveland worked hard to place his children well in the world.

Josiah's will completed the complex process of distribution.[44] His youngest sons, Ebenezer and Aaron, received the bulk of their shares in Josiah's estate at this time, and the others received small gifts. Josiah, the eldest son, was the executor and residuary legatee, and as such his share was encumbered with the cash legacies due to the other heirs. John Cleaveland, then minister of a church in Massachusetts, received 100 pounds, one of the smaller bequests, and a "Negro man named Pompie." His portion, it was understood, had been his education at Yale College.

Josiah Cleaveland well represented the strength of purpose that had brought the family from its meager beginnings in Woburn to substantial rural prosperity in Canterbury. He was, according to his son's memoir,

> . . . a Man who spar'd nor Strength nor Pains,
> What he did get, were naught but lawful Gains;
> What of the World he had or did possess,
> Were won by heavy Blows, which God did bless.[45]

His son John was not unlike him.

John Cleaveland was born on April 17, 1722, the third son and seventh child of Josiah and Abigail Paine Cleaveland. He decided to go to Yale in 1739. Until then, John had been

labouring hard with my hands, in farming-business till I was seventeen years old, then meeting with a hurt in my body by hard lifting, I was disenabled to go on with hard labour, thereupon having had for a long time before a great desire for liberal education I began study. . . .[46]

The injury came at a propitious moment, as he was coming of age and thinking about his future. His two older brothers had been given most of the family land, so that his future in Canterbury was far from assured. He would find Yale a congenial place. Most of the students there were farmers' sons from towns at least as old as Canterbury—limited wealth and ample uncleared lands kept sons in newer towns at home. John's "great desire for a liberal education" was a shrewd investment of family resources in the hope of future advancement, much as Moses's migration to the New World had been almost a century before.

CHAPTER TWO

❋

Vocation

JOHN CLEAVELAND WENT to Yale to prepare for the ministry, but the Great Awakening, which threw the college into turmoil, also exposed the contradictions between his family religious tradition and the customary preparation for the established ministry. A prudent and moderate youth, he struggled to reconcile these differing objectives until, in the fall of his senior year, he was expelled from college for attending meetings of a schismatic revivalist church along with his parents. Excluded from Connecticut pulpits by his failure to obtain a degree, he went back to Massachusetts, where he eventually found a country parish in which he was able to define the nature of his ministry in a way satisfactory to himself and to his parishioners.

I. Yale College

John Cleaveland's decision to attend Yale was only the first step in a long process of finding his way in the world. But, given his family's background, it was a bold step forward. The Cleaveland family was no longer hampered by the illiteracy that had been the lot of their emigrant ancestor; nevertheless, their educational attainments were still not very high. John's father, Josiah, came to Canterbury, "as frequently he hath his children told," at the age of four, when only a handful of settlers lived in the area.

> There he grew up thro' Hardships great enough,
> As we may well suppose; the Place was rough.
> Nor Schools, nor Time for Learning could be found;
> Nought, but to till and to manure the Ground:
> Therefore where nat'ral Knowledge was to dwell,
> No marvel, if it's Want did much prevail:[1]

However, perhaps because of his own deficiencies, this rough-hewn backwoods farmer, eager to advance his family, "had a great mind to bring up his children in good learning."[2]

John's mother's family, the prosperous and influential Paines, held public offices that called for higher educational attainments. John's great-grandfather and grandfather Paine had served in the General Assemblies of Massachusetts and Connecticut, respectively. His uncles, Solomon and Elisha Paine, Jr., had similar responsibilities. Solomon was at times both town officer and deputy, and Elisha, a noted attorney, often represented the town in provincial matters. He became the King's Attorney for Windham County and a justice of the peace, and was in 1740 chosen as a superior-court judge though the governor later vetoed the appointment.[3]

In writing of his ancestry, John Cleaveland stressed the piety rather than the abilities of the Paine family. They came from a church as conservative as that of Woburn—Barnstable on Cape Cod—and were active members of the Canterbury church. John described his mother, Abigail Paine Cleaveland, as "a woman of experimental piety," who

took a considerable deal of pains not only to teach us to read but also, to shew us the danger of an unconverted state or a state of unregeneracy[,] how we were children of wrath and exposed to hell-fire and also set forth to us the necessity of having an interest in Jesus Christ in order to be safe and happy—after this sort was I educated.

Her father, Elisha Paine, Sr., he characterized as

a pious judicious and exemplary christian, a man of great faith, . . . and one that fervently prayed for the advancement of Zion's interest, who declared just before his death to his sons, that God would speedily do marvellous things of a gracious nature . . . which has come to pass accordingly, and especially in his family or posterity, where of about forty persons give satisfactory evidence of a work of grace being wro't upon their souls.

The fulfillment of his Grandfather Paine's prophecy would have a great impact on young John's education.[4]

In September 1739, John Cleaveland began the "study of the languages in order for college." His preparation was to be the customary two years of Latin grammar, under the guidance of the local minister. His previous education was, by his own admission, deficient. His mother had taught him to read at home. For the rest, "the country was new, where my parents lived and they were obliged to work hard to get a living—and also make their children work, sooner perhaps—than was for their benefit," so that their formal education was limited to three winter months yearly. However, he "pursued" his studies "with great engagedness and constancy."[5]

In the midst of his preparation for Yale, Canterbury, and soon much of Connecticut, was "awakened." Revivals had long been a part of the New England religious experience, but this revival would shake the ecclesiastical establishment to its foundation. The unprecedented magnitude of the revival, and the impassioned preaching that brought a vast upsurge in conversions and a consequent increase in church membership, made some ministers fearful for their authority and other men contemptuous of preaching that did not bespeak an immediate religious experience. The revival reinvigorated the seventeenth-century controversies about the qualifications for church membership, the relative importance of education and religious experience in the making of a minister, and, ultimately, the right of an "awakened" laity to restructure the church according to their beliefs. The Canterbury church, with its long history of lay resistance to clerical authority, was from the first sympathetic to the revival and soon began admitting members at two or three times the previous rate. In 1740, Eleazar Wheelock, a minister from Lebanon, Connecticut, went preaching, in the new style, through Windham County. John's uncle Elisha, though converted in an earlier revival, now felt "called of God" to abandon law for the gospel "and went forth preaching . . . through the land." He was soon joined in his self-proclaimed lay ministry by his brothers Solomon and John and their nephew Abraham. On September 14, 1740, John Cleaveland was admitted to full communion in the Canterbury church. His entire family was soon caught up in the revival.[6]

He continued with his studies, and in the following September, he "was examined for and admitted as a member of Yale College in New Haven," having satisfied the rector and tutors that he was "able extempore to read, construe and parse Tully."[7] The goal that his education was to serve was now clear to him. Under the combined influence of family piety and the revival that began during his preparation for college, young John's desire for a liberal education had become a firm commitment to a ministerial career. However, the revivalist preachers were raising questions about the importance of formal education as opposed to religious experience in the training of ministers. John's sympathy for the revival and his desire to make his way in the world, both firmly rooted in his family background, would come into conflict at Yale.

The college, like Canterbury, was deep in the throes of the Great Awakening. Commencement ceremonies at the

beginning of John Cleaveland's freshman year were tumul-
tuous. On September 9, 1741, the day of the commencement, the college and community heard the Reverends Joseph Bellamy, Jedediah Mills, and James Davenport preach
in the new style. Davenport was by far the wildest, and his
performance made a lasting impact on some of his hearers,
especially those who later opposed the revival. One such observer sent an account of these meetings to the *Boston Post-
Boy:*

At *New-Haven* he [Davenport] and some other Ministers and
young gifted Brethren, held forth every Day on the Commencement Week, and generally continued to 10 or 11 a Clock at
Night; and then a great Part of their carryings on was not by
Praying, Singing and Preaching upon a Text as usual; but one
would make a short Prayer, then another give a Word of Exhortation, then another Word of Exhortation: Then one would propose
a Psalm, then another a Prayer, then another a Word of Exhortation, and so on, without any certain Order or Method . . . so
that, some praying, some exhorting & terrifying, some singing,
some screaming, some crying, some laughing and some scolding,
made the most amazing Confusion that ever was heard.

Davenport further offended the community's leaders by en-
couraging the local resentment, in college and community,
against the Reverend Joseph Noyes of New Haven's First
Church.

Mr. D_____ in almost every Prayer vents himself against
the Minister of the Place, and often declares him to be an unconverted Man, says, that Thousands are now cursing of him in Hell,
for being the Instrument of their Damnation.[8]

The commencement sermon, given on September 10 by
Jonathan Edwards, was an eloquent and sophisticated de-
fense of the revial and the new methods, later published as
The Distinguishing Marks of a Work of the Spirit of God.[9]
    The revival at Yale had begun with a visit from George
Whitefield the previous October. Whitefield, then only

twenty-five himself, "spoke very closely to the Students, and shewed the dreadful Ill-Consequences of an unconverted Ministry."[10] Other evangelists visited the college. Gilbert Tennent preached seventeen sermons during a week in March. The excited undergraduates became increasingly harder to control. Thirty of them, almost half the college, followed Tennent to Milford, "on foot ten miles to hear the Word of God," against the express orders of Yale's chief officer, Rector Thomas Clap.[11]

Clap tried hard to control the disorders caused by the revival. The trustees met on the day before the commencement to vote that if any student said that the Rector, trustees, or tutors were "hypocrites, carnall or unconverted Men, he Shall for the first Offence make a publick Confession in the Hall, & for the Second Offence be expell'd," and to deny two seniors their degrees "for their disorderly and restless endeavors to propagate" the revival.[12] But the unruly commencement that followed held out little hope of a rapid subsidence of revival spirit at the college. Moreover, developments in the town did much to frustrate Clap's efforts. A separation had begun at the First Church. In November, 112 persons petitioned for a hearing of their grievances before the church, and in December some 38 withdrew, having found "by long and sorrowful experience . . . the preaching and conduct of the Rev. Mr. Noyes . . . in great measure unprofitable to us."[13] This group provided a forum for itinerant preachers and evangelists of all types, many of whom now found the college and the First Church closed to them.

II. The Contagion of the Revival

John Cleaveland began his college career in this increasingly polarized atmosphere. In January of his freshman year, he began to keep a diary, a practice to which he reverted in times of stress throughout his life. This diary

records both Cleaveland's vocational dilemma and the rend-
ing of Yale College by the Awakening.[14]

College life in New Haven revolved around the town
green. The single collegiate building, called the Yale College House, overlooked the green and the back of the meeting house. The College House was built in 1717–1718 and
contained the library, a kitchen, the "hall," which doubled
as a dining room and a chapel, and rooms for tutors, resident graduates, and undergraduates. It could accommodate
about two thirds of the undergraduates in Cleaveland's
time. The rest of the students lived in approved homes in
the community. John Cleaveland and several other students
lived with Samuel Mix (Yale, 1720), former rector of the
Hopkins Grammar School, who owned an inn a block from
the college on the same side of the green. The students went
to meeting at the First Church, located in the center of the
green, where they heard the preaching of Joseph Noyes
(Yale, 1709), who served informally as college chaplain.
The rector's house stood next to the college building.[15]

Rector Clap was a rigidly orthodox man, as was appropriate for the man charged with training ministers for the colony.[16] His earlier attacks on the proto-Unitarian Robert
Breck established his reputation as a defender of New England orthodoxy. This was of the greatest importance to
Yale's trustees, who had, ever since the "Great Apostasy" of
1721, when Rector Timothy Cutler and his tutors an-
nounced their conversion to the Church of England, carefully scrutinized the religious principles of prospective college officers and had made them swear allegiance to
Connecticut's religious constitution, the Saybrook Platform.[17] Clap's other notable characteristic was a passion for
organization, first made manifest in the exceedingly elaborate disciplinary and pastoral routine to which he had sub-
jected his parishioners. In the college in New Haven he
found a more promising field for his talents, beginning
with the library, which he reorganized and cataloged. He

then turned his attention to the rest of the college, cul-
minating his efforts in the new charter of 1745.[18]

The college he administered contained about eighty students until 1744 and about a hundred for the rest of the decade. Until 1743, when another tutor was added, the teach-
ing staff consisted of the rector and two tutors.[19] Tutors
Chauncy Whittelsey (Yale, 1738) and John Worthington
(Yale, 1740) supervised John Cleaveland's freshman class in
the study of ancient languages—what the eighteenth century called grammar. Language study, especially Latin,
provided the tools for later studies. In the next three years,
Cleaveland and his classmates would continue to review
Latin and to study logic, natural philosophy, and meta-
physics in sequence from textbooks written in Latin.

The first four days of each freshman's week were devoted
to learning Greek and Hebrew and reviewing Latin. On
Friday and Saturday they joined the upper classes for "rhetoric, oratory, ethics, and theology." Theology was taught
with more-than-a-century-old textbooks in reformed dog-
matics, for Yale taught a sixteenth-century system of divinity well into the eighteenth century. Friday afternoon was
given to recitations from Wollebius's *Compendium Theologiae
Christianae,* Saturday morning to Ames's *Medulla Theologiae,* and Saturday evenings to the catechism of the Westminster Assembly.[20] Cleaveland's brief summary of his
three years at Yale confirms much of this formal outline.

I studied somthing upon the three special languages[,] Latin
Greek and Hebrew—and took special delight in the study of the
Greek testament[,] digging up the very roots and derivations of
words. Logick natural philosophy and history were very pleasant
parts of my study. . . .[21]

The students were taught how to make use of their
knowledge of orthodox divinity by the rector, tutors, and
resident graduate students, who supplemented the curriculum with practical instruction in scriptural interpretation

and preaching. Prospective ministers among the undergraduates, always a majority at eighteenth-century Yale, were trained in a way little changed since the founding of New England. During John Cleaveland's freshman year, though, the revivalist preachers, called New Lights, brought into question the efficacy of this traditional preparation for the ministry. The college was deluged with preaching, as Rector Clap and the New Lights vied for influence and authority over the students. Cleaveland heard at least fifty-two sermons and lectures between January 15 and March 28, when the college was closed and the students dismissed.[22]

George Whitefield, Ebenezer Pemberton, Gilbert Tennent, and doubtless many of the nineteen ministers who spoke in the college town that spring called for a converted ministry. The previous spring, Pemberton had told the students that human knowledge "puffs up the mind, raises the natural vanity of man, and is apt to fill them with scorn and contempt for others," while saving knowledge "alone renders you a Child of God and gives you a title to the Kingdom of heaven." Moreover, he warned his audience from entering upon the ministry "while you are strangers to that Christ, who you are to preach to others, [because if you do] You will in all probability be the plagues of the Church, and the Unhappy occasion of the damnation of multitudes."[23] Davenport's attack on Reverend Noyes, during the commencement ceremonies at the beginning of Cleaveland's freshman year, reflected similar convictions about the qualifications for the ministry.

Indeed, academic training for some students seemed to run counter to their spiritual development. David Brainerd found, as a freshman, that "Ambition in my Studies greatly wronged the Activity and Vigour of my spiritual Life." And again, on the eve of the revival in the college, he "grew more *cold* and *dull* in Matters of Religion, by Means of my old Temptation, *viz.* Ambition in my Studies."[24] Cleaveland's diary is a record of the struggle between his spiritual needs and his academic obligations. On January 20, in the evening, he made note that he "studied very Industriously but [was] very Cold in religion." At other times this concern is made manifest in a comparison between his spiritual deadness and emptiness in New Haven and "the blessed worke of the Lord . . . [in] in fathers family." After hearing "heavenly news from Canterbury" about "the Conversions of my brethren and sisters," he talked with his classmate James Lockwood of "Religion and our Dead Souls[,] how that we are Conforming to the world."[25] It may be that the Cleaveland family's long history of suspicion toward clerical pretension hindered his spiritual development at the college. Whatever doubts about the ministry he had inherited could only be intensified by the conflict in New Haven between the revivalist preachers and the college staff. On January 18, Cleaveland had "had Some Discourse" with several classmates "Conserning removeing out of the College if we Could See our way Clear and if we Could have some Ministers on our Side."[26] Doubts like those which afflicted Cleaveland were undermining the college.

Clap forbade the students to attend meetings with those separated from the New Haven church. On January 27, Cleaveland wrote that there was "preaching at Mr. Cooks about twenty rods from the College almost all day [but] Mr. Clapp would not let us go." Some of the upperclassmen went anyway, and Cleaveland was "allmost resolved to goe Let what would fall out, but . . . had not the Corege to do it."[27] But on the night of January 31 he went to hear a farmer named Sackett preach, and the next day "Mr. Clapp gave us a Lectour Conserning these new Lights as people Call them in a Reflecting way":

He Seemed, to talk as if these people were quakers who go under the name of new Lights. I think he Saide that [they] had taken oath against the religion of the Country, and he also Saide . . . the Colony would not bringe up Scholars to Sware against the Religion of the Colony.[28]

After this experience he went often to the meetings of the Separate Church and gradually widened his acquaintance among the members. He went to meetings at the homes of Lieutenant Joseph Mix, James Pierpont, and Caleb Bradley.[29] On February 20, he spent the afternoon with David Brainerd, who was back in New Haven two months after being expelled for saying that Tutor Whittelsey "has no more grace than this chair." On February 23, he "had Some Sweet Discourse" with Zuriel Kimberly, a shoemaker and active member of the new church. On the first day of March, Pierpont, the leader of the New Haven Separatists, and Reverend Joseph Bellamy, the revivalist preacher, came to visit Cleaveland and his friends in college, where they composed a letter to Gilbert Tennent.[30] In early March, Cleaveland left his rooms with Samuel Mix, a staunch opposer of the revival, who talked "as if the work which is in the Land was of the Divil," and after a short stay in the college house moved in with Caleb Bradley of the Separate Church.[31]

Cleaveland was not alone in his growing alienation from the college administration. One account estimates that in March thirty or forty students, approximately half of those in residence, were attending the Separate meetings. Some left New Haven altogether. At least two students left the college for Timothy Allen's "Shepherd's Tent," the recently founded school for the training of an evangelical ministry, then in New London.[32] Cleaveland, however, remained until the students were officially dismissed.

Clap, in mid-March, made an effort to accommodate the increasingly dissatisfied and rebellious students. He summoned Aaron Burr (Yale, 1735) of Newark, New Jersey, to preach to the students and to be considered as a colleague-pastor to the much maligned Joseph Noyes.[33] Burr was an active supporter of the revival, although not an itinerant or supporter of separations. He preached five times in the meeting house and four times in the college between March

19 and 28. Clap and Noyes also opened their pulpits to Jonathan Parsons and Joseph Bellamy, who were preaching for the Separates as well. Cleaveland was largely noncommittal about all this preaching, observing on March 28 that "Sence Laste Fryday I have heard thirteeen Sermons from the ministers as I trust." The next day his depleted class did not meet, and two days after that he made arrangement "for a voige home," still "in things of Religion very Dull, and Lifeless."[34]

Clap's efforts to reach a compromise failed, and he had to dismiss the students more than a month early for their customary vacation. An Old Light from Boston, perhaps Charles Chauncy, summed up the situation in New Haven:

The College in *Connecticut* is broke up. The Students would neither mind their Studies, nor obey the Rules of the College. Almost all of them pretended to an inward Teacher which they ought to follow, and several of them made Excursions into the Country, and exhorted the People from Town to Town; so that the President [Rector] was obliged to dismiss all of them from the college.[35]

This was the most serious crisis in the history of the college. The composition of the Yale student body helps to explain the college's near-fatal susceptibility to the revival. And John Cleaveland, the son of a farmer, who had come to New Haven from the hinterlands to prepare himself for the ministry, was in most ways a typical Yale student of his time.

Farmers' sons predominated at eighteenth-century Yale, but they did not represent a cross section of Connecticut farmers. More than three quarters of the students at Yale before 1750 came from towns founded before 1676. Young men from newer towns (founded between 1676 and 1713) did not come in significant numbers until the mid-1730s, and only one student came from a town founded later than 1713. A combination of plentiful land and limited financial resources kept boys in newer settlements away from higher education. Yale students came from older communities, where land was coming to be in short supply but where some families were both sufficiently affluent to afford the costs of a college education and sufficiently ambitious to desire one for their sons. The Cleaveland family, whose history in New England was strongly marked by piety and ambition, invested about 125 pounds in John's education at Yale. Most Yale students were, then, sons of the more securely established farmers, men like John Cleaveland's father, and from that group came the bulk of the Yale-educated ministers.[36]

Nearly half of Yale's graduates in the classes of 1702 to 1750 entered the ministry. The students from modest lay backgrounds, 46 percent of the 626 graduates, became ministers more than half (55 percent) of the time. By comparison, only 49 percent of ministers' sons at Yale became ministers, and only 16 percent of the sons of the provincial officeholders, both civil and military, did so. While some of Yale's candidates for the ministry were the sons of ministers, many more were young men of relatively modest background who comprised the bottom half of the classes ranked according to "family dignity"; their fathers were farmers, often prosperous farmers and local officeholders.[37]

The age at entrance into college further distinguishes the two groups of prospective ministers. Of the sons of ministers whose ages are known, two thirds entered college at sixteen or under; almost a third entered college under the age of fourteen. But two thirds of the others entered at age seventeen or older; 30 percent were over twenty years of age. The importance of these older boys to the progress of the revival at Yale was recognized in later legislation forbidding the admission of freshmen over the age of twenty-one without special permission.[38] The difference in age at entry reflected different educational experiences. The son of the minister was likely to be prepared earlier, because a minister's home was where most boys were prepared for college. Connecticut, especially in the backcountry, had few grammar schools. The minister would be more likely than others to consider a college education for his son and could more readily implement it.

A farmer's son came not so easily to the decision. Responsibilities on the family farm made it difficult to get the proper education, as did the paucity of local schools. Three young Yale students from farming backgrounds—Samuel Hopkins, David Brainerd, and John Cleaveland—have left accounts of "labouring on the farm."[39] Brainerd had actually begun to work his own farm in Durham when, at the age of nineteen, he began to study on his own "from a natural Inclination, after a liberal Education."[40] He spent the next year studying with Reverend Phineas Fiske of Haddam, and the following year with his brother Nehemiah, pastor in Glastonbury. He entered Yale in September 1739, at the age of twenty-one. The other two young men also worked on the family farm, took two years of preparation with a local minister, and then entered Yale, Hopkins at sixteen and Cleaveland at nineteen. Furthermore, farmers' sons tended to decide later, because the cost of a college education probably represented the bulk of their share in their fathers' estates. One could not make such a decision before reaching a responsible age. Nor could most young men receive their shares before their elder siblings without unduly overburdening their fathers or delaying another child's share. John Cleaveland received his portion in increments, between the ages of nineteen and twenty-three. His elder brothers, Josiah and Elisha, had received their farms at about the same age. John, like them, was expected to make his living with what he had been provided.

When the Great Awakening raised fundamental issues of conversionism and lay control, the background of a minister proved to be influential in his choice of sides. In the classes between 1702 and 1750 Yale graduated forty-nine would-be ministers who were sons of ministers, most of whom had other older relatives in the ministry as well—grandfathers, uncles, brothers. The college graduated more than four times as many future ministers without a ministerial background, most of whom were farmers' sons. Three quarters of those ministers from ministerial backgrounds whose attitudes toward the Awakening are known became Old Lights. Seventy percent of those ministers from nonministerial backgrounds became New Lights. This pattern is even more marked among students who were at Yale during the revival.[41]

The traditional ministerial role still appealed powerfully to young men bred in parsonages. They were no doubt acutely aware of the importance of ministerial prerogatives and of the long struggle by New England ministers to maintain and extend them. However, the farmers' sons who predominated at Yale found the new evangelical-style ministry much to their liking. Tenacious traditions of lay hostility to clerical pretension may have made them responsive to the idea of a ministry whose authority was based on spiritual qualities rather than on institutional power or educational advantages. As a New Light minister, John Cleaveland could advance himself while remaining true to his family's religious tradition.

Yale eventually recovered and indeed became the center of the new evangelical-style ministry. Her graduates came to dominate the pulpits of New England's hinterland, where the "zeal for the *old doctrines* and the *new measures*" was strongest.[42] But for the moment, Rector Clap mounted a fierce counterattack directed at controlling the disorders caused by the revival. Clap would make the students conform to his rules, or they would not be students at all.

III. Repression

The "break-up" of the college in March 1741 marked a change in Clap's attitude toward the revival. He would make no more accommodations but instead "applied . . . to the general Court, for power to oblige the young Fellows to keep Order."[43] Rector Clap and many other influential citizens of Connecticut had become increasingly distressed by the disruptions that seemed to follow in the wake of the revival.[44] He complained bitterly about the growing number of Separate ministers who, he believed, were conspiring against the religious constitution and the college.

They endeavour to keep up a Separation at New-Haven, and to make one in the College, and to encourage the Scholars hereunto the ministers of that Party tell them, that if they will Separate from the College they will License them to Preach without any regard to a Degree.[45]

Jonathan Law, the recently elected governor, in his address before the General Assembly directed their attention to "the unhappy Circumstances of our colledge" that "has dispersed ye students at an unusual Season." For if the "youth there . . . be trained up in Disobedience," he warned, it "will lay a foundation for Sedition and Disregard to all humane laws."[46]

A committee was appointed and, with the advice of the "Reverend Rector," reported on the state of the college. The students, they said, had fallen into the practice of rashly judging and censuring their instructors "as being unconverted, unexperienced & unskillful guids, in matters of relegion, and have thereupon contemntuously refused to submit to theire authoritie." The students also "by day & night, & Some times for Several days together" went into New Haven, or to other towns "to teach & Exhort." They were led into these evil courses "by the Instigation perswation & example of others," by which the committee meant the stream of New Light preachers drawn to New Haven by the students and the Separate Church. As a corrective, the committee recommended expulsion of those students who would not submit to the laws of the college. They also recommended that "Some experienced Grave Devins" visit the college to counteract the effect of the New Light preaching, which visits they offered to subsidize.[47]

The Assembly then turned to the problem of controlling the revival on the colonial level. In that same session they passed "An Act for regulating Abuses and correcting Disorders in Ecclesiastical Affairs," better known as the Anti-Itinerancy Act.[48] The act made it a crime to preach within another minister's parish without his express permission, punishable by the withdrawal of tax revenue for Connecticut ministers, fines and imprisonment for lay preachers, and expulsion for visitors from other colonies. Clap had a part in this legislation as well. In the following year, during the October session, the Assembly tried to destroy the Shepherd's Tent by declaring that only ministers with a degree from Yale, Harvard, or "some other allowed foreign Protestant college . . . shall take benefit of the laws of this government respecting the settlement and support of ministers."[49] In May 1743, the Assembly repealed the 1708 act that allowed toleration for those who "soberly dissent from the way of worship and ministry" established in Connecticut; the following October they strengthened the Anti-Itinerancy Act by threatening court action against those preachers from other colonies who returned when expelled.[50]

The new laws, it was soon demonstrated, were not idle threats. In the next few years, noted New Lights like Benjamin Pomeroy of Hebron, Eleazar Wheelock of Lebanon, Timothy Allen of West Haven, as well as lesser lights like Philemon Robbins of Branford, Daniel Humphreys of Derby, Mark Leavenworth of Waterbury, and Samuel Todd of Northbury lost their legal right to support. The acts of the Assembly and the excesses of some revivalists, most notably James Davenport's infamous book burning in New London, soon served to temper the revival.[51]

The college too was calmer when it reassembled in early

June. Clap wrote to the Reverend Solomon Williams of Lebanon on June 8 that "the Scholars of late seem to [be] much more cool, submissive and orderly than they were before the Vacancy, and some that I have discoursed with freely acknowledge their fault and promise Reformation." He reaffirmed his conviction "that all things would go on well" at the college if it were not for the baneful influence on the students of the ministers of "that party."[52]

There were some solid guarantees for the continuation of order at Yale. The Anti-Itinerancy Act made it more difficult for the New Haven Separates to fill their pulpit. In 1743, Samuel Finley, representative of the New York Synod and later president of the College of New Jersey, was arrested and deported for preaching in New Haven without leave from Reverend Noyes. Moreover, the Yale trustees passed and the Assembly confirmed a new regulation stating that "the members of the college shall attend on the regular stated worship of the town every sabbath, and upon no other on a week day without liberty of the Rector upon pain of expulsion."[53] The students thus were more effectively isolated from those disruptive influences that Clap so feared.

The establishment of the Shepherd's Tent in New London, in the spring of 1742, also contributed to Yale's stability. It drew away at least two students, John Brainerd and Elihu Spencer, and probably more, of the most radical students. Three others, Silas Brett, William Cook, and a student named Lord, had also left. With the expulsion of David Brainerd and the graduation of Samuel Buell and David Youngs, the leadership of the college revival was much depleted.[54]

When Eleazar Wheelock came to New Haven in early June, he was invited to breakfast with Rector Clap. He disputed with Clap about the New Haven Separates and marveled at his "remarkable faculty to darken every thing." When Wheelock returned to New Haven in late June after a preaching tour through Derby, Guilford, Branford, and

East Haven, he found that Clap would not "let . . . [him] preach in the college or to let the scholars come to hear" him. He wrote angrily that "Mr. Clap sticks as fast to Mr. Noyes as his skinn and loves him as his eyes and counts him a sound orthodox man."[55]

John Cleaveland, along with the great majority of students, returned to the college and their studies in June 1742. Cleaveland probably passed through New London on his way to New Haven, but the Shepherd's Tent was not sufficiently appealing to make him change his plans. Recent legislation made Yale the one road to the ministry for most young men in Connecticut. Licensing by a ministerial association in Connecticut without a Yale degree was nearly impossible, and a Yale degree was bought at the price of conformity to the Rector's demands. John Cleaveland and the great majority of his fellow students conformed. Much of his portion of his father's estate had already been expended on his Yale education, and the successful completion of that education was more necessary than ever for his advancement. The Rector wrote proudly to a correspondent in the fall of 1743, Cleaveland's junior year, that the "college seems at present to be . . . under very good circumstances. None of the scholars that I know of any way interest themselves in the differences at New Haven, and I hear no disputes about any thing." Cleaveland maintained a warm interest in the revival and, in October 1743, celebrated its triumphant progress in verse.

Britons Isle has catched the flame.
Many love and know thy name
Both in England and in Wales
And in Scotland grace prevails.

But Clap made the boundaries of acceptable behavior clear when he expelled one of Cleaveland's classmates for saying that "Mr. Noyes preaching had a direct tendency to lead souls to hell."[56]

It was in this atmosphere of controlled quietude that

John Cleaveland began his last year of college (1744–1745). His ministerial training was nearly complete; after graduation he would seek licensing from a local ministerial association and then begin the search for a church of his own. A permanent position would, a few years hence, allow him to marry and begin a family. His younger brother, Ebenezer, following in his footsteps, joined him for commencement in September and was admitted as a freshman. After that ceremony they journeyed home to Canterbury for the customary vacation.

Canterbury had been without a settled minister ever since May 1741, when Reverend John Wadsworth had been forced from his pulpit by a scandal involving what a nineteenth-century local historian called "a criminal charge alleged . . . by a female resident."[57] The revival in Canterbury had therefore proceeded largely unchecked, for even under the stringencies of the Anti-Itinerancy Act an individual congregation without a minister retained the right to hear preaching of its choice.[58]

The indigenous revival in the town, led by the Paine brothers, developed rapidly in this atmosphere. The revivalists soon moved beyond the church's traditional opposition to the Saybrook Platform to affirm the Cambridge Platform and congregational independence, to abandon half-way membership, and to adopt public professions of faith as a requirement for membership. The result was a sectarian church, based on adult membership and personal commitment, and shaped by the long-standing lay religious traditions of New England, and particularly of the settlers of this town. As Elisha Paine declared, "it was made manifest to him, that Christ was about to have a pure Church."[59]

The divided congregation heard several ministers but could come to no agreement, for a man pleasing to one side was to that degree unacceptable to the other. In December 1743, both groups called councils. The antirevivalists, representing the majority of the town and the minority of the church, convened the Windham Consociation. The prorevival party, representing the majority of the church and the minority of the town, did not recognize the power of the consociation and called an independent council of New Lights. The councils quite naturally differed in their evaluation of the situation, but both recommended James Cogswell (Yale, 1742) to the divided church.[60]

Cogswell was summoned to preach on probation. Within a few months the prorevival party was ready to look further. Elisha Paine pronounced Cogswell's preaching "nothing but trifling"; worse yet, Cogswell opposed public professions of faith and supported both the Half-Way Covenant and the Saybrook Platform. The town was quite satisfied, however, and began working the ecclesiastical machinery to settle him. The revival party withdrew to meet in private homes, and sent a protest to the town on September 16 against the calling of Cogswell. The protest was signed by John Cleaveland's father, his brother Elisha, and his uncles Abraham, Solomon, and Elisha Paine, and Obadiah Johnson.[61]

While at home, John and Ebenezer attended church with their parents and heard their Uncle Solomon preach. On September 22, their Uncle Elisha was arrested at the instigation of the Windham Consociation for "exhorting" the previous spring at the home of Benjamin Cleaveland, a cousin of their father's, in Scotland Parish in the town of Windham. The former attorney offered as his plea "that the court hath not jurisdiction of this case; for . . . the facts complained of are warranted by the law of God and the King, and therefore not triable by any court of law, inferior thereto." Refusing bail, he remained in jail until just before the return of his nephews to New Haven.[62]

Upon their return to Yale, the two young men were summoned to meet with Rector Clap. The Cleaveland brothers had not sought this confrontation, and their behavior toward Clap was respectful and conciliatory throughout it.

On November 19, 1744, they had the first of some six conferences with him.[63] Clap began the meeting by accusing the brothers of leaving "a Licensed and Approved Candidate for the Ministry" to attend a Separate meeting and hear a lay exhorter.[64] John claimed, in reply, that it was not a Separate meeting, being a meeting of the major part of the church. Clap then turned to the question of fitness for the ministry, that being the grounds of the Separates' rejection of Cogswell, and asked whether Solomon Paine had a divine call to preach, and whether a divine call was essential to the ministry. John parried with a show of modesty: "In case we had been called ourselves, we could be better able to answer you than we are now."[65] Clap returned to the charge of attending a Separate meeting, and John once more claimed majority status for that meeting. Clap cut him off sharply: "A few more than half makes [no] alteration; since they separated upon the same bottom (as others) of judging and censuring ministers." John then questioned the applicability of the college laws "out of New-Haven," and Clap replied shortly that "the laws of God and the laws of the college are one." Soon they were dismissed.[66]

That night, about nine o'clock, they discovered that Clap had already written up a bill of suspension and had given it to Tutor Chauncy Whittelsey to be read the next morning at chapel. They went to Whittelsey to ask for a delay; failing in that, they awaited the rector's summons. A few days later, he called the two brothers before him and asked for "as large a confession as the charge, or else . . . [they would] be wholly deprived of College privileges." In the ensuing discussion Clap once more tried to make them state a belief in the necessity of a converted ministry, and John once more claimed ignorance "of any law forbidding any member of College going just where he thinks fit when [away] from College." When Cleaveland said some of the seniors and graduates felt similarly, Clap replied ominously: "So be it. I'll make them know otherwise by my dealings with you."[67]

On November 26, John Cleaveland handed the rector a confession begging "compassionate forgiveness to an offending child." He did not, however, confess any fault other than ignorance of any law "of God, this Colony, or of the College" making his action blamable, nor did he condemn separations and lay exhorters. Clap found it unacceptable, and he and John fell into another discussion of qualifications for the ministry, in which Cleaveland affirmed and Clap denied the possibility of valid lay ordination. As the meeting was breaking up, Ebenezer introduced a new consideration: the responsibility of the brothers to obey their parents, as they had done in attending the meeting. Clap allowed that "this extenuates the crime, for it is a good thing to reverence your parents." John grasped this opportunity for compromise, offering to persuade his parents to let them avoid meetings "contrary to the mind . . . of [the] College" in the future if Clap would allow them to remain. The rector replied, "I don't know but I may." However, he continued to demand a public confession of fault. By doing so Clap placed the Cleaveland brothers, and especially John, in a painful dilemma. In order to save one part of their inheritance, the family's investment in Yale, Clap would have them repudiate publicly another part, the family's religious background. That they would not do. The conflict that John had felt as a freshman between his evangelical faith and the demands of the traditional ministry became sharper than ever in the fall of his senior year. Clap was forcing him to choose between alternatives he had long striven to reconcile.[68]

A short time afterward, John went to consult with the Reverend Samuel Cooke of Stratfield, the most outspoken New Light on the Board of Trustees. Cooke found their expulsion inevitable, "for he could not see how they could in conscience do more." Clap met with them once more to make sure "they were settled in their minds" about this decision.[69] This being the case, the rector said, in John Cleaveland's account:

I shall proceed to expel you tomorrow morning and would have you come hear it, & accordingly they did, and were commanded to depart the Hall and the limits of College no more to return— likewise were the students forbid receiving them into their chambers and of commersing with them lest they should [be] infected by them.[70]

Clap had unquestionably gone beyond the college laws in punishing the boys for their actions in Canterbury. As in the case of David Brainerd, Clap demanded a full public confession or an expulsion. In his own words, "the end and design of punishment is primarily to restrain the offender, but principally to deter others. For the good of many is more to be aimed at than the good of one individual."[71] Clap expelled the Cleaveland brothers as an example to Connecticut's New Lights, and to Yale students generally, of his continued close watch over the college.

John Cleaveland left New Haven in November 1744 and went to the parsonage of Reverend Philemon Robbins of nearby Branford. He had admired Robbins's preaching since his freshman year and so chose to prepare for the ministry with him. His future options were severely limited, because without a college degree he could not be licensed to preach in Connecticut. He was contemplating prospects in New Jersey when he wrote to Eleazar Wheelock in late March 1745. He may have intended missionary work, like that of the Brainerds, or simply a pastoral charge under the sympathetic New Side Presbyterians of the New York Synod. Wheelock promised aid but strongly recommended a petition to the Assembly for reinstatement in the college. In April Josiah Cleaveland submitted a petition in the names of his two sons, the same session in which Clap submitted his new and more authoritarian charter. The petition was dismissed; the charter passed without objection. [72]

At about the same time, John Cleaveland was offered the opportunity "to labor in the work of the gospel ministry on probation, in order to be pastor" of the Canterbury Separates. It is not difficult to understand why he refused the call. He was a prudent young man and eager to make his way in the world. He could not accept, as did his uncles Solomon and Elisha, the harassments, deprivations, and even imprisonments that were the lot of an unlicensed minister in Connecticut. His fears about the Connecticut establishment may have been confirmed by the experiences of his teacher, Philemon Robbins, who was then in the third year of a suspension imposed on him by the local association for preaching to a Separate church in Wallingford. Cleaveland had earlier resisted the temptation of the Shepherd's Tent. He had tried very hard to accommodate himself to Clap, in order to get his degree and become an accredited minister. He had stated, in their discussions, that he was "not fully determined concerning" separations and lay preaching, although he would not, as Clap demanded, publicly repudiate his family and his church. [73]

John Cleaveland's expulsion from the college brought a sudden end to his regular progress toward the ministry. Since he was without a degree, most of the pulpits in Connecticut were closed to him. In a few weeks, Cleaveland's fortunes had undergone a dramatic reversal, and his plans for the future were thrown into disarray. Therefore, when in the summer of 1745 he received an offer from a Separate church in Boston to come preach on trial for them, he responded with alacrity. [74] He soon set out for Massachusetts to learn about being a minister and to earn his way in the world. In Boston, Cleaveland would be free of the Connecticut ecclesiastical establishment and of Rector Clap. Massachusetts offered a fresh start and a more promising future, much as Connecticut had done for his grandfather in the 1690s.

IV. Boston

Separatist meetings had been held in Boston as early as 1742, in the wake of James Davenport's visit to the city, and attended by "a small number," according to Thomas Prince of the Old South Church. A church, comprised of attendants and communicants of several Boston churches, had been gathered on July 18, 1743.[75]

John Cleaveland came to Boston in the fall of 1745 and began preaching to the people of the Separate Church in the hope that they would soon offer him a permanent position. His first parish was an ideological, not a geographical, entity. Boston, whose churches were voluntarily supported and territorially imprecise, could accommodate new organizations more readily than other New England communities could. But the new church in Boston, unlike its predecessors, had no geographical base at all, no meeting house, and no gentlemen sponsors. Moreover, during its first years, a layman, Nathaniel Wardell, formerly of Old South Church, had performed the ministerial duties. Its very existence, premised on the inadequacy of the existing alternatives, was a rebuke to the churches of Boston.

The warm support for the revival among the Boston clergy had cooled with the growth of Separatism and lay preaching. Thomas Prince of Old South Church, whose *Christian History* was published to promote the revival, refused several members dismissal to the new church and suspended Wardell for preaching to them.[76] In May 1746, the venerable Benjamin Colman, dean of the Boston clergy, inveighed against

those amongst ourselves who . . . go about exhorting and preaching, grossly unfurnished with ministerial gifts and knowledge,

. . . [whose] blind censures of many faithful pastors, into whose fold they are daily breaking, . . . because of the mildness of our spirits towards them, seem to grow the more bold and fierce.[77]

Cleaveland and his church had no recognized position in the ecclesiastical word of Boston.

As a result, Cleaveland was freer in Boston to work out his own fate, but he was also at least as much of an outsider as he had been before. The hostility of Rector Clap at Yale and the Old Light ministerial association in Windham County had been replaced, in the unfamiliar urban environment, by the mingled fear and contempt of Boston's lordly ecclesiastical establishment. Two months after his arrival in Boston Cleaveland expressed his sense of his situation vividly by identifying himself, in a letter to his old advisor Philemon Robbins, with the prophet Amos.

And if the Amaziahs should rise up against me and tell me not to prophesy in the kings chaple or the kings palace; I must give them Amos's answer: . . . the Lord took me, saying go prophesy to my people Israel: and [I] am now preaching in Boston.[78]

The contrast between priest and prophet was a commonplace of Separatist rhetoric, but Cleaveland's identification with Amos reveals much of his self-perception. Amos was a "herdsman" from the southern wilderness of Judea come to preach against the softness and corruption of the city, and Amaziah, who so savagely rbuked him, was priest of the national shrine at Bethel.

A dual sense of alienation and militancy pervades Cleaveland's writings in Boston. His ragged and despised little congregation, scattered throughout Boston and Charlestown, seems to have been centered near Cleaveland's lodgings in the rapidly developing and commercial West End of Boston. As he preached in private homes throughout the city he was often beset by "scoffers" and "opposers." Once his sermon was interrupted by a "rable" led by "a great man . . . holding a very large club." On another occasion he preached from Isaiah 28:22, "Be ye not mocking," but, he noted, "mock they did in an awful manner indeed."[79]

His journal, kept between Feburary and May 1746, records the texts of more than sixty sermons preached. He increased his preaching responsibilities by augmenting the obligatory two Sunday sermons and Wednesday lecture with frequent visits to sympathetic groups in neighboring communities. He was at this time much more of an Old Testament preacher than he would be at any other point in his career. He preached only once from the fundamental text of predestination, Romans 8:29–30, and but infrequently of the promise of the gospels. He was drawn instead to the prophets. He preached from Amos, Zechariah, and Jeremiah; twice from Daniel and Ezekiel; four times from Hosea; and seven times from Isaiah.

The young minister self-consciously adopted the prophetic role and preached to his little flock as if they were a saving remnant in a sink of corruption. He turned repeatedly to the book of Isaiah for images of judgment and the survival of the elect.[80] On February 13 he preached of exclusion,

Bind up the testimony, seal the law among my disciples. (Isa. 8:16)

and on March 30 of the righteous and the wicked,

Say ye to the righteous that it shall be well with him:
For they shall eat the fruit of their doings.
Woe unto the wicked! It shall be ill with him:
For the reward of his hands shall be given him.
(Isa. 3:10–11)

The adversarial relationship between the saved and society was central to the sectarian vision of the world. Cleaveland's reliance on the grim message of the prophets, particularly Isaiah's notion of the saving remnant, reveals much about his Boston experience. This vision of the world was acceptable to the congregation, for they asked him to settle with them, but perhaps not to Cleaveland himself, for he did not do so.

On February 10, 1746, he attended a church meeting in Boston, where, as he noted in his journal, he was given "a call to settle here . . . unanimously both Church and congregation." About a month later he wrote to Philemon Robbins to tell him of the offer of a permanent position, carefully noting that he had "not given in any answer to them as yet." About the same time his father, his uncle Solomon Paine, and one of his brothers came to stay with him for a few days, presumably to discuss his future. At the end of March, still undecided, he set aside a "day of private fasting and prayer" so that he might "see clearly whether it is my duty to accept of the call to settle in Boston." Cleaveland's uncertainty seems to have consisted of doubt whether it was his "duty to take a pastoral charge of a people" and concern over his tendency to "be lifted up with pride."[81]

As late as the fall of 1746, Cleaveland was still in doubt. He set out for Canterbury with the intention of reconsidering the Canterbury church's offer of a year past, only to find his uncle Solomon newly ordained as pastor there. He wrote the Boston church on two occasions after his Connecticut trip in an attempt to explain "those difficultys which I laboured under." In the first he asked only whether they could renew their call "heartily and with unfained love" for "then I shall not fear being maintained." If he could be sure of their love and support, "we could be a happy people let the world think what they please of us."[82]

The second letter is a lengthier and more serious discussion of his difficulties. He first questioned whether he had "a particular call to take the charge of a particular Church from God as well as from man." He also wondered whether he should settle "when the people were not linked together by the bonds of divine love"—a reference to radical-moderate tensions in the church, which would lead, in

1748, to the moderates' withdrawing and founding another church. Finally, he feared that he "had not love enough to this people to stand and fall with them."[83]

Cleaveland's motives in resisting the call of the Boston Separates were a mix of the mundane and the spiritual. He worried, like a Separate preacher, about whether he was called by God to this particular church. After all, his uncle Elisha Paine and his classmate Nathaniel Draper rejected the notion of settling with one church in these corrupt times. And he worried, like most New England ministers, about his support. All of his reservations about the Boston offer, however, point to growing uneasiness about "the present strife in this littell" church.[84] The Boston church, beset with internal divisions and the hostility of the other city churches, with no meetinghouse and with members scattered throughout Boston and Charlestown, had a limited appeal for Cleaveland. This was made clear to him by a developing relationship with a Separate church in Ipswich, which offered better prospects and a more familiar, rural environment. The farming community on the North Shore was in many ways like the home he had left behind. He could share a way of life with these people as well as religious convictions, and he could expect from them a respectable maintenance.

V. Chebacco

It was in January 1746 that John Cleaveland had first been asked to preach to the "separated brethren" of Ipswich's second parish, called Chebacco, in Essex County, Massachusetts. His acceptance "was to them joyfull news." He joined them on February 17, one week after receiving the offer of the Boston church, and stayed until February 22. He preached five times, and "when I took my leave of them, the assembly was watered with tears, the good Lord be praised for what I have seen felt and heard in this

journy." When he rode back to Boston, some of the congregation accompanied him fifteen miles to Beverly.[85]
Shortly after his return, he wrote to his brother Aaron to
tell him of the "glorious time" he had had at Chebacco.[86]
Thereafter Cleaveland maintained a warm interest in their
affairs.

The course of the revival in Essex County, north of Boston, had been relatively smooth.[87] The ministers had
shared, for the most part, the lay enthusiasm for the revival
and so managed to contain it within the established church.
Ipswich, however, was more sharply divided. The first
parish was the bailiwick of the eminent Rogers clan, which
in England had produced noteworthy Puritan preachers
since the reign of Queen Elizabeth, and which had preached
in Ipswich since 1638. Old John Rogers, now nearly
eighty, and his sons, Nathaniel (colleague-pastor in the
Ipswich church), John (minister in Kittery), and Daniel
(tutor at Harvard College), were all enthusiastic supporters
of the revival and the new methods. The old man put his
imprimatur on the revival methods in a letter to the assembly of divines that met in Boston in July 1743. Nathaniel
and John preached up and down the Merrimack Valley, and
Daniel threw aside his tutorial responsibilities to travel
about with Whitefield. In July 1742, he was ordained by
his brother John and two other New Lights as a kind of itinerant minister-at-large.[88]

Theophilus Pickering of Chebacco parish was of a different mind and temper altogether. A querulous old bache-
lor from a prominent Salem family, he had served the parish
since the death of John Wise in 1725. He was from the
beginning a staunch opponent of the new revival methods,
perhaps because he had begun his ministerial career preaching to the unwilling Baptists and Quakers of Tiverton.[89]

In 1742, the difference of opinion between the Rogers
family and Pickering came out into the open. In February, a
group in the Chebacco parish wrote to Daniel Rogers asking

him to preach to them, noting that Pickering would not join in their request.[90] The three Rogers brothers then began earnestly evangelizing the parish despite Pickering's protests. In March, Daniel held meetings in Pickering's own meetinghouse, calling him a "Blind Minister" and praying "that the Scales might fall" from his eyes.[91] Unable to make the Rogers family admit the error of its ways, Pickering collected his correspondence with them, along with a letter of protest to James Davenport, and published them. Then, on October 5, he closed his pulpit to all outsiders. By these actions he gave notice that ministers should "not trespass upon" their "Neighbours Rights, by breaking into Christ's Inclosures put under the care of other Husbandmen."[92]

Pickering and his dissatisfied parishioners came to a new understanding a few months later. On January 10, 1743, he opened the pulpit to any "liberally educated orthodox pious prudent able ministers" that his parishioners might invite, provided "the people will avoid strife and contentions, and exercise forbearance one toward another . . . and will leave each other at liberty in regard of their attendance."[93] The uneasy peace thus established in the parish was broken permanently little more than a year later. On Sunday, March 11, 1744, while preaching the afternoon sermon, Pickering observed "that none knew the actings of faith, but God only." This was rightly perceived as an attack on New Light principles, and Lieutenant Daniel Gidding "loudly" or "meekly," according to various later accounts, questioned his doctrine. The meeting quickly broke up in noisy disagreement.[94]

On the following day, a group of New Lights came to Pickering's house with a list of grievances signed by twenty-six of the sixty-three male members of the Chebacco church. He stood accused, in fourteen "occasions of disquietude," with "not preaching plainly the distinctive doctrines of the Bible, with a want of interest in his ministerial work, with worldliness of spirit and conduct and with opposition to the work of grace going on among them."[95] Pickering argued with them again about his words of the day before and took down the names of three New Light leaders, Lieutenant Thomas Choate, James Eveleth, and Francis Choate. That evening Pickering wrote to Eveleth and the Choate brothers to inform them that he was

disposed to take such Measures as may oblige you to answer for your Offence at the next Court of General Sessions of the Peace . . . , unless you make a satisfactory Acknowledgement [of your error], with Promise of behaving well for the future; and also give me sufficient Security to respond all Damages, which in Consequence of your Conduct may in any wise accrue to me.

The New Lights ignored his demands, and so at the end of March, he sued them for defamation. They were eventually acquitted with costs, which Pickering later offered to pay, but thereafter the prospect of reconciliation was significantly reduced.[96]

Pickering and his opponents continued to quarrel, they complaining of his shortcomings, he of their disrespect. At first the New Lights sought a church meeting to discuss and vote on their objections to Pickering's ministry, and later a council of churches. Pickering refused both and warned them that it was "of no avail for you to keep tugging and striving with your Pastor."[97] Attempting to reconcile the warring factions, Reverend Samuel Wigglesworth of Ipswich's third parish, a moderate supporter of the revival, intervened in the fall of 1744 on behalf of the disaffected New Lights. As a result of his actions, several church meetings were held, but Pickering would not allow any votes to be taken on the issues that divided the parish. This arbitary exercise of his ministerial authority itself became a grievance.

The quarrel between Pickering and the Chebacco New Lights brought the normal activities of the church and the parish almost to a halt. Several members of the congregation withdrew from communion; church meetings grew infrequent and, when held, soon broke up in acrimonious dispute. The parish meetings were no more harmonious: from 1745 until 1747 the community was unable to reach an agreement on Pickering's salary and did little better at conducting routine, uncontroversial affairs. Even service as a parish trustee, formerly an unenviable duty, became the object of electioneering. A shaky balance of three Old Lights and two New Lights was maintained among the trustees for the rest of the decade.[98]

When Pickering offered his departure as a solution, both sides quickly agreed on terms and drew up a proposal that was signed by a majority of the church members. The Chebacco minister was not a popular man. A few days later, Pickering, perhaps startled by the willingness to do without him, withdrew his offer. No real prospect for settlement existed thereafter. A substantial body of New Lights was permanently estranged from the church, and the parish was split into two hostile parties. Pickering contributed to the atmosphere of partisan conflict by launching an attack on Whitefield, who was once again in America, finding him responsible for "the schisms, variance, emulations, strife, railing and evil surmisings . . . that have been rife among us."[99]

On January 13, 1746, sixteen members of the Chebacco church met at Daniel Gidding's home, and most agreed to separate if Pickering would not leave. Two days later, they informed the church of their resolution and, a short time after, covenanted among themselves to form a church.[100] John Cleaveland came and preached to them in mid-February, and in March they engaged his brother Ebenezer as their first preacher. Ebenezer Cleaveland served as preacher and clerk from March to July 1746. On May 20, 1746, John moderated the New Light council that approved of the separation in Chebacco and supervised the organization of the church.[101] In August, John Cleaveland, after his brother's return to Canterbury, came once more to Chebacco. He returned in the fall for a longer stay and in December was engaged for the winter. In early January he accepted an invitation to settle permanently with them. He was ordained in February 1747, just two months short of his twenty-fifth birthday.

The village was now bitterly divided into opposing camps. Although support for the revival and opposition to Pickering had been widespread in Chebacco, people who adopted these positions did not invariably join with the new church.[102] Thirty-three male church members, more than half, approved Pickering's January 1743 offer to open his pulpit to visiting preachers. Fully three-fifths of these villagers who had made public their interest in revival preaching remained with the old church. The voting (or male) church membership stood at about sixty-three in 1744; of these, twenty-six signed the list of grievances agaist Pickering in March, thirty-five demanded a church meeting from their recalcitrant pastor in May, and an un-specified majority agreed to the terms offered for his re-moval in August of the next year. However, when the decision to separate from the old church was made in Jan-uary 1746, only fourteen men agreed to do so. Over the next year or so, nine more church members joined the new church, but there were also a few men who, having sepa-rated, then returned to the old church. Like Cleaveland, the Chebacco New Lights were prudent, moderate men. For four years, from 1742 to 1746, they had sought an accom-modation with Pickering. They made the decision to form themselves into a new church reluctantly, after all hope for compromise was gone, and even then, some who were sym-pathetic to the revival or were opposed to Pickering still could not bring themselves to repudiate the church of their fathers. This deep cleavage among the villagers reveals some beliefs and practices that are basic to the community.

The economic distinctions between those who stayed

with the old church and those who joined the new church were slight. On a list compiled in 1749, the average taxable wealth of old-church adherents, both members and attendants, was a bit higher. The greater average wealth of the old-church adherents reflects a greater average age, since wealth in this rural community, as in most, was highly correlated with age. The appeal of the old church was strongest among the oldest villagers. More than four-fifths of those aged sixty or older remained loyal to the church of their youth. The older people were either resistant to the appeal of the revival, or, if sympathetic, still unable to break with the church.

The community was not divided simply along generational lines. In fact, of the twenty-five combinations of fathers and sons on the 1749 list, seventeen were on the same side of the dispute. Of the eight remaining, only four were cleanly split along generational lines, with the father on one side and his son or sons on the other. It is this family cohesiveness that best explains the impact of the revival on Chebacco. Those householders of 1749 who stayed with the old church tended to be older men and their young sons, who were still to some degree dependent, while the new church captured most of the independent, middle-aged men who were drawn to New Light principles of conversionism and lay participation. They were able to break with the old church and create a new institution to embody those principles. Although the average age among the adherents of the old church (forty-four) was only a litle higher than the new (forty-one), the averages reflect different realities. The new-church average is truly representative, while the old-church figure is only an average of ages that cluster at the nether ends of the spectrum. Respect for age and a father's control over the family property kept most young adult males in line with their elderly fathers' opinions, in this as in other matters. As to the rest of the villagers, it was hard for these eighteenth-century men to break with an institution sanctioned by long custom and, some said, divinity. Those who did break away and those who did not could not regard one another with equanimity. It was a matter too grave for tolerance. With Cleaveland's ordination in February 1747, the breach was final, and the five years of internal bitterness and hostility finally burst forth into public debate.

In March 1747, Theophilus Pickering published a pamphlet entitled *A Bad Omen to the Churches of New-England: in the Instance of Mr. John Cleaveland's Ordination so termed, over a Separation in Chebacco-parish in Ipswich,*[103] in which he told of his attempts to persuade Nathaniel Rogers, John Rogers, and Ipswich's First Church not to ordain Cleaveland. Several months later, Cleaveland and his new congregation composed a reply. In early October, the new church published *A Plain Narrative of the Proceedings which Caused the Separation.* Their strategy was revealed in the subtitle, "a Relation of the Cause which produced the Effects" (i.e., the ordination) that Pickering had "exhibited" in his "late print." In a detailed narrative of the events of the past five years, they described their attempts to resolve their difficulties "in a Way of Order," by church meeting or by council. Pickering's obstruction of those means, they argued, justified their separation. The "Judicious and Impartial" would see who was "most to blame, Mr. Pickering and Adherents, who so evilly entreated us for so many Years together, or we who by this Treatment were drove to this Pass."[104]

The terms of the debate were clear and conventional—who was at fault? Both sides argued learnedly from the Cambridge Platform and customary church practice. Both sought to determine whether the "aggrieved brethren" had had sufficient cause to withdraw from the old church. But Cleaveland, in voicing the Separates' thoughts, also explored other grounds for their separation. He began the pamphlet with a short prefatory essay on the nature of

church covenants. His description was simple: "As all Covenants, so Church-Covenants, suppose two Parties, each of
which have something to perform as a Condition dependent
on each other." The individual owed obedience, the church
owed such "Privileges and Advantages, as the Word, Sacra-
ments, Discipline etc. agreable to the Gospel." If the
church did not provide these, and blocked "Relief . . . in a
Way of Order," then a member might "seek Relief in a
Way Extrajudicial, since the main Thing in Religion, viz.
The Edification of the Person can't be obtained otherwise.
And to this all Forms however useful, must give Way."[105]

Pickering died a short time thereafter, but his death, and
the published attack by the Chebacco Separates, galvanized
his supporters into action. In February 1748, they published *The Pretended Plain Narrative Convicted of Fraud and
Partiality, Or a Letter from the Second Church in Ipswich to their
Separated Brethren.* They objected strenuously to the "defec-
tive, debasing accounts of Church-Covenants" given by
their opponents. They argued that Cleaveland's simple con-
tractual interpretation of the covenant was not founded in
tradition and provided "an unhappy Foundation of encouragement to factious and licentious Persons to trifle with so
sacred a thing as a Church-Covenant, . . . according to
their variable Humours and Wicked Lusts." It was, they
said, "destructive of Order, Peace, and Charity" to allow
"any discontented Member to judge the Truth of Facts,
from which his discontent ariseth, and also of the Nature
and Merit of them."[106]

The issue between the two factions in the parish was
expressed in the language of the covenant familiar to all
New England. John Cleaveland and his congregation, cit-
ing the experience of the sixteenth-century reformers and
the Puritans, argued for an earlier, purer version of the
tradition. This moved the men of the standing church from
passive support of their pastor to an active defense of in-

violability of the status quo against the "variable humours and wicked lusts" of individuals.

After Pickering's death, the Chebacco Separates proposed to the old church a reunion under Cleaveland's ministry. The old church refused and employed disciplinary action, church councils, and the taxing power possessed by legally established churches to punish the dissidents. Not until 1752, after six years of petitions, court trials, and General Court investigations, did they acquiesce in the legal recognition of Cleaveland's church.[107] However, the principles shared by Cleaveland and his new congregation eventually brought the community back together. During the tenure of Reverend Nehemiah Porter, Pickering's successor, the old church lost much of its membership owing to the death of the old men who had been stalwart in its defense and the departure of younger members to Cleaveland's church. When Porter was dismissed in 1766, the remaining members of the old church hired Cleaveland to preach to them as well. This arrangement continued until 1775, when the remnant of the old church joined the new under a covenant that reflected the long-standing principles of the new church.

These principles were a middle way between the vagaries of Separatism and the errors of the standing order. Using the Cambridge Platform of 1648 as its guide, the new church attempted to recapture the purity and rigor of the early church in New England. Membership became a matter of adult commitment. Prospective members were required to give public testimony of their religious experience, and the Half-Way Covenant was abandoned, although infant baptism was continued. The laity assumed a greater role in the church by the reinstitution of the office of lay elder, whose mandate was to rule "jointly and severally" with the pastor. More important, after their long struggle with Pickering, they recognized the right of members to ask for a church meeting in which they might "declare their mind, without interruption or hindrance," and they repudiated the ministerial veto.[108] This was the kind of church that Cleaveland's family had long favored. Nevertheless, despite increased lay participation, preaching remained the responsibility of their minister, who had had three years of professional training at Yale College. With Cleaveland providing the appropriate interpretation of tradition, the Chebacco New Lights designed the church to fit their notion of the venerable New England Way.

Under the young clergyman's direction, the church avowed a stricter orthodoxy than had been common in much of New England in years past. His family background, education at Yale, and associations with New Light ministers all inclined him toward the doctrines of the founders of New England. He preached the Calvinist doctrine of predestination without reservation, stressing the terrors of the damned and God's mercy to the elect. Of equal importance to the doctrine preached was the manner of preaching. Theirs was an "experimental religion" that called for preaching that grew out of the preacher's own religious experience.[109]

This middle way—reformed orthodoxy, lay participation, evangelical-style ministry—to which Cleaveland and his people adhered was the basis of the later reunification of the Chebacco church. It came, in time, to dominate rural New England. Its appeal to the people of New England gradually brought about fundamental changes in the rambling and diffuse congregational establishment, so that in 1781 a convention of the remaining Separate churches observed that "the Lord hath inclined many of the established Ministers, and Churches, to adopt the same Principles and Practice in reformation, that first influenced us."[110] Its success is testimony to the tenacious vitality of the pure-church ideal among the New England laity.

John Cleaveland's decision to settle in Chebacco was

based on shared sympathies. The pious, hardworking farm families of the village were similar in many ways to his own family. There he managed to reconcile his family religious background and his desire to be a settled, established minister. While so doing, he also helped the villagers to refashion their own religious tradition in a way satisfactory to both their awakened consciences and their sense of order. A farmer as well as a preacher, Cleaveland understood the people of Chebacco and shared their prejudices and aspirations.

CHAPTER THREE

✤

Land and Families

In CHEBACCO, JOHN CLEAVELAND, who had "labour[ed] hard . . . in farming business" as a young man, became a farmer once more. In Canterbury, the two older Cleaveland brothers had been given the family's lands, and John an education for the ministry, as their respective portions of the paternal estate. When John found a people for whom he had "love enough" to "stand and fall with them," he also found the livelihood that his ministerial education was supposed to guarantee. In a sense, then, it was the completion of his inheritance when his supporters provided him with an annual salary and, more important, a house and a forty-acre farm. The expectation of a farm and a salary made it possible for the newly ordained minister to marry, which he did in July 1747. He was now, in most respects, a member of the rising generation: young men marrying, starting families, and receiving property from the older generation. The experiences of that generation, which he would share fully and intimately as both farmer and pastor, were shaped by the village's economic structure.[1]

I. The Village Economy

In the eighteenth century, Chebacco village was surrounded by great open pastures to the north, heavily

wooded upland to the west and south, and broad marshes to
the east. The marshes were dotted with upland islands of
various sizes, the largest being Hog Island, which contained three substantial farms. The Chebacco River mean-
dered through marshy, wet lands to the sea, dividing the
parish in half. Near the coast there was a causeway across
the river, and on the north side of the causeway was the
village. Five miles further north along the coast road was
Ipswich, and thirty miles to the south lay Boston.[2]

Chebacco was settled, mostly in the 1670s and 1680s, by
the sons and daughters of Ipswich's founding generation.
Land was plentiful in the early days. The average holding
among the first settlers of Chebacco was nearly 140 acres;
60 percent owned between 75 and 160 acres. The village
population grew quickly, spurred by both in-migration and
natural increase. The most intense period of growth was between 1695 and 1718, when the population of the parish
almost doubled, because as the men of Ipswich's third generation came of age, lands in the outlying areas such as
Chebacco were portioned off to them by their fathers. These
young men moved to Chebacco, began families, and soon
swelled the village population even further. In 1720, Ipswich undertook a final division of common lands, granting
rights to more than 7,000 acres. Nearly 900 acres were in
Chebacco, mostly heavily wooded land between Chebacco
Pond and the Wenham border, which increased the available land by about 10 percent.[3]

By 1720 the great work of clearing land for farming was
well under way, aided by in-migration and the coming of
age of a new generation in the village. Early divisions of
family holdings had been advantageous, because there had
been plenty of land and not enough men to clear it. But for
John Cleaveland's contemporaries, men born in the 1720s,
this would not be so. The plain-speaking Chebacco minister
John Wise explained the plight of the old towns of Massachusetts as they approached the end of their first century:

Many of our Old Towns are too full of Inhabitants for Husbandry; many of them living upon small Shares of Land, and generally all are Husbandmen; . . . And also many of our People are slow in Marrying for want of Settlements.[4]

The people of Chebacco had to meet a serious challenge to their way of life. The growing population spurred a rapid increase in land prices. Between 1720 and 1749, the price per acre rose more than 40 percent. The rise was not even; some categories of land remained fairly stable. Much of the overall increase can be attributed to the dramatic rise in the price of homestead land, which nearly doubled in three decades. Farmers thought of their lands in two major categories, those "at home" and those outlying. The lands at home might fall into the same use categories—marsh, pasture, and wood—as lands outlying, but the convenience of closeness to the farmer's home increased their worth. The house lot itself, consisting of house, barn, outbuildings, fencing, orchard, and tillage land, increased greatly in value.[5]

However, the increasing scarcity of land in the community resulted neither in morselization nor in consolidation of the community's resources. The distribution of wealth, most of it landed wealth, changed little over the course of the eighteenth century. In part this stability in wealth structure reflected the declining rate of population growth: over 5 percent per year between 1695 and 1718, it fell thereafter to below 3 percent.* The earlier growth had been based on natural increase and in-migration, as families from within and without the parish filled its empty lands with a new generation of farmers. The later growth reflected natural increase, minus net out-migration.[6]

There were opportunities elsewhere for those who left Chebacco. The settlement of central Massachusetts, much of which took place between 1690 and 1740, opened up

*See Table 1, Appendix.

land from which farms could be made. The Cleveland family had responded to just such an opportunity in Connecticut in the 1690s. In 1735–1736, the older generation in Chebacco joined in two Ipswich petitions for land in unsettled parts. The first of these was by soldiers of the 1690 Canada expedition or their descendents. A grant called Ipswich-Canada (later Winchendon), next to grants called Rowley-Canada, Salem-Canada, and Dorchester-Canada, was made to them. John Choate, the politician son of old Thomas of Hog Island, led another group of petitioners, who likewise received a six-mile-square grant. Approximately a quarter of the proprietors in each group came from Chebacco, showing the village's interest in the open lands to the west.[7]

There were other opportunities closer to home. The men of the village had engaged in fishing and shipbuilding on a small scale since the 1660s, but the commercial development of Salem and its associated fishing ports of Gloucester and Marblehead far exceeded their efforts. The development of a substantial fishing fleet and some carrying trade on the North Shore brought young men from the inland farms to the port towns. Rapid population growth in those towns and the ratio thereby established of men to land reflected the growing importance of maritime enterprise.[8]

Maritime occupations and related trades also helped some to stay in the village. Population density suggests something of the changes taking place in the village. By 1749, Chebacco was as thickly settled as some long-settled farming towns would be at the time of the 1765 census. With nearly sixty people per square mile, some part of the population was supported, wholly or in part, by other than agricultural means.[9]

By mid-century, Chebacco had achieved stability, a workable balance of people and resources. Out-migration had slowed the growth of the population, and increased maritime opportunities helped to support some of those who remained. As a result, the price of land, which had risen more than 40 percent between 1730 and 1749, slowed to less than half that rate during the next two decades. This adjustment had been made without greatly altering the economic structure of the village. Stability and self-sufficiency were its outstanding characteristics down to the eve of the Revolution.

Chebacco as described in the 1771 valuation of property was still primarily a farming town, although the agricultural prospects of the land were never outstanding. The four most prominent soil types—tidal marsh, rough stony land, orono silt loam, and muck—were mostly unsuitable for cultivation. Much of the remaining soil was sandy or stony loams of various sorts.[10] The use made of the land tells much about the practice of agriculture in Chebacco. More than 90 percent of the improved land was devoted to livestock, either as pasturage or mowing land. The bit of cultivated land was clearly for home use only.

Chebacco's reliance on stock-raising was typical of the old seacoast towns. The farming towns west of Boston practiced more genuinely mixed agriculture with substantial acreage in both tillage and pasture. Crop raising was foremost only in the rich bottom lands of the Connecticut Valley.[11]

The poor quality of the soil and the large amounts of wet land along the coast and the river gave Chebacco farmers little alternative to stock-raising. As late as the mid-1780s, three fifths of the parish lands remained wooded and unimproved, apparently because they were not worth clearing except for firewood and building materials. The broad marshes that accounted for so much of the village land were good for salt hay and little else. But the prodigious output of these tidewater fields enabled Chebacco to support a large livestock population and, eventually, to export hay to neighboring communities.[12]

No farm in Chebacco was entirely devoted to commercial

agriculture. Farmers had to give priority to their own family's needs before thinking of the market. The bequest of
annual provisions and supplies that some men gave to their
widows can be extrapolated into the needs of a family of
five. These figures suggest a farm consisting of six to eight
acres of tillage, including a kitchen garden and orchard; fifteen acres of pasture, including fallow land, for grazing
animals; and fifteen to twenty acres of mowing land, salt or
fresh, for their winter hay. According to these require-
ments, a farm of about forty acres of improved land, plus
woodland sufficient to produce thirty or so cords of wood for
the fire, would provide a comfortable subsistence. In 1771,
farms of this size were common in Chebacco.[13] The farm
provided for John Cleaveland was, not coincidentally, just
such a farm.

Not everyone, however, was so fortunate. Fifty-six taxpayers were landless, and thirty-six of those were without
taxable property of any kind. The latter paid only a poll tax.
These men were not, however, members of a rural proletar-
iat. They were, for one thing, disproportionately younger
than the other taxpayers. Fifty-four percent were thirty
years old or younger, while only 26 percent of the taxpayers
as a whole were so young. Moreover, 28 percent of these
men were unmarried and without a house of their own.
John Cleaveland, Jr., eldest son of the minister, was listed
independently, although he was living in the parsonage and
working on the family farm.[14]

Few men in Chebacco received their inheritance before
the age of thirty.* Landlessness was a transient state for
most, a result of prolonged dependence or of old age. More
than three quarters of the landless were at one end of the inheritance process or the other. John, William, and Nehemiah Cogswell, all in their twenties, would in five years
succeed to old John's two farms, while Thomas Choate,

---

*See Table 2, Appendix.

aged seventy-eight, had passed on all his land to his sons, who in return had legally obligated themselves to provide for his support. For the remainder, landlessness was to be their "portion," and only one accumulated any property. Nathaniel Groton, an orphaned son of a landless shoemaker, in 1773 married Sarah, only daughter and heir of the recently deceased Samuel Cogswell. With the acquisition of his late father-in-law's seventy-acre farm, Groton changed instantly from a penniless artisan to a substantial yeoman. For most of the rest, death or migration ended their hard-scrabble existence in Chebacco before the next valuation in 1785.[15]

Men with insufficient lands were more often fixed in that status; only two fifths of these men were in the process of inheritance, either receiving or passing on their land. The problems of the insufficiently landed differed.* Josiah Burnham had only twenty-five acres of improved land, mostly in pasturage, but he was also a cooper, and his account books show an additional income of five or ten pounds per year. In 1760 he was paid five pounds, eleven shillings and two pence, 57 percent in kind, 43 percent in cash. The payments in kind included three and a half days' work, shoes, wood, a bushel of malt, and a couple of pigs. In this way he supplemented his income and supported his family. At the other end of the spectrum was the Emmerton family. Joseph, and his married son, Joseph, Jr., jointly owned a house, a pig, a cow, and an acre and a half of pasture. Both were fishermen, although they probably worked as farm laborers when they were not at sea. John Cleaveland recorded the sad fate of the older man:

27 Sept., 1782, Mr. Joseph Emmerton in his 70th year and Aaron Burnham in his 40th year are supposed to be drounded in the mouth of Chebacco River, as part of their boat and some of

---

*See Table 3, Appendix.

their clothes have been found; 8th November, J. E. was taken up at Bar Island and buried at Chebacco.

The little farm was mortgaged to Jeremiah Lee, Esq., a shipowner of Marblehead and probably Emmerton's employer. The estate was declared insolvent, sold, and the creditors paid from the proceeds at "ten shillings & eight pence three farthings & a half on the pound." Life was hard for the poor minority in Chebacco. They had to work much harder than the majority for their living, and could not retire or provide adequately for their children.[16]

Still, more than three quarters of the Chebacco farmers had, once had, or would have lands that could provide a comfortable subsistence. Some had more than that. Since stock-raising was the dominant type of agriculture, the distribution of livestock indicates the potential surplus for market. Only sheep were raised in numbers sufficient for commercial purposes. The population of cows, swine, horses, and oxen was sufficiently small and widely dispersed to forbid other than domestic consumption and use.[17] But there were 1,040 sheep in Chebacco in 1771, 40 percent more than in the entire town of Concord, and part of the great Ipswich flock of 5,000. Sheep were raised for wool and mutton, often for domestic consumption, since mutton could not be preserved by eighteenth-century means. Sheep were exported live, usually to the West Indies. By Cleaveland's time, sheep-raising was a declining enterprise. Between 1735 and 1767 in Massachusetts, the per capita holdings in sheep had fallen 25 percent. Between 1768 and 1772, the provincial exports of sheep also declined 25 percent, while exports of beef and other commodities remained stable. By the late 1760s, Chebacco's investment in sheep was, per capita, more than twice the county average.[18]

Ownership of sheep was widely dispersed in the village. The average flock consisted of sixteen sheep, at most twice that required for domestic needs. Many Chebacco farmers, then, raised a few extra sheep for a declining market, but no farmer was dependent on them for his livelihood. The continued investment of Chebacco farmers in sheep in the face of worsening economic prospects may be the result of their hay supply. Chebacco's best and most productive mowing land was marsh, and nearly 80 percent of its hay was salt hay. This was fine for the omnivorous sheep, but it made the milk produced by dairy cattle taste sour.[19]

Commercial farming was widely, if thinly, spread throughout the village, while nonagricultural commercial pursuits were narrowly restricted in number and kind. There was a small fleet of locally owned vessels, mostly small fishing boats of twenty tons' burden or less. Investment in them was confined to a small coterie that shared Choate connections and New Light principles. Elder Francis Choate, his sons Jacob and John, and his nephew Thomas owned 70 percent by tonnage. The next-largest lot was owned by Mary Eveleth Rust, daughter of Lieutenant James Eveleth, a New Light leader. Her recently deceased husband, Joseph Rust, an innkeeper, was also a nephew of Elder Choate. The remaining tonnage was owned by Abijah Wheeler, an old Gloucester shoreman turned Chebacco farmer and a New Light stalwart in the village's time of troubles.[20]

The other major commercial enterprises were three sawmills, a gristmill, a tannery, a brewery, and a tavern. The oldest of these was the Burnham sawmill, the rights to which had been granted by the town in 1667 to Thomas Burnham (d. 1694), a carpenter born in England. It passed from him to his son John (d. 1704), and then to his grandson Thomas (d. 1748). Thomas Burnham left the mill to his three sons. In 1771 it was owned by his son Jeremiah (one-fourth share), and his grandsons Joseph (one-fourth), son of Nathan, and Thomas (one-half), son of Thomas. Five generations and 104 years had passed since the privilege was granted to the first Thomas Burnham.[21] The second sawmill, owned jointly by the Story and Eveleth families since at least 1715, had been set up in 1671 by William Story, like Burnham a carpenter. In 1771 it was owned jointly by Seth and Zechariah Story (one-half) and James Eveleth (one-half), now all in their eighties. Another Story-family saw-mill, of more recent origins, was owned by Lieutenant Jacob Story and his son Jonathan, son and grandson of old Jacob, who was Seth and Zechariah's cousin.[22]

The gristmill had been in operation since before 1687, when it was moved from its first location to a spot near the Chebacco Falls. John Burnham, who also owned the saw-mill, passed it on at his death in 1704 to his three younger sons, Jacob (one-fifth), Jonathan (two-fifths), and David (two-fifths). They still owned it in 1771, although their great age had put it effectively in the control of their sons.[23]

The "mault-house," or brewery, was well established at the death of Deacon Thomas Low, aged eighty, in 1712. It was owned in 1771 by his grandson Samuel. The tavern in Chebacco was established by Lieutenant Nathaniel Rust, Jr., the first schoolmaster, sometime before his death in 1711. His widow, son, and grandson after him were inn-holders. The tannery was begun in the 1720s by Francis Cogswell; in 1743, he sold it to Joseph Perkins and Thomas Choate, Jr., who were brothers-in-law. In 1754, Perkins became sole owner.[24]

The structure of business in Chebacco was very stable. From 1720, or even 1700, to 1771 the ownership, number, and kind of businesses had changed very little. These enterprises were conceived less as commercial opportunities than as family rights and communal responsibilities, and there were no more of them than the community required. The public grant that brought them into being conveyed rights as secure as those in property.[25] For their owners these enterprises were, moreover, secondary and supplemental to farming. They owned farms well above the community average in value. Trades and crafts were also supplemental. Some relied on the income from a craft more than others did, but the possession of such skills was widespread in the village. Francis Choate, an elder in the church, justice of the peace, and owner of 180 acres, was a practicing blacksmith.[26]

Stock-raising is not a labor-intensive kind of agriculture, so time remained, particularly in the winter, for the practice of a trade. Young men, in the prolonged dependence brought about by late marriage and later inheritance, learned shoemaking, fishing, carpentry—useful and profitable occupations. These too were passed along in families. Chebacco had several generations of blacksmiths named Choate or Foster, carpenters named Low, Story, or Burnham, and shoemakers named Perkins.

And yet, identification with a trade was rare. Most men called themselves yeomen, although inventories often listed the tools of a trade. This is a key to their self-perception. They might make shoes or build buildings, but while they owned land they saw themselves as yeomen farmers, not tradesmen. It was around land that their lives were built.[27]

The men of John Cleaveland's generation engaged in a great many land transactions, mostly with fellow townsmen and mostly for land in Chebacco. There were forty-three nonresident taxpayers in 1771 who lived in neighboring towns such as Wenham, Beverly, Gloucester, and Manchester. Their holdings averaged less than five acres each; together they owned 190 acres of marsh. There were similar holdings in the untaxed and abundant woodlands. The outside holdings of Chebacco farmers were similar—mostly marsh and woodland in adjacent villages. Since the original land grants had been made by town governments, family properties tended to be concentrated in one jurisdiction or another. Furthermore, the practical necessities of farming required the concentration of most of one's property in one area.[28]

Almost every member of Cleaveland's generation dealt in

land at one time in his life. Much of this activity occurred within families. Many dealings involved transferring land from father to son, dividing it among brothers, or selling the wife's share in her father's estate to her brothers. Nearly half of the dealings of men with fewer than ten land transactions were with other family members. John Cleaveland, whose forty-odd acres of improved land were just a few acres shy of the average, was involved in the land market in precisely this way. His first four transactions, in the late 1740s and the 1750s, were with his wife's family, and were made, apparently, to secure control of his farm.[29]

The opportunity for more ambitious investments in land was restricted. About a quarter of Cleaveland's contemporaries had eleven or more transactions, and this group had half again as much improved land as the average. Moreover, only a quarter of their dealings were within their families, leaving a much higher margin for more commercial transactions. Almost all of their investments were local. They bought land from out-migrants, often from sons left with insufficient land. Sometimes financial crisis brought land onto the market, as when William Goodhue's inherited debt forced the sale of his farm, 120 acres in all, in eight transactions between 1726 and 1740.[30] In fact, the probate court frequently made land available, since the executors of 25 percent of all estates had to sell at least some land to meet obligations. Much of trade in land, however, was not in homestead land, but in unimproved land, woodlots, or marsh.

Investment in land for most Chebacco farmers was closely tied to the life cycle of their families. These men bought land during the years after they received their inheritances but before their children came of age. Then, in their late forties and fifties they would, as Cleaveland's father had done, sell off land to provide capital for daughters and younger sons. This pattern of behavior was most marked among the men, a majority, who had fewer than ten land transactions during their life; more than two thirds of their dealings in land before age forty-five were purchases, while three fifths of their later dealings were sales. The investment of excess capital in land, and the sale of it to provide for the rising generation, helped to keep the distribution of land stable. More important to the stability of the village, though, was inheritance. Most people got most of their land, especially the more valuable homestead land, from the older generation, rather than from the open market.[31]

Like that of his ancestors in Woburn and Canterbury, John Cleaveland's future was to be shaped by the scarcity of land. In a populous and long-settled village like Chebacco, it was a concern for every family. The men of Cleaveland's generation lived in a crowded but stable and predictable world.* Their fate was determined by the tough and adaptable family networks that, guided by custom and communal sanction, passed and distributed scarce resources from one generation to the next. These families, although seeking primarily their own self-preservation, were the means by which the community balanced men and resources and attained stability.

II. Marriage

Not marriage but birth itself began the process by which a generation was pared to fit available resources. Even with the relatively healthful conditions typical of colonial New England, perhaps as many as one child in three died before the age of twenty. In this generation, migration from Chebacco removed nearly another third, since children migrated with their parents. But for the hundred or so young men of Cleaveland's generation who remained, marriage marked the first step toward their destined position in the adult world.[32]

---

*See Table 4, Appendix.

John Cleaveland began his courtship of Mary Dodge in the fall of 1746. In February 1747, he was ordained by the Separate Church in Chebacco and accepted in matrimony. In his proposal, Cleaveland stressed spiritual affinity and free choice in marriage. "We are one," he wrote upon her acceptance, "in judgement affection and by a free choice of each other for the most near social union." As awakened Christians and descendants of Puritans, they were aware of the dangers of earthly affections. She was concerned that her reply "shewed too fond a temper" and he asked "to be righted" if "you do think I discover too much fondness towards you." There was, he added, "some danger thereof . . . seeing my mind is so strangely engaged in real affection towards you."[33]

The place of affection and the play of free choice in marital selection can be seen in their previous experiences of courtship. Mary Dodge had first been fervently courted by her cousin Ezekiel Dodge, who was preparing for the ministry at Harvard College. He said that "if rivaled or repulsed" he would "leave the university for a silent wood" and become "a right down hermit." Cleaveland too had courted a cousin, Olive Johnson of Canterbury, who wrote in September 1746 to say that she was "no longer halt between two opinions," although she loved him "as a cousin and brother," she would choose another.[34]

Cleaveland mentioned judgment as well as affection, which in context may have meant shared religious conviction but which may also have stood for more practical limitations on freedom of marital choice. Cleaveland, "considering his profession and station," sought a bride both pious and well placed. Olive Johnson was the daughter of Colonel Obadiah, Canterbury's wealthiest and most influential citizen. Mary Dodge offered comparable dowry and local connections.

Twenty years after his own marriage, Cleaveland told his daughter to "chuse for yourself" one "most agreable both to your judgment and fancy" to be "your nearest and dearest friend." Despite this romantic prescription, he took care to make the elements of choice clear to her: "character, parentage, [and] worldly estate."[35] The same attitude was more directly expressed by Zechariah Story, Jr., a young sailor of Chebacco who compiled a list of marriage maxims. The marital calculus of cash and chastity was well put in his fifteenth and seventeenth maxims "For the Woman":

In love you shall successful be if you
Retain your chastye,

Your husband makes you a rich wife
And happy too shall be your life.[36]

Character is not susceptible to measurement but wealth is, and its measurement in this instance suggests the influence of family wealth on marital choice. Eldest sons, entitled by custom and the law of intestacy to a larger share in their father's estate, were less than half as likely to marry a woman from a family less wealthy than their own than were their younger brothers. Persistence, continued residence in the community, also bespeaks economic wellbeing. Eighty-two percent of the men remaining in Chebacco married a woman from a family equal or superior to their own in economic standing, while only 20 percent of their more mobile brothers did.[37]

In his own marital bargaining, Cleaveland, unlike most men, traded on his professional status to secure a well-dowered and well-connected bride. His wife's mother belonged to the wealthy and influential Choate family, leaders of the New Light faction in Chebacco. Doubly bound to Cleaveland by ties of religious conviction and kinship, the family of Mary Dodge Cleaveland drew upon their resources to make him a kind of joint heir. When a farm in the village came up for sale consisting "of 45 acres of land[,] a double house (not quite finished) and a barn upon it," Cleaveland appealed to his father for a loan. Later that month (September 1748), the price was met without the help of the elder Cleaveland. One third was paid by Mary's brother Nehemiah Dodge, another third by her uncle, Elder Francis Choate of the new church, and the remainder by another Choate uncle, several Choate cousins, and a few other Cleaveland supporters. Ninety percent of the purchase price was met by his wife's family.[38]

Most men in Chebacco married in their mid- to late twenties, most women in their early twenties. When John Cleaveland and Mary Dodge married in July 1747, they were, at twenty-five and twenty-four, closer in age thàn most couples. Marriage ended a long adolescence of labor on the farm for young men and women. It began or furthered the transfer of property to the rising generation, the expectation of which shaped marital choice. Marriage did not, however, end dependence.[39]

Although aging fathers would come to rely more and more on their sons to manage their farms, and some even surrendered ownership, most men remained dependent until their fathers died. Only 16 percent of Cleaveland's generation received all their property before their fathers' death, although another 16 percent received some part beforehand. Two thirds, then, of Chebacco's sons coming of age in the 1740s and 1750s had to wait for their fathers' deaths to receive their property. While most sons inherited by age forty, more than 40 percent did not.* Twenty-five percent were age fifty or older when they inherited.[40]

Favored sons experienced their dependence most directly by sharing the homestead with their fathers. More than 11 percent of all taxpayers in 1749 lived and worked in such an arrangement. The twenty-four sons involved ranged in age from seventeen to forty-two, although two thirds were between twenty-one and thirty. Three fifths were married. The life span of these arrangements varied according to the

---

*See Table 5, Appendix.

longevity or charity of the father. Nathan Burnham, aged about thirty, received the rest of his inheritance late in 1749 after his father's death. More than half of them had succeeded to the property by 1760, but a few waited until the 1770s. Jacob Goodhue was twenty-six in 1749, with a wife and two children. His father, John, was sixty-four. Jacob did not assume full control of the property for twenty-five years more, until John's death in 1774.[41]

The coresidence of householder and heir was more common than the figure 11 percent would indicate. Seventeen out of eighteen parents listed with their sons were at least fifty years old, comprising almost 40 percent of the total number of taxpayers over fifty in the community. The coresidence of a farmer and his adult son was a stage in the history of many families and not simply an alternative living arrangement.

The overall level of coresidence was high in the long-settled areas of New England. According to the 1765 census, one third of the families in the eastern countries, excepting Essex, shared a house. In Essex County and in Ipswich, more than 50 percent did so. The simple but ample house of the sort John and Mary Cleaveland moved into in the fall of 1748—with two chambers above and below, a central chimney, and kitchen in the lean-to—was described by him as "a double house." Finding a place meant more than housing for the young men of the village. They faced resources unequal to their numbers, as had their fathers before them. The problem, while communal in its implications, was resolved individually.[42]

III. Inheritance

The adult experience of the generation of which Cleaveland became a part can be summarized simply. Nearly two thirds remained permanently in Chebacco; the rest migrated. The result was an acceptable ratio of men to resources. It was achieved by means of the inheritance system, a complex amalgam of law, custom, and personal preference.[43]

The law of inheritance in Massachusetts was promulgated in 1692 and remained largely unchanged throughout the provincial period. It reflected the experience of land-poor seventeenth-century Englishmen in land-rich New England. It contained, however, a new provision that offered an alternative to division of the estate among the heirs, if to do so would risk "spoiling the whole." This bespeaks an awareness of scarcity that looked back to the English past and forward to the provincial future. The act also protected the widow's dower, which was a one-third share of the real estate "for life" and of the personal property "forever," from the deceased's will or his creditors. In the absence of a will, the children were guaranteed equal shares, with the exception of a double share to the eldest son.[44]

Customary prescription was also compelling. The daughter's share, whether defined by her father or the probate court, seldom included land. Her right in the estate was realized as movable, personal property: household goods and money. Land descended in the male line.[45]

Despite these limitations, the farmer who chose to distribute his property in his lifetime retained considerable freedom, especially in dealing with his children. He could divide his property among them in any way, entail it to the next generation, even pass over them entirely. The choices made by individuals are a useful indicator of personal and social goals.

There were several ways for a man to pass his property on to his children. He could grant or sell it, bequeath it by will, or allow a settlement to be made after his death by the probate court. The first two alternatives involved planning, the last a passive reliance on the law of intestacy, the heirs, and the judge of probate. The great majority—80 percent—of estates in Chebacco were settled by one of these methods. Of the unrecorded remainder, more than two thirds involved less than ten acres of land; more than half involved no land at all. Most of the rest were of unknown size. Very little real property passed through this system unrecorded.[46]

Of those estates whose transfer was recorded, three quarters were divided by will or deed, only one quarter by the posthumous process of the probate court.* The choice of one means or the other was influenced by the amount of property involved. Nearly half of the estates settled by the probate court had fewer than twenty acres, while only one of those divided according to parental will had so few acres. These figures, along with the small size of estates without record of disposition, suggest that property below a certain size did not merit careful planning. The heirs most probably made an informal division of what remained after the debts were settled. Some of these smaller estates may have been probated only because of pressure by the creditors, since many were absorbed by debt.

Among the posthumously settled estates that had more than twenty acres, there was a different pattern. Most of the original owners died between the ages of forty and fifty-five; two thirds left minor children. The cause of death was seldom recorded, but one at least died "suddenly"; another died at sea. Some of these men undoubtedly intended to do by law what others did by will, that is, leave the estate in the widow's hands during the children's minority. Some, with ample opportunity to plan, had little incentive to do so. John Cogswell, aged sixty-six at death and without wife or child, simply allowed his small landholding to revert to his siblings. The overall pattern is quite clear. Most farmers with adult children and at least moderate-sized holdings took upon themselves the task of distribution.[47]

This task was often made difficult by an overabundance

---

* See Table 6, Appendix.

of heirs. Yet the reverse situation could be even more trou-
bling. The choices made by men without heirs, or without
male heirs, offered a contemporary definition of family
boundaries and obligations.

Farmers invested much of their energies and resources in
providing for their children. It was the great task of most
lives, and an important measure of success or failure according to community standards. A man without heirs was incomplete, for he had no one to carry his name and property
into the next generation. Naming patterns reflect this understanding of the child's role. Virtually every husband and
wife named a child after themselves, repeatedly if necessary,
and then turned to other relatives. Mary Cleaveland, herself
bearing her mother's name, explained the function of naming in celebrating the birth of a nephew:

December the 28: 1742
This day at won o clock was born to my brouther a sone to bare up
the name of my dece'd father glory be to God that he has not left
us with out name and memory.

Naming placed a child socially in relation to the older generation; the considerations involved were pecuniary as well
as pious.[48]

A man without children might endow some charity, give
to his relatives, or do nothing and allow the estate to revert
to his siblings. In almost every case such men chose a principal heir from among their brothers' sons. In lieu of children, they acknowledged by bequests the next degree of
relation—brothers and sisters, nieces and nephews—but
concentrated their estate on one member of the younger
generation, usually a male who bore the same last name.
The fortunate young man might also carry his uncle's first
name, since most hard-pressed farmers would gladly offer
up a namesake to a childless brother or brother-in-law.
After the death of his children in the throat-distemper epi-
demic, the next male child born to each of Colonel John

Choate's two younger brothers and to his younger sister was named for him. Benjamin Proctor likewise had three namesakes, and Grover Dodge had one. The young man, when selected, assumed the heir's role in running the farm.[49]

Men without sons, a more common occurrence, had different options. When faced with the choice of keeping the land in the patrilineal family or passing it on through their daughters, they invariably chose the latter alternative. So it was that Nathaniel Cogswell got the bulk of his grandfather Jonathan Wade's land, as Grover and Nehemiah Dodge did from their grandfather William Grover, and as Gifford Gouldsmith did from his grandfather Gifford Cogswell. Abijah Haskell might have been similarly advantaged had not his grandfather Abijah Wheeler changed his mind. Wheeler halved his eldest daughter's share in his estate because "she and her husband have behaved undutifully towards me in taking away from me their son Abijah which I bro't up from a infant." He turned instead to his second daughter, Lucy, and her husband, Samuel Proctor, offering their "eldest surviving male heir . . . when of age . . . the right of redeeming all of my real estate." In these arrangements the son-in-law fulfilled the role of principal heir, eventually holding the land in trust for his own sons.[50]

These men ostensibly violated the customary bias against female inheritance, but in fact they simply reached through their daughters to a male descendant of the next generation. Because these farmers understood family in a fairly narrow sense, blood descendants were always preferred over collateral kin, even of the same name. In an extreme case, Samuel Cogswell passed over a Cogswell nephew, grand-nephew, and several great-grand-nephews, one of whom was thoughtfully named for him, and gave his entire property to his only living child, a daughter unmarried and childless. Within two months of his death, she married, at age thirty-five, a propertyless artisan four years her junior, doubtless to the dismay of the expectant nephews.[51]

Most farmers, however, suffered no shortage of heirs. In making necessary choices among these descendants, they were governed by laws and by customs generally recognized and agreed upon by the community. These laws and customs, moderated by individual idiosyncracies, determined the future makeup of the community.

Daughters were provided for differently from sons. Their shares or "portions" of the estate were usually equal, regardless of seniority, and paid in personal property, usually household goods or money. In posthumously settled estates, their portion was theoretically equal to that of any other sibling, excepting only the eldest brother, but even then they were seldom given land. Indeed, this agricultural society thoroughly and effectively separated women from the ownership of land. Widows were almost never accorded more than a life interest in land, whether by wills or by the law of intestacy. Daughters were seldom given or bequeathed land, especially if they had living brothers, and they fared no better in the settlement of estates. In most cases they agreed to monetary compensation in lieu of land, but even if the estate was fully divided, daughters held land only at the pleasure of their brothers, who had a right of redemption, that is, the right to repurchase the land at the original valuation in order of seniority. Law and custom combined to keep land within the patrilineal family, excluding daughters and widows, because at marriage a woman's property became her husband's. In this sense, in the eyes of the community a daughter was less a part of her father's family than was a son. She owed primary loyalty not to her father, nor, in the case of a widow, to her children, but to her current husband. The right of a woman in the family lands was determined by this understanding.[52]

It was the sons, not the daughters, who contributed farm labor, support in old age, and, eventually, a successor to carry on the family name and position in the village. For nearly 13 percent of Chebacco farmers, this progression was not a matter for concern, because they had only one male heir. A somewhat higher percentage of men with only one son, rather than directing the distribution of the estate by will and deed, allowed the allocation to be settled after their death. In a time of fairly high childhood mortality and little conscious birth limitation, to have only one male heir was as much a cause of concern for the parents as it was good fortune for the heir. The parents involved must often have felt anxious about the single life that separated them from the plight of those without male heirs. Mary Cleaveland described her late brother as the "staff" of her mother's "old age on which she hoped to lean."[53]

Most fathers, however, were forced to make hard choices, to give land to some sons and not to others. Nearly two out of five of those who settled their own estates, and half of those whose estates were settled after their death, left one or more sons without any land. This decision was at once the most difficult and the most important that most men ever faced. It was just such a decision as this that brought the Cleaveland family to Connecticut and John Cleaveland to Chebacco. These farmers had to balance the conflicting demands of their children, of their desire to maintain the family's position in the community, and of the practical necessities of life in an agricultural community.

From a strictly economic perspective, it would have been best to give all the land to one son. The farmers of Chebacco, however, made little use of impartible inheritance. In the eighteenth century, only 10 percent of men with sons to choose among chose to endow one with all the land. Time did not strengthen this tendency. The highest percentage of such transmissions before 1790 (17 percent) occurred between 1730 and 1749, the transitional decades after the early days of abundant land. Hence, 90 percent of men who disposed of their own land by deed or will did so to two or more sons; 48 percent did so to three or more sons. About 60 percent of all farmers stretched their resources so that all of their sons might have some land. The father was influenced to some degree by the amount of land he had to divide among his sons. In an overwhelming majority of cases, however, the family lands did not pass intact to the next generation.[54]

This prodigality of the Chebacco farmers seems to negate the careful planning done in their wills and deeds. The picture is misleading, however, since some men found ways other than exclusion to preserve the integrity of family holdings in Chebacco. A fortunate 10 percent were able to provide sons with land outside of the village, usually in central Massachusetts or southern New Hampshire. Captain David Low, who died in 1746, and Jonathan Cogswell, Esq., who died in 1752, left some of their sons with lands in Ipswich-Canada (later Winchendon), land that they had petitioned for in 1735. Others, more than 20 percent, gave some sons relatively small bits of land in Chebacco, obviously inadequate for their entire support. William Gidding, the long-time parish clerk, left his son Thomas a house and forty-acre farm, while his son Daniel got only eleven acres of upland and marsh on the north side of Gidding's Island.[55] These bits of land could, in combination with a trade, enable a son to remain in the village.

This pattern of behavior suggests the dilemma of the aging farmer with several sons. He wanted to keep them about him to be the "staff of his old age." Their support was both psychological and economic; the old man relied on their hard work as well as their love and companionship. Yet he also wanted to maintain the family's position in the community, and in any case was reluctant to divide his holdings beyond that which would support a family. The dilemma could not easily be resolved. Most men worked out an accommodation between the poles of impartible inheritance and equal division of their real estate. Only two men, William Cogswell and James Eveleth, approached the extremes. Cogswell, who died in 1762, passed over his four oldest sons and endowed Jonathan, the youngest, with his six-room "mansion" and 178-acre farm. Jonathan came to be a town officer, a deacon, and, at his brothers' expense, the second-richest man in the village. Eveleth, on the other hand, divided his 205-acre "upper" and "lower" farms among his five children, one son, and four daughters, two of whom lived in Connecticut. The estate was soon absorbed by the surrounding farms, and the family disappeared from Chebacco within a generation. The harsh consequences of decisions such as these indicate why most men sought the middle ground.[56]

Posthumously settled estates were handled differently. The participants in these settlements included the heirs, the widow, three weighty and substantial local men as assessors, and the judge of probate, a position held from 1756 to 1765 by Chebacco's Colonel John Choate. According to the 1692 "Act for the settlement and distribution of the estates of intestates," the judge appointed three "sufficient freeholders" to assess and divide the estate, unless the heirs could "mutually agree of a division among themselves beforehand." In 1749 the male heirs of Thomas Burnham divided their father's lands among themselves "by mutual agreement" and compensated their sister. Once the division was made, the awarding of specific shares was referred to the heirs, although theoretically the judge could do as he wished. The judge could also, on advice from assessors or heirs, decide that the "estate in houses and lands" could not be divided "without great prejudice to, or spoiling of the whole" and give it all to the eldest son, who would compensate the others for their shares. This was a very flexible and subjective principle much dependent on the will of the parties involved. In the mid-1730s, William Butler's ninety-six-acre farm was granted to the oldest of his sons, while John Foster's sixty-acre farm was divided evenly among his three sons. The widow's participation was based on her dower rights, which could be divided off from the rest of the estate for her lifetime at her request, and her supervisory authority over minor children. The settlement process was conciliatory in nature and aimed at peaceful agreement among the parties involved. The wider spectrum of interests represented and the more direct input of community sentiment through the judge and the assessors resulted in more strictly settled estates. In comparison with paternally divided estates, they were more likely to deny one or more sons a share in the real property, and more likely to settle all the land on one son.[57] This pattern was even more evident in the distribution of middle-sized estates, those between 40 and 100 acres. In these cases, fathers were only half as likely to leave a son without land as the assorted interests that assumed his responsibility after his death.

Paternal decisions, when measured against the practice in probate for intestacy, inclined toward division rather than impartibility. The greater strength of the heirs, the judge, and the assessors in resisting divisions suggests that community opinion and economic realities called for a somewhat sterner attitude than most fathers were willing to adopt toward their own sons. Especially in the case of the more than 20 percent who concentrated their land on one son but still carved out a piece for one or more of the others, paternal fondness led men to stretch their resources to the limits of economic feasibility. It is important to note that while resources in land may have been stretched to the limits, they seldom went beyond that point. In the end, only a handful of the men who devised their estates before the Revolution failed to leave at least one son with a house and forty acres. Almost every man whose own lands were adequate left a successor with an agricultural competency.

Adherence to the principle of seniority among sons, solidly based on custom and the law of intestacy, helped to reduce some of the inevitable tensions. So too did the fact that younger sons, left without land, could expect other provisions from the paternal estate. The inheritance of land,

and hence the ability to continue in the community, were strongly affected by one's place in the birth order.* Nearly three quarters of the men in Cleaveland's generation who remained in Chebacco were either first or second sons. In Canterbury, Connecticut, Cleaveland's own family conformed to this pattern: his two elder brothers were given the family land, and the three younger went with family support to seek their fortunes elsewhere. In Chebacco, John Cleaveland's "mobile" inheritance, his education, and his training for the ministry won him a place in the ranks of the young farmers who were gradually assuming control of the community's resources and responsibility for families of their own.

IV. Family Responsibilities

Land or the expectation of land sufficient to justify remaining in Chebacco entailed a complex series of familial obligations, first to the older generation, then to one's siblings, and finally to a new generation altogether. Children arrived to confirm the new marriages, although sometimes too soon for respectability. The young Cleavelands, by inclination and necessity models of proper social behavior, were married a full year before their first child was born.[58] The baby girl was named Mary, a name she shared with her mother, grandmother, and great-grandmother. After eighteen months there was another child, a son, who was given his father's name, which in turn had been given to his father in memory of a childless uncle. John sent word to his family in Connecticut, and his mother, still caught up in the Awakening, sent her blessing:

When I red your letter and came to that passag where you say his name is John my soul lept with a suden glimps it was one that should lean on Jesus Crist pray for Zion they shall prosper that love him.

---

*See Table 7, Appendix.

That done, she passed on the news that "your brother Elisha hath another son a fat one and his name is Josiah." She concluded: "Bless the Lord O my soul and forget not all his benefits."[59]

John and Mary Cleaveland had seven more children in the next sixteen years. The names of the younger children were mostly given in remembrance, more often of Dodges than of Cleavelands.* The relatives so honored were quite close, parents and siblings for the most part. Only the fourth child bore the name of a living relative. John's younger brother Ebenezer had been expelled from Yale with him and had also become a New Light minister, settling in a neighboring Gloucester parish.[60] The fourth child's name commemorated those special ties. Mary Cleaveland, in her journal, took special notice of the children born to her. The journal, which she kept from January 1750 to December 1762, contains only thirteen entries. Eight deal with childbirth or baptism, four with the death of people in the community, and one with George Whitefield's visit to their home in 1754. She marked out these events as milestones in her life.[61]

Her theme was the radical contingency of human existence. Her principle of inclusion for deaths was suddenness, not family ties, for she passed over the deaths of her brother and father-in-law. Instead, she took note of those torn from life without warning by a bolt of lightning, a fire, or a rapid fever. The solemn message to be drawn from these misfortunes was always the same: "Be ye allso raddey for in such an hour as yee think not the son of man cometh."[62]

Childbirth carried a similar message. After each she thanked God for "appearing . . . in the perilous [work?] of child baring" and making her "the liveing mother of another liveing child." Each confinement was a reminder of mortality, each live birth an instance of mercy. After her third, she asked, "May I never forget the goodness of God

---

*See Table 8, Appendix.

85

to me and mine . . . that when God is taking others away by death I am stil spar'd." Children were cause for rejoicing. After her fifth she recalled "the goodness of God . . . who has apered for me so often," but childbirth, like death itself, carried a somber message for the Christian woman. She expressed this mixture of fear and faith most fully in the last entry, written after her seventh delivery, just a few months before her fortieth birthday.

December the 28th 1762
I was safly delivered of annother child[.] Her name is Abigail[.] The Lord was better to me than my fears and better then to some others and much better than my deserts[.] May I in return give up my self and all my children to be the Lords to be for him and for no other.

She was grateful for her fertility, especially so when she produced sons, and twice thanked God that she was not cursed like the barren fig tree in Mat. 21:18–22. She celebrated the baptism as well as the birth of her sons, recognizing their entrance into the Christian community because of their greater importance in the eyes of the world.[63]

John and Mary Cleaveland had reason to be thankful, for God had vouchsafed them both her life and the lives of their first seven children. The children survived the rigors of childbirth and the dangers of adolescence; in fact, all but one saw their father to his grave in 1799. In a society where one might expect to lose one child in three before the age of twenty, the minister's family enjoyed great good fortune. Soon, however, the parsonage came to know the sorrows that had afflicted other households. In 1767 Mary Cleaveland, approaching forty-five and nearly five years past her last pregnancy, gave birth to twin girls, who died within ten days. It was still a large, and on the whole, healthy family of a size typical among couples who survived the childbearing years together.[64]

In the early 1760s, John and Mary Cleaveland, now

middle-aged, were responsible for a large and complex household. Besides themselves and their seven children there was a slave, Pompie, a servant, Hannah Bear, and Mary's niece, Elizabeth Dodge. Pompie had come to the Cleavelands by inheritance. Hannah Bear was a forty-year-old spinster from the fishing village of Manchester, who underwent conversion in the revival of 1763 and joined the Chebacco church. Elizabeth Dodge had been left in her aunt and uncle's care by her father, whose death in 1758 made her an orphan. The little girl, although placed in her aunt's young family, was "not debar[red] . . . from staying sometimes with her grandmother," who had raised the motherless girl. She remained with her aunt until her marriage in 1770 to Jonathan Goodhue, a young man of Chebacco.[65]

Elizabeth Dodge's experience illustrates the working of the family network in times of crisis. While John and Mary were her "overseers," they had her share of the household goods, to use or sell for her support, and 5 pounds annually from the rental of Nehemiah's estate. When Elizabeth reached age eighteen, she could claim living space in the Dodge homestead and a dowry of 200 pounds paid in annual installments of 40 pounds by her three older brothers. It was a handsome dowry, equal to or better than that which Mary Dodge brought to John Cleaveland in 1747, better by far than what Cleaveland could do for his own daughters. She was absorbed, no doubt warmly, into her aunt's household, but economically she remained separate, dependent on her father's estate.[66]

The other additions to the Cleaveland household have a different significance. Pompie, a solitary slave in a white household, was representative of blacks in rural New England. Cleaveland inherited Pompe from his father in 1751. Thereafter he usually had a slave in the household. It is questionable whether slavery on this basis made economic sense, since one could hire day labor more cheaply, but it may have rewarded him in other ways. In 1771, the six other slaveholders in the parish, owning eight slaves among them, came from the uppermost strata of village society, with landholdings more than twice the average. Slave owning may have been for Cleaveland a way of making manifest his high position in the community.[67]

Hannah Bear, spinster, also represented a marginal social position, although one whose numbers were growing rapidly. Throughout eastern Massachusetts, the selective migration of young men had reduced the marriage chances of young women. By 1765 in Essex County, there were only 85 men over the age of sixteen for every 100 women. Hannah Bear, the daughter of a poor fisherman, was one of those who did not marry. She does not seem to have been, like many of her kind, a poor relation, but her position in the household was probably similar to that of one.[68]

The Cleaveland household, though large, had only two generations in residence. Mary's mother lived on the Dodge homestead in the Hamlet Parish, first with her husband, then with her son and his wife, and, after 1758, with her three adolescent grandsons. John's widowed mother lived in Canterbury, Connecticut, with her eldest son and his family. The Cleaveland farm in Chebacco came to them because of his position, not in the usual way through inheritance, so the care of their widowed mothers devolved on others in the family.

Because wives were usually younger than their husbands, most men (four fifths in Chebacco) left widows. Twenty-four men in Cleaveland's generation, more than one third of those who remained in Chebacco, lived for a time with their widowed mothers. The widow's dower rights assured her one third of the real estate for life and one third of the personal estate forever.[69] These dower rights inextricably intertwined the widow with the management of the estate. Her husband could not, by will or other means, alter this in any way, except with her consent. The working out of these rights in practice took many forms. Some husbands outlined the widow's share in minute detail, as did Gifford Cogswell, who made an impressive list of "annual payments and privileges" that his wife might expect. He carefully listed her annual provisions of meat, corn, and vegetables and gave her two pigs, eight sheep, and half the poultry "kept," as well as a little money and all of the flax "from the swingle." He also assured her the choice of rooms in the house, house repairs, and a "convenient" garden "dunged and dug," and placed a horse at her disposal. Others focused on the protocol of joint living arrangements, carefully allotting living space by assigning rooms and granting cellar, kitchen, well, and barn rights, as well as delineating common areas where anyone might pass through unmolested to his own area of the house. These remarkably specific arrangements show a fundamental suspicion of human motives that transcended even family ties. They also show, however, a quixotic faith that somehow every contingency could be planned for, every right and privilege so carefully described that conflict would not arise.[70]

Most men, however, simply gave their widows "such privileges in my estate as the law directs," relying for an equitable sharing of resources on custom and the natural affection between mother and child. As the more detailed directions suggest, the widow's rights translated into a guarantee of adequate provisions, living space in the house, and a kitchen garden nearby. This was probably the least burdensome of the obligations assumed by the new landowner.

The new landowner found himself at the center of a network of rights and obligations. Land was the basis of life in the village, and most rights in the land were based on kinship ties. Widows, wives, heirs, and also creditors all had claims, whether legal or customary, on the estate that would be realized under certain conditions and at certain times. The claims of the children began to fall due as they came of age. Daughters needed dowries and sons a start in life. Marriage was usually the catalyst for the initial transfer of property, as daughters took away household goods to start their own homes. Sons without expectations of a landed inheritance were given some cash or training in a trade.

The son who inherited most of the land also inherited these obligations. The 1749 will of John Burnham illustrates well the process of property transfer. His daughters were each entitled to 110 pounds as their portion of his estate, of which 18 pounds was still owing to the eldest, 35 pounds 10 shillings to the next, and 72 pounds 3 shillings to the youngest. These payments were spaced out over four years. The two eldest sons had "been paid already" their "portion in my estate" to their "full content and satisfaction," but the third son was still owed 164 pounds, or almost 60 percent of his portion, half of which was due within two years, and the other half within the next three. The son remaining, Samuel, inherited the "rest and residue" both "real and personal," after paying all debts and legacies. Samuel Burnham inherited a going concern. In anticipation of changes between the making of the will and his death, John Burnham inserted a clause stating that "anything paid after the making of the will, as part of their portion, on account, shall be accounted by the executor against their legacies."[71]

The will, or even the posthumous settlement, provided a kind of intergenerational accounting. As control of the land passed from one generation to the next, account was taken of what each heir "has already had" and of what remained to be paid to fulfill each one's "portion" of the estate. Samuel Burnham assumed, besides the care of the widow, his stepmother, a financial obligation to the other heirs, payable in the next five years, amounting to nearly 22 percent of the total value of the estate.[72]

The obligations that new landowners owed to the other heirs varied widely. Heirs whose fathers had already paid

each child his or her portion before their death owed nothing; but most began their new life in debt to their siblings—one such owed payments to his brothers totaling 85
percent of the value of the farm. In posthumously settled estates the other heirs' rights were interpreted more literally.
Each child's share of the assessed value of the land was es-
timated, and the son, or sons, who received the land had to
buy out the other shares. Most men, however, bore a burden no heavier than Samuel Burnham's.* The amount owed
to the other heirs was influenced by the father's age at
death, the value of the estate, and the number of heirs. Of
those men whose principal heirs owed less than 10 percent
of the estate in legacies, 81 percent were over seventy at
their death and 91 percent owned over 100 acres of land.
The lighter burden may have been some compensation for
the longer wait for inheritance.

The inherited obligations reached beyond the family into
the community. The transfer of land to a new generation
entailed an accounting and settlement with extrafamilial
creditors as well. The burden of debt was, in the aggregate,
somewhat heavier than that of the legacies.† These public
debts had legal priority over legacies. The average number
of debts was thirty-three, usually owed to as many creditors, mostly local, in a village of no more than 150 householders.‡ Nearly two thirds of the estates owed more
than twenty debts. Cumulatively these debts made up a
complex web of debtor-creditor relationships crisscrossing
the community. The debts were of various kinds, some
bonds and notes, some unsettled book debts. The latter,
predominant in number and value, were individually small
and locally owed. Almost one-quarter of the estates had to
sell some land to meet these obligations, but only a very few

---

*See Table 9, Appendix.
†See Table 10, Appendix.
‡See Table 11, Appendix.

estates collapsed into insolvency as a result, perhaps because of the dispersed and local character of the debts.[73]

The internal economy of the village was based on credit and a sophisticated barter system. The accounts of the Story-family sawmill, Joseph Perkins's tavern and tannery, Jonathan Burnham's farm, and Josiah Burnham's coopering business all show that the majority of the income was in kind, either goods or services. Accounts with individuals usually ran from one to three years, until the flux of service and payment was ended, settlement made, and a fresh account begun. These "book debts" technically fell due at death, but the judge of probate and the local creditors seldom pushed for a quick settlement, because they favored the farm's survival as an economic unit. In that way, debts were eventually paid and the family's livelihood preserved. For example, Joseph Goodhue, who died in 1768, left a ninety-acre farm burdened with a debt amounting to 45 percent of its value. Nearly twenty-five years were allowed to pass before all debts were paid.[74]

Bonds and notes were more formal obligations. They carried interest and were often secured with land. Bonds guaranteed the performance of an action. A few parents, after passing on their land, secured their own support by bonds from their children. Probate courts required bonds to insure the payments of debts and legacies. Notes, on the other hand, were a way of making the scarce cash resources of the community more available. They reinforced the primary power relationship in the community, from the older and wealthier to the younger and poorer. When David Low died, the assessors called the three notes of hand in his possession "his annuities." Jonathan Cogswell had, at his death in 1752, thirty-seven notes and seventeen bonds outstanding, worth more than 700 pounds. Only one of the notes was for more than 5 pounds, two thirds were for less than 1 pound. The bonds were for somewhat larger sums, but none was for so much as 20 pounds. These instruments provided secure investments, enforced by law and communal sanction, for older farmers with income beyond that needed for subsistence and working capital for younger men, particularly for those hard pressed by the obligations of a landed inheritance.[75]

The Cleaveland farm was burdened with different kinds of family obligations. The farm was purchased for Cleaveland by his wife's family and a few other supporters. They bought it from the previous owner in three separate transactions for 3,600 pounds Old Tenor (O.T.), the inflated currency in use in 1748. According to one of Cleaveland's successors, it "became his, as from time to time he paid the original value, without rent or interest." Like many another young man, John Cleaveland was a long time clearing out the various rights and interests in the land he controlled.[76]

Nehemiah Dodge, sometime before his death in 1758, gave up his one third interest to his sister Mary Cleaveland. The money originally used to purchase that share included part of her dowry of 700 pounds O.T. Cleaveland had at that time decided "to lay out the little that I am to have by my wife to help buy this farm."[77] The remaining two thirds came more slowly. Thirty years after the purchase, about 20 percent remained outstanding, scattered about the village by sale and inheritance. He slowly gathered these in, so that at his death in 1799 only a fragment of a share remained outstanding.[78]

Cleaveland paid off obligations worth two thirds the value of his farm. It was a heavy burden, but it was comparable to that borne by the average Chebacco landowner, who started out owing legacies amounting to 20 percent of the value of the estate, debts amounting to another 20 percent, as well as the widow's dower. Moreover, he had time constraints in the payment of these obligations, which Cleaveland did not.

Cleaveland now had "some interest to leave to wife and child, in case I should dye before them."[79] It was precisely this hope that moved forward the lengthy and complex process of inheritance. There was, moreover, no pause. Barely had the obligations to one's elders and siblings been cleared away when the rising generation, marrying and starting out into the world, began makings its needs felt. Cleaveland's education, his "portable" inheritance, had earned him a modicum of security in the world, but soon he would face, with limited resources, the responsibility of providing for his children. This responsibility, in Cleaveland's striving family as in others, was the major economic motive in rural New England.

For most men in Chebacco, time and inheritance, not entrepreneurial ability, was the key to their advancement. Periodic tax lists record the communal transmission of property from one generation to the next. Between 1749 and 1770, when Cleaveland's generation was coming into its own, most of those whose worldly possessions increased were, in 1749, under thirty-five years of age, and most of those whose decreased were over forty-five. It was for the men of Chebacco a stable world of finite resources, and one's place in it was largely determined by birth. Most men would not ever own much more than they inherited.[80]

On the eve of the Revolution, John Cleaveland and his contemporaries in the village had come into their inheritance. They controlled most of the community's resources and its positions of responsibility. And most of what they owned, values a well as wordly advantages, had been passed down from their fathers.

CHAPTER FOUR

✦

World View

CULTURE, LIKE PROPERTY, must be passed on from generation to generation. And the means of cultural transmission
in rural New England, education both formal and informal,
were conservative. There were few outside influences to disturb the passage of fundamental attitudes and assumptions
from parents to children. The villager inherited most of his
mental world, from craft skills to religious and political
beliefs, from his forebears. Formal institutions such as the
school and the church reinforced this conservative world
view.

The political crisis of the 1760s brought forth a response
from rural New England based on the historical understanding of God's dealings with His "New English Israel."
A crisis of this magnitude could only be interpreted by the
villagers of New England in these cosmic terms. Their education encompassed no alternative means of comprehending
human history. John Cleaveland in that period, as in the
religious controversies of the 1740s, helped the villagers to
refashion and articulate their political beliefs in a time of
change.

JOHN CLEAVELAND

I. Education

Informal education, private and domestic, was of great importance in the world of John Cleaveland. About 40 percent of the men in Cleaveland's generation in the village identified themselves with a trade at some time in their lives, either in their youth, before they came into their inheritance, or by means of their share in a family business. At least half shared a trade with their father and received from him both tools and training. Most of the rest practiced lesser crafts, such as shoemaking, a skill that was widely diffused in the community. There was an impressive concentration of skills among the descendants of the seventeenth-century emigrant carpenters William Story and John and Thomas Burnham, who passed on sawmill rights, tools, and craft training from generation to generation.[1]

The conservative means of craft transmission had a marked effect on the appearance of the village. Some of the surviving colonial houses in Chebacco are examples of late English Gothic domestic architecture, with steeply pitched roofs, asymmetrical facades, and massive central chimneys. The transplanted English craftsmen and their descendants preserved styles in New England that the homeland had long forgotten. The symmetrical, classical ideals of Georgian architecture spread only slowly into the countryside. When Jonathan Cogswell, who as justice of the peace from 1733 until his death in 1752 held the highest civil rank in the village, built his house in the 1740s, he incorporated the cellar and cavernous seventeenth-century chimney from the original Cogswell homestead. The new house, though it sported end chimneys, paneling in the new style, and the gentler Georgian pitch of the roof, still had the slightly asymmetrical facade and long, sloping back roof of a much older house. The Cogswell house represents the cautious adoption of the new style by the village leadership some sixty years after the Foster-Hutchinson house introduced neoclassical architecture to Boston.[2]

The use of land, too, was shaped by these conservative tendencies. Almost all of the men in Cleaveland's generation were raised, like Cleaveland himself, as farmers. The "apprenticeship" in farming began at an early age, and passing years brought increased responsibilities, until finally most of those who remained in Chebacco got the tools, stock, and land necessary to operate a farm. The agricultural practices of colonial New England were venerable and little influenced by conscious innovation. The village moved out of the settlement stage, when the land was being divided and cleared, into a stable system of agriculture based on livestock raising that remained essentially unchanged through the end of the colonial period.[3]

Other, less tangible aspects of village culture were also learned outside of formal educational institutions. A significant, though elusive, part of the inherited culture was the folk tales and songs. Hundreds of identifiable versions of English folk songs survived, though often changed and adapted, in the New England countryside, illustrating the continuity and vitality of an oral culture with roots deep in the English past. This traditional culture was embodied in more fundamental attitudes as well.[4]

The supernatural was still very real to these eighteenth-century villagers. Both their religion and their understanding of the natural world encouraged and appreciation of "the wonders of the invisible world." Beliefs in witchcraft and other profane supernatural phenomena survived, although the civil authorities no longer took cognizance of them, and it remained more compelling to these men and women than to their antiquarian descendants in the nineteenth century, who recorded evidence of these beliefs as quaint "folk tales." Essex County spawned a rich supernatural lore, ranging from simple image magic and fortune-telling to demonic visitations. Ipswich had its share of these supernatural manifestations, such as old Harry Main, the moon cusser, whose voice could be heard calling ships to their ruin, and the devil's footprint on the ledge in front of the First Church. In 1729 the *New England Journal* reported the story of an Ipswich man haunted by "an apparition in blood and wounds" who told him of his murder in Rhode Island and urged vegeance on the murderer. The survival of these oral traditions, and the attitudes they express, suggest the conservatism of informal, nonscholastic education.[5]

Public education began in Chebacco in 1695 with the appointment of Nathaniel Rust, Jr., as the first schoolmaster. He taught in a room in his own house, which also served as the village tavern. In 1702, the first schoolhouse was built on a site near the center of the village.[6]

The educational facilities mandated by the province were simple—a reading-and-writing school for every town with more than fifty families and a grammar school for those with more than one hundred—but the local attempts to meet them were remarkably complex.[7] The schools of Ipswich were supported by a variable combination of public and private means. The Latin grammar school, which capped the local educational hierarchy, was founded in 1651 and endowed with 300 acres of common land near the center of Chebacco, as well as with some private donations. The school and its funds were initially managed by self-perpetuating feofees, or trustees. By 1720, however, the selectmen had taken control of the school, added English to the curriculum, and were supporting it with rental income, taxes, and tuition.[8]

This model of mixed support for education also prevailed in the less ambitious parish schools. Chebacco gave its first schoolmaster one quarter of an acre for a house lot and the "improvement," or use, of six acres of pasture. The town's attempt in the 1720s to adjust the school-farm rents upward was denied by the court, but 100 pounds in back rent was collected and divded among the town's schools, with 20 pounds going to Chebacco. Thereafter the town assessed a school tax, which later was combined with other income, totaling 150 pounds by 1740, and divided among the town's schools. In 1742 the Chebacco parish meeting also assessed annual tuitition at two shillings three pence per child.[9]

In the mid-1750s, the town established a schedule for moving schools, or more accurately schoolmasters, among the parishes. The final stage in the evolution of the school in eighteenth-century Chebacco came in 1757 and 1761 with the establishment of district schools in the parish. These were administered by groups of proprietors who built and maintained the schoolhouse, hired the teachers, collected the appropriate share of the town's school money, assessed tuition, and provided room and board for the schoolmaster when necessary. The town, which continued to provide land for the schoolhouse and administer the school rate, and the parish gave over most of their authority to these semiautonomous bodies of householders. The proprietors of the district schools were, in effect, semipublic corporations, much like the parish excepting only the right to tax.[10]

These schools, after 1740 at least, were open only for the four winter months. A few of the teachers who conducted them were recent college graduates from outside the town, such as those who passed in rapid sequence through the master's chair at the grammar school in Ipswich-town, but more were local residents. Only four of the twelve teachers whose names are known had college degrees, and two of those came in the mid-1760s, when an attempt was made to add Latin to the parish curriculum. More typical were local men like the first teacher, Nathaniel Rust, Jr., an innkeeper, or, many years later, his great-grandson Parker, a doctor. William Gidding, the parish clerk, taught in the

1710s. Thomas Burnham, deacon in John Cleaveland's church, writer of wills and deeds and farmer of more than sixty acres, taught during most of the 1760s.[11]

The education of these teachers is unknown, but most were probably themselves products of Chebacco's schools. Their occupations, however—innkeeper, parish clerk, country lawyer, doctor—demanded writing and speaking abilities above those of the average farmer. They may have been graduates of the Ipswich grammar school who chose not to attend Harvard, but if so, this training, like that offered by the college, based as it was on mastery of Latin, was largely irrelevant to the purposes of a reading-and-writing school. Even in Boston, only three, or 13 percent, of the eighteenth-century writing-school masters had college degrees, while, necessarily, all of the grammar-school masters had them. The purposes of the English and Latin curricula were different even if they were, coincidentally, taught by the same man.[12]

In 1702, the parish clerk laboriously and revealingly spelled out the parish's intention to use six acres of common land, provided by the town, "for the incorigmant of a riting scoll heare in Chabaco and to larn the children to wright and reade: hear in this place." In 1740 "cyphering" was mentioned as well, but otherwise the parish devoted little thought to the curriculum. It was generally understood what the children should learn and how they should learn it.[13]

The basic text of most New England writing schools was the famed *New England Primer,* most often printed with the Westminster Assembly's *Shorter Catechism.* It included the alphabet, a syllabarium, and the alphabet of lessons ("In Adam's fall / We sinned all"). Between 1740 and 1760 the alphabet of lessons was "evangelized" by replacing secular doggerel, such as "The cat doth play / And after slay," with more spiritual rhymes, such as "Christ crucify'd / For sinners dy'd." This provides some evidence of the influence of the intenser piety of the Awakening, the extracommunal movement that Cleaveland represented in the village, on education in New England. Following these elementary exercises in the primer were the Lord's Prayer and the Apostles' Creed, which were probably used as elementary reading texts.[14]

Printers added a variety of uplighting verses and stories to their editions of the *Primer,* but the story of the Marian martyr John Rogers, accompanied by a woodcut of Rogers at the stake surrounded by his wife and children, was most often included. Rogers's story, which was loosely based on the account in Foxe's *Book of Martyrs,* introduced the children to the fires of Smithfield, the reign of "Bloody" Mary, and the history of Protestantism's struggle against Catholic tyranny. The story might have had a more powerful impact locally, because the Rogers clan, ministers in Ipswich's first church from 1638 to 1775, proudly though erroneously traced their descent from the martyr.[15] The fusion of education with religious instruction was reinforced by the use of the *Shorter Catechism.* A touchstone of New England orthodoxy, the *Shorter Catechism* was not really adapted to the abilities of children; it served as the basis of Samuel Willard's *Complete Body of Divinity.* Its use meant that educational growth was equated with the mastery of doctrine.[16]

This curriculum was taught to classes comprised of very young boys and girls. There was much local variation in the matter of admitting girls, but the Chebacco records always refer to children, not boys. There was likewise great variation in the ages of the students, but the records of several towns indicate that most students were between six and twelve. Older children had more important work to do; apprenticeships began at age fourteen.[17]

Although the province required that children be taught to read and that towns of a certain size maintain schools, it did not require attendance at those schools. The placing of one's child in the Chebacco school called for a decision on the part of the parents, since it was not required and they lost the child's labor as well as the tuition paid, over and above taxes. In 1760, twenty-four parents in Chebacco, about 16 percent of the householders, paid four shillings six pence in tuition for each of thirty-six children, comprising about 10 percent of the boys and girls under sixteen. Roughly the same proportion of the under-sixteen population attended public school in Boston at about the same time.[18]

Yet the school, with its variable attendance record and short term, managed, according to available measures, to be fairly effective. In the seventeenth century, before the establishment of school in Chebacco, about 25 percent of the householders were unable to sign their names. The figures for their wives are fragmentary, but perhaps as many as 75 percent were illiterate. By 1771, literacy, at least as measured by the ability to sign one's name, was virtually universal among the householders and had reached almost 75 percent among their wives.* The literacy of the villagers of 1771, born between 1690 and 1750, testifies to the local commitment to education. Moreover, women continued to improve their position throughout the eighteenth century; 85 percent of Chebacco women born after 1731 were able to sign their names.[19]

The demands of a more complex economy undoubtedly played a part in the growth of literacy. Most of the householders of 1771 had transferred property by deed, made or accepted a loan, taken part in the probate process, or served as a witness. All of these tasks, requiring a signature or mark, were more easily comprehended by a man who could read the documents involved. An illiterate man was at the mercy of literate ones in such dealings. However, as the impressive rise in women's literacy would suggest, these practical ends may not have been the most important factor

*See Table 12, Appendix.

in the rise of literacy. The schools trained young people to read and, with the aid of the *Shorter Catechism,* properly to understand the Bible. The centrality of the word of God in the reformed tradition far outweighed any utilitarian motives in influencing the school's curriculum.

Formal education in Chebacco, though widespread, was narrow and limited in practice. Education in the village school was, for the most part, terminal and self-contained. No Chebacco boy went up to the college at Cambridge between 1720 and 1775; and few, during those years, had gone on from the village school to the Ipswich grammar school, which drilled college-bound boys in the classical languages.[20]

The number and kind of books owned by Chebacco householders suggests the range of their interests. Only 13 percent of wills and inventories mention books at all, although other estates may have contained them. Religious books predominated, mostly Bibles and works by evangelical authors such as Isaac Watts and John Flavel. A few people owned copies of the province law book, one of the many editions of the *Acts and Laws of His Majesty's Province of the Massachusetts-Bay in New-England.* The ownership of law books was, however, limited to people with special interests, among whom were Francis Choate, justice of the peace, and Daniel Gidding, a local lawyer.[21]

Chebacco had few ties to the sources of cosmopolitan culture. Before 1768 there was no press or newspaper in Essex County, or indeed anywhere in Massachusetts outside of Boston and Cambridge. The provincial elite, shaped by the classical education considered essential for an eighteenth-century gentleman, was sensitive to the drift of English culture. The liberalization of Harvard College and of the Boston clergy and the elaborate political and commercial network stretching across the Atlantic—these were the sinews that held an Anglo-American world together, a world far removed from the daily concerns of the countryside.[22]

The classical education that sensitized one to the drift of cosmpolitan culture was less frequently encountered in the countryside. In 1765 there were more Harvard graduates living in the town of Boston than there were in either Essex, Middlesex, or Plymouth counties. There were, in 1765, only about 160 Harvard graduates in all of Essex County, and almost a third of those were ministers, out of a population of more than 40,000. Moreover, two thirds of those graduates lived in the cluster of port towns. Classical education in the farming villages of Essex and the rest of the province was limited to the minister, and perhaps the schoolmaster and local squire. Even for these, their way of life offered only limited opportunities for participation in the more cosmopolitan culture of the provincial elite. In Chebacco, in 1771, there were no college graduates except for Cleaveland himself, and he had been educated at Yale, which was more conservative and insular than the Bay Colony college.[23]

These were the elements of education for the people of Chebacco. Both domestic and public education combined to preserve and pass on a world view that was conservative, insular, and religious. But education did not end with adulthood; Cleaveland, as minister in the village, lectured his people weekly on matters of morals and doctrine.

II. Religion

At Yale, John Cleaveland had received a thorough grounding in Calvinist theology as interpreted by Puritan commentators of the sixteenth and seventeenth centuries. He combined this conservative theology with old-fashioned Congregational-church principles imbibed at home and a stress on religious experience. He exemplified the evangelical Calvinism that would soon dominate the hinterland of New England.[24]

Cleaveland was, by virtue of his education and position,

the most important extrafamilial source of moral authority and instruction in the village. Books were few, and these few mostly religious; and newspapers were a product of far-off Boston, full of foreign news and commercial information alien to the concerns of the countryside. Much of the villagers' education, from childhood to old age, was found within the confines of the church.

Cleaveland preached in the meetinghouse that his congregation had built in 1752 and also, from the mid-1760s onward, in the old meetinghouse, built in 1718. The buildings were essentially similar, built four-square with pews along the sides and benches in the middle. The pulpit was raised and faced down the broad center aisle to the door. The older church also had a turret and a bell.[25]

The New England meetinghouse was an ideologically inspired architectural innovation with few precedents in English church architecture. It was simply a gathering place for the village, for affairs both religious and civil. It had been stripped bare of all "churchly" trappings that smacked of popery, save only the pulpit. Country churches like those of Chebacco also rejected later cosmopolitan innovations such as choirs, organs, and even wood stoves. All was calculated to direct attention to the pulpit, which mirrored the centrality of the sermon in the liturgy.[26]

The liturgy, too, was stripped bare of the distracting "corruptions" of the Anglican service. Set forms of prayer, homilies, Bible reading without commentary—all were cast aside in favor of the "word expounded." The order of service was starkly simple: long prayer, psalm, sermon, short prayer, psalm, and benediction. In Chebacco the psalms were "lined out," or spoken first line by line, in the old style by the deacon, until the deaths of Cleaveland and Deacon Thomas Burnham in 1799.[27]

The prayers were supposed to be informal and spontaneous, in reaction to the set forms of liturgical prayer in the Anglican service. The prayer grew in length and impor-

tance during the colonial period. The free form and emo-
tional content of these "adapted supplications," as Cotton
Mather called them, made them particularly popular
among New Lights. These prayers were often "improve-
ments" of mundane village happenings in which the
preacher sought out and explicated the divine message behind the commonplace earthly reality. The result was a rhe-
torical style and, more important, a habit of mind that
shaped the villager's perception of the world.[28]

Cleaveland's prayers cannot be recovered, but something
of their structure and style can be seen in surviving journals
and letters. They were later described as being "without a
careful and orderly arrangement of topics . . . the effusions
of a heart in close communion with God."[29] In a letter to
his father written in the fall of 1748 asking for help in financing his farm, Cleaveland made this improvement:

O what a favour it is that a right to the heavenly country is already purchased and made sure to all those that are free born in re-
generation; but that was purchased not with corruptable things as
silver and gold, but by the precious blood of the son of God. Here
was an infinite price laid down for poor reched self-ruined finite
creatures, surely they are not capable of making amends for it. O
why then was all this cost lay'd out upon finite creatures? Why
because He would display His own glory hereby: yea such mysteries, as otherwise would have been for ever kept hid from the
creation are now made manifest to such as believe God. Grant
that we may have a fellowship with the hidden mysteries of the
gospel of Christ for Christ's sake—Amen.[30]

Years later, in 1780, he began a letter to his son Parker
about the wartime death of his son Ebenezer with "my dear
son, how fading are all things here below!" He described
the circumstances of Ebenezer's death in minute detail and
then began an extended meditation: "Your brother being
dead yet speaketh, and preacheth a lecture, be ye also ready,
louder than ever your father preached, or than we ever hear
thunder roar!"[31] One's earthly portion suggests the heav-

enly portion, one's dead son suggests the biblical Elijah, and so by analogy the divine pattern in worldly matters is made clear. This habit of mind had roots in the exegetical technique by which sermons were made.

Cleaveland was responsible for providing his congregation with three sermons a week—two on Sunday and a mid-week lecture—for fifty-two weeks a year. This meant more than 150 sermons a year, but as the numbering on his surviving sermons indicated, he wrote no more than 60 or 70 a year.[32] This he was able to do because of the cooperative network of ministers who regularly exchanged pulpits with one another. About 50 of Cleaveland's sermons have survived for the period 1750 to 1775, and he preached from them about 100 times. Half of these deliveries were from his own pulpit in Chebacco, and half were given elsewhere. About a third of those given elsewhere were given in neighboring parishes in Ipswich and Gloucester; another third in Essex County towns to the north, such as Rowley, Newbury, and Haverhill; and the remainder in various towns in New England and New York.[33]

Reverend Cleaveland had a voice that carried, in the summer when the meetinghouse windows were thrown open, across the whole village. He was described as "by no means a graceful preacher. His manner sometimes bordered on the rough and even the boisterous." But if the cosmopolitan clergy regarded him as a rude enthusiast, the country saw him as a warm, affecting preacher. There is little doubt that this burly, barrel-chested farmer-preacher was a commanding figure to his parishioners.[34]

Little remains of those soul-shaking, rafter-rocking sermons. Of the nearly 2,000 sermons he probably composed in the first quarter-century (1750–1775) of his Chebacco pastorate, only a handful have survived. And those few are only skeletonlike outlines of the sermons that were delivered. As a New Light, he could not simply read his sermons, because that would lessen the warmth and spontaneity that was expected of his preaching. Instead, he carried to the pulpit only "very brief and imperfect notes."[35] But these notes were in fact careful outlines of the venerable Puritan sermon form.

First came the biblical text with a literal explication, then the major doctrinal points suggested by the text, and finally an application to the lives of his congregation. In November 1775, he delivered a sermon to his congregation on Matthew 3:10: "And how also the axe is laid unto the root of the trees: therefore every tree that bringeth not forth good fruit is hewn down, and cast into the fire." These, Cleaveland explained, were

the words of John Baptist to the Sadducees and the Pharisees who came out to him with the multitudes which came out to be baptised from Jerusalem, all Judea and the regions roundabout.

John the Baptist's sermon, later echoed in Christ's Sermon on the Mount, was directed to these groups because the Pharisees trusted "in themselves that they were righteous" and the Sadducees "did not believe there was any wrath to come or future state of rewards and punishments."

Cleaveland then explored the deeper, more general significance of the text. The method of investigation was interrogatory, like the catechism on which his parishioners were raised.

Q.1. What are we to understand here by trees at whose root the ax is laid?
A.   Men or mankind[,] the children of our past parents, frequently called the children of men and the sons of men, are all understood.

The trees are mankind, the axe is the "rebellion against God" by "our first parents," and the good fruit "benevolence to being in general, . . . to Christ superlatively[,] to my neighbor as myself, it is full of self denial." And "what is signified by every tree being cut down and cast into the fire that brings not forth good fruit?" That, as his listeners doubtless understood only too well, meant that man deserved "not only [to] die but [to] be damned, . . . [to be] destroyed soul and body in hell forever." Original sin was a familiar, if not a comforting, doctrine, and one perhaps all the more easily understood by an agricultural people whose earthly fate was much shaped by the folly or prudence of past generations.

Finally came the application. This was the practical import for the lives of his listeners of the message that Cleaveland had drawn out of the text. And the meaning in this case was simply "meeting the commandments of God and of Jesus Christ the son of God." One who brought forth "good fruit" was one who "worships God in that way and manner God requires," who "does not curse and damn and swear profanely," and who "loves his neighbors not only such as love him[but] as are his enemies with a benevolent affection." The burden of his discourse was an orthodox justification of good works. Obedience to God's ordinances could not save a man—that was the error of the Pharisees—nor could it be perfect, he cautioned. Still, good fruit came from good trees, corrupt fruit from corrupt trees, and, as Christ had said, "by their fruit we shall know them." While good behavior was not an assurance of salvation, its presence or absence strongly hinted at one's future fate.[36]

This was a typical pastoral concern. Cleaveland had, within the confines of the reformed religious tradition he shared with his congregation, both to justify and to encourage good behavior. Other concerns had once been uppermost in his ministry. In his first post, as minister to a despised and beleaguered congregation of Separates in Boston, he had been drawn to the prophets. There he found texts that expressed the mingled defensiveness and self-righteousness of the Separates. He had been particularly drawn to Isaiah's notion of the saving remnant that was to be gathered before the destruction of Israel. As a settled

Cleveland
o/-

An Epicedium.

O R A

Poetical Attempt upon the Life & Death

O F

Mr. *Josiah Cleaveland,*

LATE OF

C A N T E R B U R Y.

Who departed this Life (undoubtedly)
to a better, *February 9th* 1750, 51.
Aged Sixty Years, four Months,
and two Days.

[John Cleaveland]

Zech. i. 5. *Your Fathers where are they?* .
Pfal. lxxxix. 48. *What Man is he that lives, and shall not see
Death? Shall he deliver his Soul from the Hand of the
Grave?* Selah.
Rev. xiv. 13.— *Write, blessed are the Dead that die in the
Lord,* &c.
Luk. xvi. 22.---*The Beggar died, and was carried by the Angels
into Abrahams Bofom.*
2 Sam. i. 17. *And David lamented with this Lamentation over
Saul and over Jonathan his Son.*

B O S T O N: Printed by S. KNEELAND, 1753.

Cover of *An Epicedium* . . . (Boston, 1753), John Cleaveland's poetical biography of his father, Josiah. The title is an anagram of the
author's name. (Courtesy of the American Antiquarian Society)

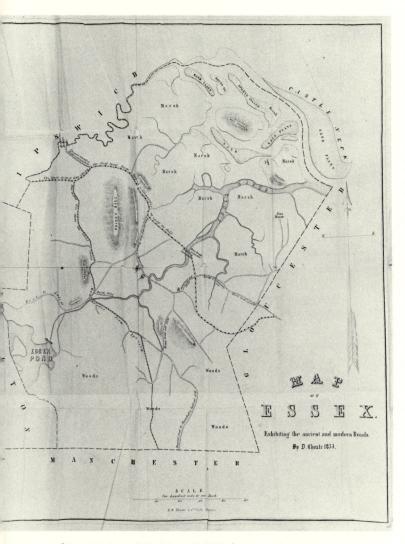

A map of Ipswich Second Parish, called Chebacco, and since 1819
the town of Essex. The map was drawn by David Choate in 1853
and published as an insert in the 1868 edition of Reverend
Crowell's town history. (Courtesy of the Essex Institute)

Chebacco May. 17. 1769

Dear Daughter,

Last night I had a Line put into my Hand with your Name to it, expressing your Thoughts and desiring my Advice relating to a Matter of great Importance in this Life. —

And in Reply, I say, I would have you chuse for yourself. I would not have you accept of this or that man's offer for fear you should not have another, and so trye to make the best of him you can, but to accept such an one because he appears upon all accounts to be most agreeable and suitable to stand in that Relation to you, this is chusing: and not to accept of any one that does not appear most agreeable both to your Judgment and fancy. your mother had divers offers before she was of your age but she would not accept of any one, but when the right came, she did it appeared to her to be the right, every way agreeable to both her Judgment and fancy. So it was with me as to her. and it is my Prayer to God that I may find another that I may chuse after that manner. and it is my prayer that you may have a most lovely, agreeable and Suitable Person for your Companion in Life, and I would have you also make it your Prayer to God. — As to that man chose, it is a mistake that I dislike him because he is a Black-smith; and I know nothing either for him or against him, I know nothing of his character, Parentage or worldly Estate. I have only seen him transiently, and all that ever I said of him that would ... to any determination, was to this purpose; that he did not cut a more agreeable figure than the Woods ...

A letter, dated May 17, 1769, from John Cleaveland to his daughter Mary. The letter concerns her marital prospects. (Courtesy of the Essex Institute)

The Cogswell House, built 1730–1740 by Jonathan Cogswell, Esq. (Courtesy of Nina Fletcher Little. Photo credit: Martin Friedlander)

John Cleaveland's pulpit from 1793 to the end of his life. (Courtesy of the First Congregational Church, Essex, MA. Photo credit: Martin Friedlander)

pastor, his concerns gradually changed. He preached more often from the gospels, especially Matthew, and from the apostolic letters, especially Corinthians.[37] He sought to lure or to frighten people into accepting Christ. He preached often, six times in five years, on a famous hellfire-and-brimstone text:

Enter ye in at the strait gate; for wide *is* the gate, and broad *is* the way, that leadeth to destruction, and many there be which go in thereat: (Matt. 7:13)

But he preached as often from Christ's promises:

I am the light of the world: he that followeth me, shall not walk in darkness, but shall have the light of life. (Joh. 8:12)

He tried, as an evangelical pastor, to guide his flock, in Solomon Stoddard's words, between the Scylla of false assurance and the Charybdis of despair.[38]

It is easier to appraise the contents of Cleaveland's sermons than it is to understand the mentality of his audience. Some evidence of his people's religious consciousness can be found in their conversion relations. Revivals were a normal part of the religious experience in the village, with one major upheaval in each generation. Most of the villagers who joined the church in the eighteenth century joined during the revival years of 1727–1728, 1742–1743, or 1763–1764.[39]

The last of these began, according to Cleaveland, when "in the Spring and Summer of the Year 1763, two or three young Persons appear'd to have some Concern and Conviction upon their Minds." It went on into the autumn of the following year. Church membership swelled in Chebacco and the surrounding towns.

The whole number of those we admitted in the Space of *Seven* or *Eight* Months was upwards of *Ninety;* but above two Thirds of them were Females. I have heard, that the Rev. Mr. *Parsons* of *Newbury-port,* admitted about that Time, upwards of Fifty; and the Rev. Mr. *Jewett* of *Rowley,* about Thirty; and the Rev. Mr. *Chandler* of *Gloucester,* a considerable Number, but I have not heard how many.[40]

The accounts of the conversion experience necessary for admission to the church have survived for fifty-three of the ninety new members. These thirteen men and forty women were among the prospective members who "signified their Desire to make a public Profession of Christ, and to be admitted into the Church in full standing." They gathered at the parsonage where the "Pastor and Ruling Elders" examined them "as to their Knowledge, Principles and gracious Experience," after which Cleaveland took "down in Writing the Relation of their Experience, both as to a Law-Work and Gospel-Faith and Repentance, which is read to the Church in public Congregation."[41]

The relations followed a set formula. These short statements, mostly between 250 and 1,000 words, were part of a venerable tradition rooted in the spiritual biographies and autobiographies of the Elizabethan Puritans. Edwards's *Life of Brainerd* was the great work in the genre in their own day, but for most of the laity, the tradition was an oral one. Most New Englanders listened for a lifetime, in private and "in public congregation," to one another or to their ministers "laying down the marks of being born of God." It was with this noble aim in mind that the young John Cleaveland had attempted an autobiography, "that I might leave somthing which by the blessing of God, hereafter shall minister conviction to sinners and consolation to such as are passed from death to life."[42]

In these relations, the sinner is first "awakened," usually by means of a sermon or personal tragedy, to the nature of his sin. Then he realizes that good behavior or "righteousness" is a "sandy foundation" upon which to build his salvation. This leads him to despair. But then, in the depth of despair, the sinner is brought to understand the "sufficiency of Christ" for his salvation, and is comforted. The pattern was the same, whether in Edwards's subtle and complex "personal narrative" or in the simple and unreflective relation of a village girl.

Martha Andrews, while at a meeting at Deacon Craft's, saw that she "was a perishing sinner" with "no power to help" herself. She realized that God "was under no obligation to save" her, and saw "the justice of God in casting [her] immediately into hell." Only when she discovered that Christ was an "all sufficient saviour" was the burden of guilt and fear lifted from her, and she "found love of delight in God's word and in his people." And so, in just over two hundred words, was the spiritual pilgrimage of young Martha recorded.[43]

But for others in the village conversion was, if not more deeply felt, at least better articulated. For Benjamin Marshall, a middling farmer and shopkeeper of about Cleaveland's age, conversion and joining the church capped a lengthy spiritual odyssey. Marshall, who had had a "religious education" and had "begun the practice of religion" young, had "hopes" at age eleven but could not give a "particular account" of his experiences. Cleaveland came to the parish some years later and said that "persons might experience in religion and yet stop short of a saving change." This made him cautious. His concern fluctuated in later years, but he remained sensible "that my feet stood in slippery places and that text, their feet shall slide in due time, followed me."

He had lately been put "under concern" by the death of a young man in his family while he was at Casco Bay. He returned to Chebacco during the height of the revival, Thanksgiving 1763, and there he recognized his "actual sins." Later, during a lecture by Reverend Rogers of Gloucester, he was "brought to see" his "original sin" and the justice of God "in my condemnation." But when Cleaveland called on sinners to give up all to Christ, he drew back,

afraid. Then, the next day at the quarterly fast, when Cleaveland, "lining" the psalm, read the words "my God, my
soul shall fill, with most peculiar joyes," Marshall's "mind
was in sweet calmness." Afterward, he feared self-decep-
tion, knowing "God will not be mocked," but at last he
was comforted.[44]

Each of these relations expresses a belief in predestination. This belief was among the most fundamental of the
villagers' assumptions about the way the world worked. It
is even reflected in the grammatical construction of their
relations, in the careful use of the passive voice to describe
their religious experiences. Cleaveland, like his many New
Light brethren, had sharpened his people's awareness of this
venerable doctrine, still central to the reformed religious
tradition. As an orthodox Congregational minister, supported by public rates, it was also his duty to point out the
social implications of this belief, that is, the sovereignty of
God over the life of the community as well as over the lives
of individual men and women. The idea of God's covenant
with New England was thoroughly intertwined with other
elements of the villagers' education, and although it had
little to do with the everyday business of politics, it shaped
their perspective on the world beyond their borders.

III. Politics

Political education, like other kinds of education in the
village, was acquired informally. Local politics was politics
of family and connection, smaller in scale but not essentially different from the imperial politics with which the
provincial great occupied themselves. One's place in this
political system, as well as one's understanding of it, was
shaped by the wealth and family connections received from
past generations.

Authority over Chebacco was exercised by a variety of jurisdictions. There were civil, military, and judicial jurisdic-

tions at the parish, town, county, and provincial levels. The officers in these jurisdictions can be further divided into elective and appointive, as well as those who served inside and those who served outside the village. The latter distinction was, if not the most important, at least the most evident to contemporaries.

At the top of the provincial hierarchy was the governor, since 1692 a royal appointee. The distance of this august personage from the towns and villages he ruled over was accentuated by the fact that from Jonathan Belcher's dismissal in 1741 to Thomas Hutchinson's appointment in 1770, the governor was an Englishman. In his hands lay the power of appointment for all militia offices, from colonel to ensign, and all judicial offices, from justice of the Superior Court to justice of the peace.[45]

The only elected official who served outside the town was the representative to the General Court. While most representatives were merely prosperous farmers, far beneath the governor's notice, in the assembly they cumulatively controlled the disbursement of provincial funds and the salaries of appointed officials, including that of the governor himself.[46] The character of local appointments was faithful to the local political structure. The governor's appointments were so well guided through the thickets of village politics that his choices were the same kind of men, and often the same men, that the village chose for its elective offices.

The major officeholders in Chebacco, elective and appointive, were with few exceptions over forty and in the first or second quintile in wealth ranking. But these are only crude indicators of the character of village leadership. The contemporary understanding that these factors reflect was that the village leaders should be men who had come into their inheritance and succeeded to their father's place in the community. The eighteenth-century belief in a congruence between political power and socioeconomic position, and the delayed-inheritance characteristic of farming communities, combined to give shape to this political system. Independence did not come for most Chebacco farmers until their forties, or later, because most had to wait until their father's death for the property that made officeholding possible. A dependent son could not be a leader, any more than a propertyless man, or more aptly, a servant, could be a voter.[47]

As these were offices of some honor and responsibility but no profit, eligibility was fairly widespread. Most Chebacco men would have the minimum requirement, an agricultural competency, at some point in their lives. The five parish trustees were elected annually, and the positions rotated frequently. On the 1771 board, Robert Burnham was serving his ninth term, John Choate his seventh, Ensign Humphrey Choate and David Low their fourth, and Deacon Thomas Burnham his second. Two of them had not been on the previous year's board, and one would not be on the next one. Other positions were more stable. Militia appointments were for life, though at the pleasure of the governor. The offices of parish clerk and treasurer were elective but seldom changed hands. Joseph Perkins held both offices in Cleaveland's parish from 1752 until his death in 1805. One of his predecessors as clerk, William Gidding, had served for most of the first half of the eighteenth century.[48]

Beyond the minimum qualifications, a complex mixture of personal and family qualities influenced one's chances for office. In 1771, the Choate family, prosperous and energetic farmer-artisans, held seven of sixteen possible positions in the parish government, church, and militia, far more than any other family. The Cogswells, large landholders, wealthier than even the Choates, seldom took the positions in local affairs that they could have commanded. Daniel Gidding, though a man of small estate, was a capable country lawyer and zealous New Light, a combination that brought him election as an elder of the new church, several terms as a parish trustee, and even a term in the assembly. The Choates had substantial wealth and interest in village affairs, the Cogswells lacked the latter, and Gidding made up in ability and commitment for his lack of the former.

The most prestigious local appointment was that of justice of the peace. Here the politics of family and connection operated at a higher level. Jonathan Cogswell was second in taxable wealth on a 1749 list and at his death in 1752 owned 354 acres in Ipswich and Gloucester, two rights in Ipswich-Canada, and a total estate worth 3,288 pounds. His mother was a Wainwright from Ipswich-town, and his maternal uncles were colonels in the provincial militia and successful merchants. His Wainwright cousins married into the Dudley and Winthrop families. His cousin John Wainwright, the Ipswich partner in the Boston- and Ipswich-based family mercantile firm, was a justice of the peace and of the Inferior Court of Common Pleas, as well as being clerk of the house. Cogswell's wealth and connections to the province's great families brought him in 1733 an appointment as Chebacco's first justice of the peace, which he held until his death in 1752. The next justice of the peace was Elder Francis Choate, who, though wealthy by village standards, had only half as much land as Cogswell. His brother, however, was Colonel John Choate, an insider in Governor Shirley's administration. The criteria of wealth and family connections for the highest of village appointments were, though humble enough by provincial standards, well beyond the reach of all but the very top of village society.[49]

The village occupied the lowest level of a complex hierarchical system that stretched from the parish meetinghouse to Whitehall. It was, by virtue of the elected assembly's power, a well-integrated system in which degrees of office, elective and appointive, were congruent with wealth and social position, or society's "natural" leadership. Moreover, the system provided much local autonomy. In parish and town, the villagers chose their officers, taxed themselves, and sent a representative to the assembly, which, along with the councillors they elected, legislated for the province. Only the governor was beyond their reach, and even he was not beyond their influence.

Still, the provincial government's intrusive powers were potentially, if not actually, great. The militia, though little more than a social organization in peacetime, was in wartime a potent combination of civil-defense unit and draft board, all under the command of the governor as captain-general. Of wider influence was the judicial system, appointive from the local justice of the peace, who judged "small causes" in his own community, to the county-level courts of General Session (civil and administrative) and Common Pleas (criminal), and finally to the Superior Court of Judicature of His Majesty's Province of Massachusetts-Bay. The most powerful and inclusive provincial prerogative was that of taxation, which was still safely in the hands of elected representatives. The power of converting private wealth to public wealth was a very great one, as the provincial tax bill annually reminded the villagers.

It was, from a local perspective, a stable and equitable system. The parts of it most influential in the daily lives of the villagers were either under local control or, if appointive, at least congruent with the local power structure. When change came, it stemmed from imperial motives at best dimly understood within this local frame of reference. The local experience of imperial politics was limited to war.

Some eighty men from Chebacco fought alongside of the King's armies in the French and Indian Wars. Small numbers of villagers, five to eight in any one year, took part in the conquest and occupation in the mid-1740s of the French stronghold of Louisbourg on Cape Breton Island. Much to the Yankees' dismay, the Treaty of Aix-la-Chapelle in 1748 handed their hard-won victory back to the French. The renewed French threat on New England's northern coast was a reminder that the War of the Austrian Succession, as it was called in Europe, was an imperial war. Larger numbers, as many as twenty-eight in 1758, took part in the assaults on Canada in the late 1750s, and a few more fought in sea battles in the West Indies. The great victory of the British empire over the French, resulting in the almost total elimination of French sovereignty over American soil and a vast expansion in the British Empire, according to the terms of the Treaty of Paris in 1763, was to some extent, they felt, theirs. In 1771 there were in the village thirty-five veterans of this conflict, almost a quarter of the adult male taxpayers.[50]

The military experience of the Chebacco soldiers was unhazardous: almost all of them survived to return to Chebacco, but it was also menial, for almost all were common foot soldiers. Of the six officers, only one held a command rank. John Choate went to Louisbourg as colonel of the 8th Massachusetts Regiment, but he arrived after the fall of the citadel. He came with a commission as judge advocate of an admiralty court, accompanied by occupation forces, not as a military commander. Another Chebacco officer was John Cleaveland, chaplain in Colonel Jonathan Bagley's regiment; of the other four, two were lieutenants and two ensigns. Chebacco's local perspective on the imperial war was not unlike their perspective on the imperial political system. And yet eighty men risked their lives, most of them voluntarily, presumably with some notion of the broader issues involved.

Two Chebacco soldiers who took part in the conquest of Louisbourg in 1745 left journals and letters that tell of that experience. Benjamin Craft, thirty-nine, was a soldier, and Daniel Gidding, forty-four, a lieutenant in Colonel Robert Hale's regiment. They sailed from Boston in late March and landed on Canso Island. On April 30, they made their landing on Cape Breton Island under French fire and began the siege. On June 17, Louisbourg surrendered and was oc-

cupied by the provincial troops. Their journals are filled
with accounts of camp routine, illness in their company,
and their desire to return home. The imperial schemes of
Governor Shirley, or General Pepperrell and Commodore
Warren, the joint commanders, meant little to them. The
movements, much less the motives, of these great per-
sonages were mere rumors floating about the camp. So the
conflict was interpreted in New England terms, which is to
say according to the traditional understanding of God's covenant with His "New English Israel."[51]

Both soldiers resigned themselves to the divine will.
Craft hoped that the Lord would "enable us to be contented
with all the Allotments of his providence." This reflects the
acceptance of divine intervention in human affairs, in which
good fortune was His "Blessinge," and failure the "frowns
of his providence."[52] Lieutenant Gidding interpreted their
fate in battle in these terms. On May 27, the French attacked, and Gidding wrote:

About one of ye Clock this morning I heard ye gons [guns.] [O]ur
people ware Ingaged in Battle & a heavy, sorrowfull Battle itt was
to us[.] [A] Great Number of our Brave soldi[ers] ware Kild,
taken & wounded[.] [Y]e Lord our God frownd upon us: I Believe
there is an accu[rsed thing] in our Camp. [O] Lord help us to
search Each man his one hart and Pray father lett thy holy Spirit
be with Each of us in ye search that the accursed thing may be
found out & we obtain Pardon.

But God soon smiled upon their efforts again, and on June
17, Gidding reported that "this Day things ware agread
upon[,] the Gates war oppened & we Entered into the city I
Know not ye terms: ye City is Exceeding Strong but God
has Brought us into itt."[53]

The occupation brought other signs of divine favor. On
June 22, he saw with satisfaction that "the mas[s] house
[Catholic Church] was clensed out . . . [and] was told that
Mister Moodey was to Preach on ye morrow." His account

of the "cleansing" of the "mass house" and the installation of a Protestant preacher was in language appropriate to a man educated in New England, one who only a few weeks before had been reading "Mr. Bunyan upon ye two Covenants" and finding him very satisfactory. Even the housing of the troops revealed God's intentions toward New England:

This Day many of ye Inhabitance moved out[.] [O]ur company movd into a Very comfortable house we Built not, thus our God makes us to Posses our Enemies housses.[54]

Craft, Gidding, and their compatriots saw the events at Louisbourg in light of their New England education. Since the imperial perspective was foreign to their experience, they saw the conflict in terms of God's covenant with His people, and they tried to make out the divine pattern in the welter of events. John Cleaveland, who was to spend a lifetime instructing the people of Chebacco in this way of looking at the world, himself went on a later expedition against the French in North America.

Cleaveland received his commission in March 1758 from Governor Thomas Pownall, who made him chaplain of the Third Regiment, commanded by Colonel Jonathan Bagley. In the early summer, he rode off across the province with his brother Ebenezer, also a chaplain, and the regimental surgeon, Caleb Rea of Danvers. On June 9, they arrived in Albany, where they waited for the regiment to join them. At the end of June, the whole regiment marched north to Fort Edward near Lake George, joining other provincial troops from Massachusetts and Connecticut, as well as British army regulars, all under the command of the British general James Abercrombie. They were to be part of a two-pronged attack on French Canada, with Abercrombie to take the French outpost of Fort Ticonderoga and Brigadier General Amherst to retake the stronghold at Louisbourg.[55]

There were uneasy relations between the provincials and

the regulars from the beginning. New England sensibilities were shocked by the regulars; Cleaveland later wrote that "profain swearing seems to be the naturalized language of the regulars." He prayed "that God would remove wickedness from the camp" that stemmed mostly from the regulars' propensities for "Gaming, Robbery, Thieft, Whoring, bad-company-keeping, etc."[56]

Tensions increased after the failure of the expedition. In early July, the army rowed across Lake George and landed at Ticonderoga. In a preliminary skirmish, Lord Howe, Abercrombie's able and popular second in command, was killed. Abercrombie's subsequent mismanaged attack on Montcalm's forces at Ticonderoga resulted in heavy losses, and it was abandoned on the edge of success. The dispirited troops returned to make winter camp on the south shore of Lake George.

The provincials were disturbed by dark suspicions of the general's motives. The losses were grievous, six men had been killed in Cleaveland's regiment, including Lieutenant Nathan Burnham of Chebacco, and eleven more wounded. A while later came information from French deserters that Montcalm's troops had been about to flee northward, but as Cleaveland observed, "we returned and saved them a deal of trouble!" Cleaveland complained that Abercrombie listened to none but his "ReHoboam-Counsellors":

Our field officers have not that equal rank . . . [with the regular army officers], which was promised, never was one of our provincial colonels called to counsel before we went down [to Ticonderoga] nor while there nor since our return, and know no more what is agoing to be done than a sergeant 'till the orders come out.

"We begin to think strongly," he wrote, "that the Grand Expedition against Canada is laid aside and a Foundation is going to be made to . . . impoverish our Country."[57]

But the search for fault turned, inevitably, inward. Cleaveland wished success on the rangers led by Major Robert

Rogers and his captain, Daniel Gidding of Chebacco, in these terms:

The Good Lord enable them to go forth in His Name and crown them with remarkable Success and wipe off the Reproach which lies upon us and defend our Land and Privileges. Amen and Amen.

God ordained all things and so this "reproach" was, ultimately, not because of British betrayal but was instead a divine judgment on New England. They must "purge the Army from Wickedness" because "our sins [are] the procuring cause of his righteous Judgment." Mary Cleaveland, his wife, writing of the local reaction to the "strange defeat" at Fort Ticonderoga, said that it was thought to be "one of the greatest if not the very greatest jud[g]ments we [have] ever seen, I fear the glory is a departing from New England." In referring to the "I-chabod," as she earlier called it, she linked the defeat to Increase Mather's famous jeremiad of that name, and to the historical understanding of the New England experience that it represented.[58]

The defeat, however, was soon followed by victories at Louisbourg and Fort Frontenac. Amidst the celebrations over the former, Mary Cleaveland wrote to her husband:

I think that we are loudly cal[l]ed upon to sing of mercy and of jud[g]ment. The reduction of Cape-Britten is mercy greater than we are senceable of and far greater than we deserve.[59]

The tide turned in 1758, and within a few years the French were driven from North America. Cleaveland returned to Chebacco in October 1758, went with occupation troops to Louisbourg the next summer, and then returned to his domestic and pastoral responsibilities. But imperial politics would soon disturb both his life and the lives of his parishioners again.

The imperial wars left Britain burdened with debt, which encouraged schemes for reorganizing the empire that

would produce more revenue. Each stage of colonial resistance to these schemes made the British ministry lean toward punitive, instead of merely pecuniary, measures. The
empire, which had played such a limited role in the lives of
the eighteenth-century villagers, had suddenly, in little
more than a decade, become an intrusive and threatening
force. The stable system, based on cooperation between the
royally appointed governor and the elected assembly, was
put under unprecedented stress by Parliament's postwar
policies. The parliamentary acts drastically reduced the
governor's discretionary powers, his ability to negotiate and
compromise with the assembly. The acts themselves attempted to extend the arm of the imperial bureaucracy into
each community and to create a new power of taxation
beyond the power of their elected representatives. Equally
serious were the punitive acts in the 1770s, which altered
the structure of government in Massachusetts and violated
the now venerable charter of 1692. Moreover, these acts
were to be enforced by royal troops. The final outrage, in
colonial eyes, was the Quebec Act, which created a Catholic, absolutist counter-empire in Canada and the Mississippi
valley.[60]

There are two ways of assessing local reaction to these
events. The first is on the basis of the official pronounce-
ments of the town meeting. The Stamp Act first roused the
meeting to action, when they instructed their representative that

As our subordination to our mother country had its foundation
intirely in our charter, . . . any measure not consistent with those
charters, and that deprives us of any right in them, is neither consistent with such subordination nor implied in it.

Thereafter, they voiced support for the "worthy 92 gentlemen" who refused to rescind the circular letter at Lord
Hillsborough's demand, protested the remaining Townshend tax on tea, responded to the call of Boston's commit-

tee of correspondence, and commended the "noble and spir-
ited" actions at the "tea party." The second source for
gauging local reactions to the revolutionary crisis is the political essays of the Reverend John Cleaveland. Though similar in many ways, they are fuller and more personal than
the town's responses.[61]

Before 1768, Cleaveland had not often felt called upon to
comment upon political affairs. In 1758, he and his fellow
chaplains had talked about drawing up a "Vindication of
the Army" for the newspapers, and in 1767, in his pamphlet on the revival, he praised the "SONS OF LIBERTY."
It was not, however, until the fall of 1768 that he wrote his
first political essay for the newly founded *Essex Gazette*.[62]

The *Gazette* had started publication the previous spring
in Salem and was the first newspaper in the province outside
of Boston. The editor, Samuel Hall, was a product of the
familial network of colonial printers. He had apprenticed
with his uncle, Daniel Fowle, and then worked for Ann
Franklin, the widow of Benjamin's brother James. Hall's
paper was committed to the Whig cause from the first. His
move to Salem may have been encouraged by Richard
Derby, the city's foremost merchant, who was much vic-
timized by "customs racketeers." The paper relied mostly
on the Boston papers for its material, especially for commentary on the current crisis. The other products of his
press reflect the intensification of political conflict in the
late 1760s and early 1770s. In 1768, three out of five of his
publications besides the newspaper were sermons on religious subjects; by 1775, sixteen out of twenty publications were on political subjects.[63]

The *Gazette* was part of an expanded network of political
communication. On publication days, a post rider carried
the papers to towns between Salem and Newburyport; in
1774, the route was extended northward to Haverhill. Hall
also employed a messenger to bring news and newspapers

from Boston, whose papers were involved in a network that stretched southward to Baltimore.[64]

The flow of information and commentary was most often from city to countryside. Cleaveland's essays were often the sole country voice in a mass of political writings imported from the metropolis. His self-perception may be revealed by the pseudonym under which he wrote most of his eleven essays: Johannes in Eremo—John in the Wilderness. The Latin phrase both echoes his own given name and refers to Matthew 3:1: "In those days came John the Baptist, preaching in the wilderness of Judea." The biblical John had come preaching repentance in anticipation of Christ's coming. Cotton Mather had used the phrase for the title of his memoirs of John Cotton, John Norton, John Wilson, and John Davenport, four English Puritans who had come to preach in the wilderness. And in 1773 Eleazar Wheelock, Cleaveland's old friend and patron, used "vox vociferantis in eremo" (Matt. 3:3) on the seal of his newly chartered college, located in the "wilderness" of New Hampshire. The prophet's role was an attractive one to evangelicals, and John's message, "Repent ye: for the kingdom of heaven is at hand" (Matt. 3:2), expressed a sense of urgency and crisis appropriate to the times. Cleaveland also used the phrase in a political sense, to express his community's relationship to the body politic. Though he lived "in quite an obscure corner" of the province, yet he wrote "as a true Member of the political Body, tho' placed at a local Distance from the Metropolis or Head."[65]

His first essay, protesting the Townshend Acts, was published in the October 25, 1768, issue of the *Essex Gazette*. Cleaveland feared imperial taxation because it threatened the rights in property that made the colonials free men.

Is it not the Birth-Right of Englishmen to be free? Can they be free, if they are taxed, to raise a Revenue, without their Consent?

JOHN CLEAVELAND

What Privilege of Englishmen is left us,—and wherein do we differ from mere *Slaves,* if the British Parliament may lay a Tax upon us, and will do it, without our Consent, for the Sole Purpose of raising a Revenue? —Is there not Such a Thing belonging to Englishmen as *Property?* Can one man dispose of the Property of another without his Consent and not be Guilty of Robbery? —Is *North-America,* with all its numerous Inhabitants, the Property of the House of Commons . . . ? If we are their Property, we are not the free sons of *Britannia* but the Slaves of that respectable house!

He was, as he had been after the "strange defeat" at Ticonderoga a decade before, suspicious of British motives. Might not these acts, he suggested, be a design by the King's ministers to provoke the colony into acts of rebellion so "that they may have Occasion to send the Force of *Britain* against us to take from us the Titles of our Lands and Possessions . . . which our worthy Predecessors with great Hazard and Expence obtained for, and have transmitted to us?"[66] Cleaveland here echoes his own "worthy predecessor," John Wise, who some eighty years before had also striven to protect the property of his farmer-folk from British encroachment. Given the centrality of land to the lives of these people, the anxiety about land titles and extralocal taxation here expressed is easily understood.

Cleaveland next wrote early in 1771, questioning the motives of the new governor, Thomas Hutchinson. He strongly suspected Hutchinson of being "a *meer tool* of an arbitrary minister of state" because he valued his royal instructions above the charter. This violation of the charter brought him back to the historical argument he had alluded to in his first essay. The immigrants to New England, he maintained, were free of the King's sovereignty once beyond his borders and had taken the land in the new world in their own name. Therefore, the charters had established a new relationship.

The political Union, Connection, Dependance and Subordination of the original unconquered Colonies of North-America to the

British empire and government . . . *are entirely founded in the Covenants and Compacts between Great-Britain and these Colonies, which
are contained in their Charters.*

The charter was a *"voluntary compact"* formed "for the End of
protecting, defending and promoting the natural Rights
and Properties of all the Individuals in each Confederation"
and a "Breach on either Side necessarily infers a total Dissolution."[67]
    This was the language of natural-rights philosophy, but
it was also very similar to the language used in his attempt
to define the nature of the church covenant some twenty-
five years before. His definition then was that "as all covenants, so church covenants, suppose two parties, each of
which have something to perform as a condition dependent
on each other." Cleaveland had also written that if relief "in
a way of order" was blocked, then one might seek "relief in
a way extra-judicial, since the main thing . . . can't be obtained otherwise. And to this all forms however useful,
must give way."[68]
    Cleaveland had pointed out the fundamental similarity
between the civil and ecclesiastical covenants in his 1767
pamphlet on the revival in his church. Stoutly maintaining
the ancient principle of congregational independence, he
drew a parallel with the contemporary political situation:

Pray, what *has roused up the spirits of the SONS OF LIBERTY at this
Time,* but an apprehended, or supposed unreasonable *Encroachment
upon their civil Rights and Liberty!* And ought we not to esteem our
sacred Right and Liberty as dearly?[69]

He elaborated upon the comparison in the second part of
the fifth Johannes essay, published on April 14, 1772.
Cleaveland compared the relationship of colonies to the imperial government with that of ministers and congregations, making clear the voluntary nature of such compacts
and the connection between Protestantism and liberty.
Whether made by empires or churches, the fundamental

nature of covenants was the same, and they were valid only so long as both parties were enjoying that for which they had contracted.[70]

Discussion of church covenants was common in New England, especially during the Great Awakening and its aftermath, when more than 200 churches in New England divided, nearly 90 in the province of Massachusetts alone.[71] Cleaveland adapted the language of the covenant to the current political crisis and in so doing helped to justify resistance to British authority for the rural majority. His analysis of the British violation of the secular covenant with the colonies helped him to interpret the conflict in light of God's covenant with New England. For if the people of New England were in the right, innocent victims of unlawful encroachments on their liberties, then God would protect them, as He had in the past. The intensifying crisis soon pushed him to this conclusion. Cleaveland's May 1774 essay expresses the ancient understanding of New England's relationship to the deity.

What shall we do to save ourselves from the Distresses brought upon us by an untoward Generation? I answer, Be not cast down, oh AMERICA! Be not discouraged, oh BOSTON! . . . Let all Ranks and Orders of Men reform from every Immorality and vicious Practice, and pray to the God [of] Heaven [and] Earth, *the preserver of men,* . . . to break every Weapon formed and forming against us,—to maintain our Rights and Privileges, civil and religious; and above all Things, to make us a holy and truly virtuous people, and to preserve us pure from the growing Pollutions of the World.

Here Cleaveland has quite literally assumed John the Baptist's role, and was crying, "Repent ye: for the kingdom of heaven is at hand."[72]

It is this understanding of the imperial conflict that accounts for the verbal violence of Cleaveland's attacks on General Gage and the Tories. If God was on the side of the colonists, then their opponents were, if not positively satanic, at least in defiance of His will. It is with full faith in the absolute rightness of his cause that Cleaveland called Gage "thou profane, wicked-monster of falsehood and perfidy" and advocated the confinement of Tories to the *"Simsbury-Mines."* With the certainty of a prophet, he warned Gage that "Heaven is armed with vengeance against you, . . . together with all those *parricides,* those monsters in human bodies, who have fled to your wing for protection."[73]

In 1775 he matched actions to words in defense of his cause. According to old accounts, "he preached all the young men among his people into the army and then went himself, taking his four sons with him."[74] Having alerted his people to the threat to their liberties, the militant old parson marched them off to war.

CHAPTER FIVE

✤

Revolution

THE PEOPLE OF the village were spurred to resistance, and eventually to armed struggle, against British authority because they saw in it a fundamental threat to their way of life. The war would change their way of life in some ways, though in others it would leave it much the same. The responsibility and the means for providing for the rising generation were not essentially changed, though Cleaveland would try to use the war itself to advance his children.

I. The Village at War

In late December 1774, John Cleaveland wrote a charter for a militia company in Chebacco "agreeable to the advice of the late provincial congress." In a scene typical of those being enacted throughout the province, the newly formed company elected its officers, then solemnly promised to defend "our constitutional privileges, whensoever there shall be a manifest call for it against our common Enemies."[1] Local control quickly replaced the governor's authority over the militia. By mid-April 1775, the Provincial Congress had reassumed the old royal government's power of appointment over officers and was preparing to organize an army. But before that plan was executed, General Gage sent troops to Concord to collect the rebels' stores. The minutemen were called out.[2]

News of the movement of royal troops out of Boston and the bloodshed at Lexington and Concord did not reach Chebacco until mid-day on April 19. The new militia company, led by their elected captain, Jonathan Cogswell, Jr., who at thirty-five was already the wealthiest farmer in the village, went to join the other Ipswich companies. They assembled and began a hurried march through Danvers and Salem, stopping for the night in Medford. They were too late for the skirmishes in Lexington and Concord, too late even to hinder the British retreat. The next morning, April 20, they headed home, reaching Salem the first night and Ipswich the next day.[3]

Before the troops returned, however, Ipswich was swept by a panic. The townspeople of Ipswich, having heard that the regulars had fired on the farmers of Middlesex and having sent more than 300 of their own into the fray, were jittery and ill-defended. On the morning of April 21, two ships were sighted off Great Neck and thought to be British men-of-war come to take British prisoners from the Ipswich jail. Conjecture became rumor, and rumor fact; soon the story of the regulars landing and attacking the town spread throughout Ipswich and the surrounding towns. By the time the tale reached Newbury, the messenger was crying,

For God's sake, turn out! Turn out! or you will all be killed! The regulars are marching this way and will soon be here. They are now at Ipswich cutting and slashing all before them.

The "Great Ipswich Fright," as J. G. Whittier later called it, spread rapidly northward. Many people, fearing for their lives and property, fled up the Merrimac Valley. Thomas Burnham, the grammar-school master, mustered the remaining men to defend the town.[4]

The townspeople's grim and bloody expectations grew out of a decade of strife. The use of British troops in armed combat against Massachusetts farmers confirmed the darkest suspicions of a conspiracy to enslave America, in progress since 1763. The bloodshed at Lexington and Concord thoroughly aroused the countryside and brought forth from John Cleaveland an impassioned valedictory:

King George the third adieu! no more shall we cry to you for protection! no more shall we bleed in defense of your person, —your breach of covenant! your violation of faith! your turning a deaf ear to our cries for justice, for covenanted protection and salvation from the oppressive, tyrannical and bloody measures of the British parliament, and putting a sanction upon all their measures to enslave and butcher us, have DISSOLVED OUR ALLEGIANCE to your crown and government! your sword that ought in *justice to protect us,* is now drawn *with a witness* to destroy! —O George see thou to thine own house.[5]

The intensity of the local commitment to the defense of their rights is most clearly reflected in the record of enlistments. Almost three quarters of the males in Chebacco eligible for military service, between the ages of sixteen and fifty, went on active duty at some time during the war. About forty villagers served in Colonel Moses Little's regiment, under the command of Captain Abraham Dodge of the Hamlet Parish. Their own minister, John Cleaveland, was regimental chaplain. Little, a Newbury farmer fifty years of age, commanded the 24th regiment of the provincial army, stationed in Cambridge during the siege of Boston. The Chebacco company saw action during the Battle of Bunker Hill. One of their number, a boy of fifteen named Jesse Story, was killed; another, Francis Burnham, was wounded.[6]

In 1776, many Chebacco soldiers served under Captain Daniel Gidding, son of the late church elder of the same name and a farmer and lawyer like his father before him. The intense fears of invasion by sea that had flared into the "Great Ipswich Fright" still troubled the citizens of the North Shore communities, so in January 1776 the Provin-

cial Congress established a seacoast-defense unit in Gloucester and Beverly. The men of Chebacco served in Gloucester,
just a few miles from home, in the regiment of Colonel Foster, a Chebacco native turned Gloucester merchant.

In the fall of 1776, other villagers marched off to Long
Island, and later the Battle of White Plains, with Jonathan
Cogswell, Jr., once captain of their minutemen company
and now colonel of his own regiment. Cleaveland, then in
his mid-fifties, took one last tour of service as chaplain with
this regiment. In the fall of 1777, volunteers from Captain
David Low's militia company went to reinforce General
Gates's army, then struggling with Burgoyne in upstate
New York. After "Gentleman Johnny" 's surrender, Che-
bacco men helped to escort his defeated army back to
Charlestown and Cambridge and then guarded them until
they could be transported to England.

As the theater of war shifted southward, the participation
of Chebacco men decreased but did not stop altogether.
Some, under the command of Captain Joseph Hodgkins of
Ipswich, stayed with General Gates's army from the spring
of 1777 through the great victory at Saratoga to the bitter
winter at Valley Forge.[7] Others, over 20 percent of those
who served in one of the revolutionary armies, enlisted in
the Continental army. Most enlisted in 1777 or in 1779
under the command of their fellow villager, Captain John
Burnham, and fought the long, wasting war from the middle colonies to the final battle at Yorktown. In the end at
least nine villagers, including Captain Burnham and
Cleaveland's eldest son, had served out the entire war. Eleven men, nearly 10 percent of those who enlisted during the
war, died in the army, though more often from camp dis-
eases than in combat.

The war—in its political, military, or economic
aspects—touched the life of every villager. The impact,
however, was not uniform. Most influenced by the war were
the young men, who bore the brunt of the fighting. More

than 60 percent of the soldiers from Chebacco were under thirty at the time of their enlistment; more than 80 percent were under forty. Of those who fought outside the Commonwealth, in the later stages of the war, the pattern is even more marked. More than 70 percent of those who served out of state were under thirty. Almost all of those who enlisted in the Continental army or who served out the entire war enlisted in their twenties. Only seven men in their forties took up arms beyond Massachusetts's boundaries. Two, Daniel Gidding and David Low, were officers, and the rest were landless laborers and artisans.

Middle-aged, landowning farmers served during the alarm of April 19, 1775, and in the seacoast-defense unit in nearby Gloucester. Thereafter they confined their military service to the reserve "alarm list," which was to be called out in case of sudden enemy attack on the village. For the rest of the war, fought as it was in distant places, the burden fell upon dependent men, the young, and the poor. Those who bore the burdens and enjoyed the privileges of property remained behind to tend it.

But the war also affected those who stayed home. The village was not torn by internal dissent. There were only two avowed loyalists in Ipswich, Dr. John Calef and Samuel Porter, a young lawyer with a small farm in Chebacco. Both fled. The intolerance of the local patriots is best shown by the experience of Jonathan Stickney, Jr., who was an undergraduate at Harvard College. In April 1776 he was arrested, sent to the General Court, and sentenced to solitary confinement in the Ipswich jail for

having in the most open and daring manner endeavored . . . to encourage & introduce Discontent, Sedition, and a Spirit of Disobedience to all lawful authority . . . by frequently clamoring in the most impudent insulting and abusive Language against the American Congress, the General Court of this Colony and others who have been exerting themselves to save the Country from Misery & Ruin.

The unfortunate young man, having made an abject apology to the authorities, was remanded in early June to his father's custody.[8]

The village was mostly free of external threats as well. No battles were fought in Essex County; no hostile troops occupied her towns or disturbed her citizens' property. Unlike many middle-colony communities, Chebacco was spared these most tangible and distressing of wartime experiences. Yet the war still had an important effect on Cleaveland's community.

Most immediately, it brought severe dislocations in the local economy. The provincial army drew off manpower necessary for the operation of family farms. The agricultural-labor force in the village was properly allocated by the hiring of dependent young adult males by farmers with insufficient indigenous manpower. It was this flexible labor supply that was drawn on so heavily by the revolutonary army.[9]

The maritime industries that provided the most important source of supplementary income were even more hard hit by the war. In 1771, about seventy-five men and boys found part-time employment working the twenty-five fishing boats that sailed out of Chebacco, and others doubtless worked on boats sailing out of nearby Gloucester, Marblehead, or Salem. Most men in the village, especially young men, went on fishing expeditions to the Grand Banks during the "fall fare," after harvest, or the "spring fare," before spring planting. Some villagers were full-time sailors; others had substantial maritime investments. Chebacco also built boats. The three-man fishing boat so popular locally was called a Chebacco boat because of its supposed origin in the village. The extent of the local involvement in boat building is hard to estimate, although the existence of three sawmills in a village of perhaps 150 families may be some indication of its importance.

These complex maritime enterprises were hampered, if

not actually curtailed, by the war. Loss of labor to the army, especially from the pool of young dependent or semidependent males, was harmful. Of equal importance was the danger from a hostile Royal Navy. David Choate, a young man fishing out of Chebacco in these troubled times, described his experiences in a journal entry of 1779.

We got down to Dammerils Cove; can make no hand of fishing here[,] there is so many cruisers about, we were drove up Kennebeck river, got down again after a few days & made the best of our way home, . . . conclude not to go to the Eastward again on account of the English Privateers being so thick on that shore.[10]

This added to the risk of oceangoing enterprises. Some men served on American privateers, but generally the war greatly reduced the maritime commerce that had played such an important part in the village economy.

Curtailment of trade soon resulted in shortages and rising prices. The outcome was inflation far more virulent than any in the previous history of the Commonwealth. A staple like Indian corn, quoted at 4 shillings per bushel in January 1777, sold for 8 pounds by Janaury 1780. The value of the currency printed by the new state government depreciated rapidly in relationship to specie. By April 1780, one dollar in hard money, silver or gold, was worth forty dollars in paper. Various attempts at price fixing were made, based on appeals both patriotic and practical, but despite all efforts the inflationary spiral continued—further spurred by an influx of depreciated continental paper.[11]

Most internal transactions in the village were based on credit and eventual payment in kind, and thus were little affected by inflation. Still, the community was far from self-sufficient. Some foods and manufactured goods had to be imported at inflated prices. The complex web of debtor-creditor relationships that crisscrossed the community was also threatened. Debtors were tempted to pay off old debts with paper currency the face value of which was increasingly at variance with its depreciated exchange value.[12]

The demands of the tax collector grew during wartime as well, as both state and local governments struggled to meet the expenses of recruiting and supporting an army. In 1780 alone, according to the local historian, Ipswich

furnished . . . as its required proportion, 106 shirts, 106 pairs of stockings and shoes, and 33 blankets; raised 60 men for six months, and 12 horses for the public service; voted £1200, to hire soldiers for the continental army; [and] furnished 31,800 pounds of beef.[13]

These staggering demands on local resources were made, and met, year after year. Cleaveland, as a salaried man paid by public taxation, felt the pinch early and severely. In his salary request for 1780 he complained that

what my people have raised for me ever since they have acted as the united parish [1775] has fell far short of affording me a comfortable and honorable subsistence owing very much to the depreciation of the currency; and as the regulation of prices last made is now laid aside as a rule of buying and selling, I would humbly move to the parish to take under consideration the raising of my salary this year in species—in corn for instance.[14]

Although the parish made a heroic effort on his behalf, raising his salary nearly 350 percent, the rate of inflation that year was 500 percent.

The pastor's economic travail was compounded by the coming of age of his sons and daughters. His resources would be stretched to their limits, and sometimes beyond, by his efforts to find good places for his children. The wartime world was different from that which he and his generation had known, but war or no war, each family still faced the problem of financing the rising generation from available domestic resources. John Cleaveland, like old Moses before him, had too little land to divide among his sons, and so he had to find other ways to provide for them.

II. Domestic Economy

During the Revolution, the Cleaveland household underwent fundamental changes. Its structure altered as the children came of age and went out into the world. Other relatives and servants took their places as Cleaveland strove to meet both family responsibilities and the manpower needs of his farm. The family circle was first broken in 1768 by the death of his wife, Mary Dodge Cleaveland.

Mary Cleaveland died of breast cancer in April 1768, at age forty-six.[15] One of her last acts, less than a month before her death, was to divide, at the behest of her "beloved husband," her bedding, clothing, jewelry, silver, and other household items among her daughters, thus starting the division of personal goods that would comprise their portion. She had other property in her own right, including a one-third interest in the family farm and an outstanding bequest from the estate of her uncle John Choate, but these remained in the hands of her husband.[16]

For Cleaveland, with a farm to run and seven children between the ages of six and twenty to raise, remarriage was a certainty. When he wrote to his oldest daughter about her marriage prospects, less than a year after his wife's death, he also commented on his own. He was, as he wrote a little later to his old patron Eleazar Wheelock, now president of Dartmouth College, "lonely and the care of my family [is] doubled upon me." "I am ready," he wrote,

to think never man was blest with a better wife than I was, her price was above rubies; and I desire to be thankful, that I have been made to acquiesce in the sovereign good pleasure of God in taking her away as being as wise holy and good as His giving her to me was, and I believe God can make up the loss not only in

Himself but also in giving me another companion as good as she was, tho' at present I can't see the person that appears likely to supply and make good her place.

His sternly orthodox acceptance of her death (God was "as wise holy and good" in "taking her away" as He was in "giving her to me") was joined with a candid prayer for compensation ("supply," as in a ministerial replacement, and "make good her place," in the language of office-holding). Cleaveland's affection and admiration for his late wife did not preclude an immediate and active interest in finding a successor.[17]

His search came to an end some seventeen months later in September 1769, when he married Mary Foster, the widow of a merchant from nearby Manchester. She was born Mary Neale in Salem in 1730 and had returned there after her husband's death in 1766. There were no surviving children from her marriage, and the responsibility for her step-children fell upon her late husband's family. It is not clear how Cleaveland came to know her. She was, ironically, a niece and an heir of Cleaveland's old rival, Theophilus Pickering.[18]

Mary Neale Foster Cleaveland was, like her predecessor, a woman of some property with impressive family connections on the maternal side. The Pickering family were prosperous farmers with commercial interests, much like the Choates, and her uncle, Deacon Timothy, was a leader of the Salem community. His son—her cousin, Colonel Timothy—would play a part on a much larger stage in years to come.[19] Mary's father had left her a half-interest in a house in Salem, and her husband had left her the whole of a larger house just across the street as part of her share in his estate, which was valued in the whole at almost 4,000 pounds. But the family properties were heavily mortgaged, and in the end all she salvaged was about 160 pounds in money at interest, 40 pounds in household goods, and a

Negro servant named Violet, valued at 26 pounds 13 shillings 4 pence. Although her resources were modest by Salem standards, in Chebacco they were worth nearly three times Cleaveland's annual salary.[20]

The material advantages of his second marriage capped a prosperous decade for the Chebacco minister. His salary had steadily increased during his ministry in Chebacco, reaching a peak in 1770. Between 1747 and 1752, his salary was paid by voluntary donation. In 1752, the province made his supporters into a separate parish, and thereafter the tax collector gathered his salary, which rose from about 40 pounds to 65 pounds in 1765. After 1766 he preached to, and was paid by, both parishes, and his combined salary reached 90 pounds in 1770. It fell off in the hard times that followed but stayed within the range of 60 pounds to 65 pounds for the rest of his long ministry.[21]

His income and expenditures were part of the complex network of credit that shaped the internal economy of the village. His salary was voted at the parish's annual election meeting in March, after which the trustees of the parish apportioned that sum among the householders in the village and drew up the tax lists. The taxes, however, were only slowly collected. The parish accounts indicate that between 1776 and 1797 it took, on the average, more than four years to collect all the taxes and close the accounts for any one year. In the most extreme case, the taxes for 1780 were not finally collected until January 1796. Cleaveland, then, did not receive his salary in a lump sum. Instead, it was more like an account on the parish against which he might draw for necessary expenditures. As in most local accounts, money changed hands only in the final settlement or when Cleaveland borrowed money from villagers against his tax revenues.

This use of his salary is well illustrated by his running account with John Choate, his first wife's cousin and the son of Elder Francis Choate. Between 1771 and 1777, Choate provided Cleaveland with 9 pounds 9 shillings 11 pence worth of tools (spade, scythe), supplies (molasses, fish, salt, sugar), and clothes (shoes, cloth, buttons). In 1774, he also paid Ebenezer Mansfield, a laborer, 1 pound 16 shillings, presumably for work on Cleaveland's farm. In return, Cleaveland give Choate orders on individual taxpayers for rates owed for specific years. The taxpayers would then pay Choate on their own accounts and their receipts from him would be duly credited by the parish tax collector.[22]

The running accounts of Cleaveland, the parish, and individual creditors of Cleaveland and debtors of the parish tax collector grew enormously complex over time. Thus, in 1770, Cleaveland and the parish negotiated a mutual forgiveness for the years between 1747 and 1768. He forgave them the accumulated arrearages on his ministerial rates, and his creditors in the parish—thirty-four farmers, fishermen, shopkeepers, and artisans—forgave him "all demands, charges, accounts and book-debts whatsoever, that we have or may have made and kept against him."[23] His salary was not his sole means of support. He also had a farm, which had been purchased for him in 1749, after his ordination and marriage.

According to the title deeds, the farm, purchased on his behalf for the most part by his first wife's relatives, consisted of "about thirty-eight acres" of "upland and salt-marsh" with a "dwelling house, barn, smith shop, [and other] edifices" as well as an orchard. The house was on the road to the old Cogswell homestead, now Spring Street, and was probably built by Adam Cogswell in the last decade of the seventeenth century.[24] Cleaveland later accumulated other holdings. In 1760, he purchased, in common with his wife's uncle Francis Choate and two of Choate's sons, fifty-two acres of woodland near the Gloucester line. Two years later he bought four more acres of woodland in the same area. With a forty-acre farm and twenty-odd acres of woodland, Cleaveland had holdings that equaled the median for

Chebacco farmers.[25] The farm was, in the manner of family properties, heavily burdened by obligations, in this case to his wife's family. His wife's death in 1768 left him in control of her third share in the farm, which had been purchased by her brother (partially out of her unpaid dowry) and given to her some time before his death in 1758.

The 1760s were a time of accumulation for Cleaveland. An account sheet of 1762 indicates that Cleaveland had by that time managed to clear nearly 100 pounds over his living expenses. His chaplain's wages, earned in 1758–1759, were an important supplement to his regular income. About 52 pounds had gone into the purchase of woodland and about 45 pounds into paying off the proprietors of his estate. This, along with his wife's share, increased his right and title in the farm to about two fifths. By 1777, that had increased to about four fifths. He made, however, little progress in clearing off the encumbrances during the war. Times were harder then, of course, but the greatest strain on Cleaveland's resources came from his responsibility for launching his children into the world. This effort absorbed much of his energy in the 1770s and 1780s. His hopes and ambitions for his children were the moving force behind the steady accumulation of the years past.[26]

Family and property were always linked for John Cleaveland, as they had been for previous generations in his family. His appeal to his father for help in purchasing a farm in Chebacco had been based on the necessity of having "some interest" in the world to leave to his family.[27] But his ambitions for his children were more than merely material. In 1759, Cleaveland, then serving as chaplain in Louisbourg, had written a letter in wretched verse "to all my children together."[28]

All you my children dear, in knowledge young,
Attend unto the counsels of my tongue;
You are your father's hope, your father's joy,
Let pious thoughts, not toys, your minds employ;

If you desire a length of happy days,
Obey your parents—walk in holy ways;
If joy and peace to crown your mortal state,
Restrain your lips from slander and deceit;
If happy you would be, when time's no more,
Believe in Christ our Lord, and Him adore.

After the opening stanza, he devoted one stanza to each
child and one to Hannah Bear, the family's spinster servant.
Piety and obedience were enjoined on each child by their
absent father, but otherwise his ambitions for his daughters
and sons were quite different. From his eldest son and
namesake, then nine years of age, he expected serious preparation for a career.

Now John, my eldest son, your father's joy,
While you are young, your time and thoughts employ,
Good learning to procure, and not in play;
. . . .
If you a minister design to be,
Avoid all sinful ways, your book study:

His eldest daughter, Mary, then age eleven, was not coun-
seled as to education or career. Instead, Cleaveland directed
her attention to domestic responsibilities and social graces.

Love your brothers, sister and kinfolk near;
Courteous and modest be to neighbors all,
Civil to rich and poor, to great and small.

The daughters of the house were prepared in the home for
their future lives as wives and mothers and were consequently less of a drain on family resources. But the standing and resources of the family strongly influenced their
prospects in the marriage market, which in turn shaped the
rest of their lives. His daughters had fears of spinsterhood,
fears that were well founded. Many young women in the old
towns of eastern Massachusetts would not find husbands, as
increasing numbers of young men left for less settled parts

of New England. Though Cleaveland's genteel profession gave his daughters high social standing in the village, they were still women of limited fortune and uncertain prospects. He could manage dowries of only sixty pounds for his daughters, and that mostly in personal items and household goods. This was less than a third of what their mother's dowry had been. And spinsterhood for them meant a lifetime of dependence, without ever having the privileges and responsibilities of married women.[29]

Mary was the first of Cleaveland's children to contemplate matrimony. While on a visit away from home in May 1769, she wrote to her father about her marital prospects. She was then two months away from her twenty-first birthday and had borne her mother's responsibilities in the household for more than a year. Cleaveland wrote a long, cautionary reply, beginning,

Dear Daughter,
    Last night I had a line put into my hand with your name to it, expressing your thoughts and desiring my advice relating to a matter of great importance in this life.
    And in reply, I say, I would have you chuse for yourself. I would not have you accept of this or that man's offer for fear you shall not have another, and so try to make the best of him you can.

He then went on to review her current suitors.

As to Mr. F———R, it is a mistake [to think] that I dislike him because he is a blacksmith. I know nothing . . . either of his character, parentage or worldly estate. I have only seen him transiently, and all that ever I said of him that would bear any degree of deminution, was to this purpose, that he did not cut a more agreable figure than Mr. Woodman if so much.

Despite his reservations, Cleaveland insisted that she must "chuse her [own] mind" according to the dictates of "judgment and fancy." Then he ended the letter on a final note of caution.

When you have an offer, that shall appear to you upon all accounts quite agreable and suitable, I give you leave to accept of it,
but don't be hasty in coming to a determination,

> From your careful and
> affectionate father,
> John Cleaveland[30]

Cleaveland exercised his paternal authority in an oddly
backhanded way. The choice, he said, was hers, but he
managed to make his opinions about suitability of "character, parentage [and] worldly estate" quite clear. He was, to
all appearances, persuasive. She married neither the black-
smith nor the faintly praised Woodman. When she did
marry, some two years later, she chose Jonathan Proctor,
who was the son of a well-to-do farmer.

Mary Cleaveland's father-in-law, Isaac Proctor, owned
more than 400 acres, consisting of two substantial farms,
one in Chebacco and one in Manchester. He was also a pious
man who joined Cleaveland's church during the revival of
1763–1764 and who began his will with a lengthy spiritual
narrative. In Cleaveland's eyes, it was probably an altogether "agreable and suitable" match.[31]

His youngest daughter, Abigail, did as well, if not better, when she married Joseph Cogswell. His father, Jonathan Cogswell, was a deacon in Cleaveland's church who
owned about 300 acres in Chebacco. The Cogswells, moreover, were connected to some of Ipswich's "best" families,
the Appletons and the Wades. Deacon Cogswell, whose
total worth was perhaps twice that of Isaac Proctor, called
himself a gentleman, while Proctor never claimed more
than yeoman's status.[32]

Neither daughter married the eldest son or principal heir
of these distinguished local citizens. But both married into
goodly and godly families, and both were established by
their fathers-in-law on substantial farms in southern New
Hampshire. As in their father's case, clerical gentility, not
wealth, helped them to make good marriages. The middle

daughter, unfortunately, had less happy experiences.[33]

Elizabeth Cleaveland was born in January 1757, the fifth child and second daughter of the Chebacco minister and his first wife. In the late 1770s, she gave birth to an illegitimate daughter, who was named Lois. Some years later, the story reached William Bentley, a liberal minister of Salem unfriendly to Cleaveland, who wrote in his diary after a ministerial association meeting in Chebacco that Cleaveland was "a man of small abilities . . . [whose] daughter in the zeal of night meetings was overtaken by temptation, and fell."[34]

Premarital conception of children was not uncommon at this time. Cleaveland regularly admitted such couples to his church after they made a "sincere apology" for their sin. But he did not like what necessity forced upon him. When writing to his son in 1769 about local news, he observed,

Molly Foster is like to have a child, I suppose by Gage, Pat Holmes by Mo' and Betty Giddinge by one Allen of Manchester. Satan rules. Be sober[,] be vigilent[.] For the devil is your adversary, watch and pray.

In any case, his own daughter's situation was far worse. Not only was she the minister's daughter, but for some reason marriage did not follow her transgression. Whether the father of her child was grossly unsuitable or had simply taken the high road out of town, it is impossible now to know.[35]

It is hard to say what Elizabeth Cleaveland felt about all this, or how her family treated her. Her only surviving literary record is a relation of her conversion experience, written in July 1782. It was a conventional statement of religious experience with an oblique reference to "trouble . . . in the family," which she wished "to be sanctified" or turned to her eventual good. In her petition to God to turn earthly pain to spiritual advantage, she expressed an orthodox attitude toward misfortune. There was also, perhaps, a hint of her experiences as a pregnant and unmarried young woman in her description of hell as that "yonder region of horror and despair! O that is insupportable, the thought of a never ending eternity, to be upbraded by devils." From this odd, seemingly personal image, one can sense something of the family's treatment of her.[36]

She and her child long remained a part of the Cleaveland household as dependents under the rule of her father and her stepmother. The tone of that relationship and her restlessness within it is captured by a letter written to her by Cleaveland, when she was past thirty and all of her sisters and brothers were married and established on their own. He urged her, in his absence, to

[s]trive to be a very good girl, daily pray to God for the pardon of your sins[,] that God would bless you with an obedient temper of heart to all Gods commands, that you daily read the Bible and be sure you keep the Sabbath, and at all times obey your mother with chearfulness.

Since she was not a married woman, she was, in her father's eyes, still a "girl." As his stress on "chearful" obedience suggests, she was perhaps still a somewhat willful "girl."[37]

Perhaps these restraints led her, when she was nearly forty, to marry against her father's will. She accepted a proposal from one Abraham Channel, a peripatetic and penniless tailor with a batch of children from a previous marriage. It was a much poorer match than those that her sisters had made, as her father was quick to point out. He tried to dissuade her by telling her what support she might expect from him both during his life and after his death, if she did not marry. He would, he wrote, "rejoyce" to see her married, "provided, you can better yourself by it, and be in a situation to serve God and your generation with christian reputation."[38]

The same words could have been used to express Cleaveland's hopes for his sons, though with careers, not marriage, in mind. It was more difficult and more expensive to set up his sons in the world. His farm would not admit of a division and would not, without a ministerial salary, support even one son in the "comfortable and honorable" manner to which Cleaveland aspired. He hoped to send them to college, in preparation for a profession, preferably his own. He had always intended John, his eldest son and namesake, for the ministry, but

> tho' he had advanced so far in learning, that he might enter college, yet as close study hurt his health and bro't him almost into a consumption, he has laid aside his books and betook himself to husbandry-labour, which suits his health much better.

This he wrote to his old friend Eleazar Wheelock, who, as president of Dartmouth, conducted an institution along evangelical lines satisfactory to Cleaveland. In place of young John, he offered Wheelock his second son, Parker, who "has a great mind to come to your school." Parker, he wrote, "has activity and sprightliness enough but no appearance of saving grace." It may have been these spiritual failings that kept Parker out of college, but it was more likely his father's economic failings. "My circumstances," Cleaveland wrote, "are such at present that I could not carry him thro' college" without help.[39]

Cleaveland's third son, Ebenezer, was trained as a cooper; but Ceaveland had not lost his ambition to educate his sons for a genteel profession. He tried again, a few years later, with his youngest son, Nehemiah. While visiting his family in Canterbury, old John had been inspired by the sight of two nephews, who were "promising candidates for the gospel ministry," to make Nehemiah "an offer, if he chose it, to give him what learning I could in the languages etc. and he might get a degree at college by tarrying one or two years." Whether Nehemiah chose not to, or the family finances forbade it, neither he nor any son of John Cleaveland ever attended college. Lack of funds was the persistent problem, but his sons may also have felt some reluctance to follow so closely in their father's footsteps.[40]

They did have professional ambitions, however. Parker Cleaveland spent two years (1769–1770) studying medicine with Dr. Elisha Lord of Pomfret, Connecticut. Pomfret was near the old Cleaveland family homestead in Canterbury; Parker, who was only eighteen when he began his studies, was under the supervision of his uncles. At the conclusion of his first year of study, his father "consent[ed] to your living with [Dr. Lord] a twelvemonth on his last terms, provided you will try, as soon as that term is out, either by keeping school or some other honest way, to be getting the money to pay the Dr."[41] The "tuition" of twenty pounds per year represented about a quarter of Cleaveland's salary, and Cleaveland still had a wife and six children at home. He was feeling the pinch acutely when, in another letter, he urged Parker to be prepared to make his own way in the world.

My wants are so many on every side and my income so small, that I know not what to do. —You must therefore strive to get your learning as soon and as cheap as possible so as to get into some lawful way of earning something as soon as may be.[42]

The expenses were met, his education was completed, and in 1771 Parker Cleaveland settled in nearby Byfield, a parish lying between Rowley and Newbury. Less than two years later, just before his twenty-second birthday, he married Elizabeth Jackman, the daughter of a neighboring farmer. He was, at that early age, independent. He was a doctor, a husband, and, after a while, a father.

Parker's older brother did not fare so well. As late as 1773, John Cleaveland, Jr., was still working on his father's farm. In a sense, Parker had assumed some of John's prerogatives as oldest son, which caused some bad feelings between the two brothers. An incident in the fall of 1772 had brought John's feelings of resentment out into the open.

Earlier that year Parker had persuaded his father to allow him the use of a pasture on the family farm to fatten some cattle. The ambitious but inexperienced young entrepreneur chose unwisely. His appeal to his father for aid provoked a reply that revealed his father's anger and his brother's jealousy.

I hope these steers turning out so poorly will make you more guarded in buying cattle for the future. —And as to their being no damage to me, they prevented my taking in two or three creatures to pasture, and you ought to consider, as you have had almost two years for yourself, before you were 21, and your brother John lived with me not only till he was 21, but almost two years since to carry on my farming business, and I have not been able to let him have so much, by half as yet, as your horse, bridle, saddle and books amount to, which I have purchased for you, he thinks hard of it, and would no doubt have been glad to have filled up the pasture for himself. I love all my children and should be glad to do for all of them abundantly more than I am able at present to do.[43]

The final act in this domestic melodrama came several months later. In April 1773, after John had finally left his father's farm, he returned to visit Chebacco. John and his father were firm in insisting that Parker come to him to pay his respects. A more open confrontation between the brothers was averted, as this note from the father to Parker would indicate.

Your brother John has taken back his letter and burnt it so that he has not seen mine and I would not have you say anything to him about it.[44]

The older brother had gone to stay with his father's family in Canterbury. In February 1773, he married his cousin, Abigail Adams, after which he lived and worked on the Adams family farm. From there he sent lugubrious letters to his family in Massachusetts expressing his religiosity and his general dissatisfaction with life.

He played rather hard, in this correspondence, on the theme of life's transitoriness. In a note to Parker, written on a visit to Chebacco, he requested his company but then observed, "If you cannot come and if we should never see each other any more in this world," he would ask God's blessing for him.[45] In a later letter to his father, he explained why a planned visit had to be postponed, adding,

whether or no I shall ever come down to see you again, or whether I shall ever see any of my relations down there, any more in this world, is very uncertain, for we have no lease of our time, no not of one hour.

Moreover,

in case I should live any considerable time in the world my circumstances are such at the present that I do not think it my duty to tarry in these parts much longer . . . if I do go it is likely I shall go to some distant country . . . therefore . . . it is very unlikely that ever I shall come to see you any more.[46]

But the war intervened to thwart the unhappy young man's plans to go to "some distant country." By the summer of 1775, the male Cleavelands were reunited in the service of their country. The three older brothers all enlisted in the revolutionary army besieging British-occupied Boston and were stationed in Cambridge. Their father served as chaplain to the troops and their younger brother Nehemiah as his aide. The war would give direction to the lives of the young Cleavelands for a time.

III. Places in a Revolutionary World

The revolutionary war enlisted Cleaveland's deepest sympathies, for he saw it in the context of God's providential plan for his people in New England. He also came to see it as another stage in his campaign to find good places in the world for his sons. During their first enlistment, he devoted much energy to finding suitable places for them in the army. An officer's billet was appropriate for a gentleman. To the Cleavelands, it seemed both prestigious and lucrative.

For Cleaveland's eldest son, without profession or prospects, the war provided an honorable, if temporary, occupation. Cleaveland made an appeal to his younger brother, Colonel Aaron, that "if you should have a regiment I bespeak the adjutants' birth in it for my son John."[47] The best his uncle was able to arrange for him was a sergeant's billet. Young John was happy enough in the army, though, and rose in time to the rank of lieutenant, spending most of the war riding post between Connecticut and New York or serving guard duty in Danbury, Connecticut. He was, as befit a parsonage-bred boy, somewhat priggish about the "bad company" with which he was "surrounded," whose "ideas rise no higher than the grogg-shop." But, as he assured his brother Parker, he had

the agreeable satisfaction to converse with gentlemen of genius, taste, and education in the army, and you may be assured there are many such here notwithstanding the contemptuous idea, the city, and country gentlemen conceive of the army.

The war rescued young John Cleaveland from an enervating period of drift and gave his life some purpose: "I esteem it a high honor, to be employed [in pro]moting the good of my country."[48]

For the second son, Parker, the war presented different opportunities. The war was only another episode in old John's vigorous attempts to win professional advancement for his second son. Apparently Parker's humble practice in the backwater parish of Byfield did not satisfy his father, who before the war had advised his son of opportunities in Ipswich and in Moultenborough, New Hampshire. Old

John watched the careers and lives of other local practitioners with almost ghoulish interest.

> If Dr. Rust should not live thro the small-pox, and as Dr. M——
> has put a finishing stroke to his being improved again in Ipswich,
> you may perhaps, think the door opened in divine providence to
> move in, especially, if any of the Ipswich people of influence,
> should speak encouragingly of it.[49]

Despite his father's best efforts, Parker was still in Byfield when the war broke out. In early June 1775 old John cornered Dr. Joseph Warren, who was acting as surgeon-general, and eventually finagled a surgeon's berth for Parker in the 16th regiment, commanded by Colonel Paul Dudley Sargent.[50] In December 1775, Parker lost his place to another, although the Cleavelands had thought it guaranteed to him. The hot-tempered old parson sent off a scorching letter to Colonel Sargent, which ended with a lecture on the behavior expected of a gentleman.

> Nothing, I suppose, will touch a person of honor to the quick like
> a conviction of acting out of character.—He feels it, if he under-
> stands [that] any person of credit thinks he has acted out of char-
> acter, and especially, if they complain that their character or in-
> terest is affected thereby—and won't rest till he has righted and
> made all things easy.[51]

The next day, he sent a much more soothing letter to Colonel Edmund Phinney, appealing for a surgeon's berth for his son, but to no avail.[52] Parker was destined to spend the rest of the war in private practice.

Cleaveland's two younger sons, Ebenezer and Nehemiah, were still boys living at home when the war broke out. They first saw military service as aides to their father or brothers. The war was for them the beginning of adulthood. Ebenezer first served in 1775 as a waiter to his brother Parker in his post as surgeon of the 16th regiment. His father tried at least twice to arrange a lieutenancy for him, including an appeal to his brother Aaron, but without success. Most of Ebenezer's later military service was as a common seaman on a privateer. Ebenezer was less favored than most of Cleaveland's children. He bore facial scars and was missing an eye, as the result of a childhood accident. He was also, unlike any of the other sons, raised to a trade, that of cooper. In 1777, though, fortune seemed to smile upon him. In that year he married Mary Rust Cogswell and moved to "Little Cambridge" (now Belmont), where he probably practiced his trade. His bride was the daughter of the late Joseph Rust, a prosperous innkeeper and farmer, and the recent widow of Jonathan Cogswell, son of Deacon Jonathan. It was a good marriage by village standards.[53]

Soon the young couple had a son, who was called John in his grandfather's honor. The little boy was the first male grandchild in the Cleaveland line. This was a cause of some anxiety for the two older brothers, both married four years and still childless. John, Jr., whose prerogative regarding his father's name was now lost, wrote to his brother Parker:

I am informed that our brother Ebenezer Cleaveland has fairly beat his two elder brothers in the business of procreation—tho I have not heard lately how the case is with you, in this respect, yet as I have not been informed to the contrary, I suppose you still possess the same barren desert as heretofore—we ought not to be discontented under the allotments of providence.[54]

The child died, but was replaced in less than a year's time with another son, who was also named John.

In 1778, Ebenezer had hopes of leaving Little Cambridge and "taking a tavern in Boston . . . called the Green-Dragon and the Free-Masons-Lodge."[55] These plans may have fallen through, for in the autumn of 1779 he moved his wife and child to his father's house. Wracked by persistent ill health and fears of consumption, he signed on to a merchant ship sailing from Salem to the West Indies, in the hope that an ocean voyage would be beneficial to his health.

His voyage was very unhealthful. The merchant ship was

stopped by an English privateer, and Ebenezer, whose scarred face suggested that he was a deserter from the Royal Navy, was taken. He escaped from the English privateer in the West Indies and signed on a Dutch merchant ship bound for St. Eustatius. The Dutch ship was taken by a French ship for carrying contraband and the crew thrown into prison at Guadeloupe. Many were "seized of the jail-fever and dyed like rotten sheep," but Ebenezer and the other survivors were rescued by a continental privateer. The privateer carried them back to St. Eustatius, and there Ebenezer signed on the ship *Eustis,* another privateer. He worked for a time but then fell ill again with "jail-fever" and died on March 30, 1780, a little more than two weeks sailing time from home.[56]

His father heard the news and sent his youngest son, Nehemiah, to ask how Ebenezer had "expressed his mind about dying." Old John was comforted to hear that Ebenezer "rejoyced or was glad the time was come," which could be interpreted as a hopeful sign of a "good estate." The Reverend Cleaveland's own temporal estate was much encumbered by his son's death, since he was now saddled with the responsibility for his son's widow and child, as well as for a note of Ebenezer's for 100 pounds, which he had countersigned. Mary Rust Cogswell Cleaveland, now twice widowed by the war, married again nine months later, but the child remained with his father's family.[57]

The wartime experiences of the youngest son, Nehemiah, were relatively more peaceful. Reverend John Cleaveland served twice as a chaplain during the war, in Cambridge in 1775 and on Long Island in 1776, and Nehemiah accompanied him as an aide. Otherwise he assumed John, Jr.'s responsibilities on the family farm. In June 1780, Nehemiah enlisted for a six-month term in the Continental army, during which he served as a private in an artillery company stationed at West Point. When he returned in December 1780, he had passed his twentieth birthday. He began

preparation for a career in medicine, living for a year with
Dr. Manning in Ipswich and afterward with his brother
Parker in Byfield. In 1783, the death of a Dr. Dexter
created an opening in nearby Topsfield, and the family was
able to muster sufficient resources to buy his equipment and
establish Nehemiah in practice.[58]

With two of the three surviving sons of John Cleaveland
established, family attention turned to the oldest, still un-
placed. Leaving the army, now in his early thirties, John
Cleaveland, Jr., faced an unpromising future once more.
An offer from his younger brother Parker to train him as a
doctor rekindled old resentments, and he rejected it sum-
marily. Late in 1782, before his final discharge from the
army, he entered into his diary a covenant that reflected his
ministerial ambitions.

Permit me, O Lord, to restore to thee those powers and faculties,
which I have ungratefully alienated from thy service; and receive,
I beseech thee, thy revolted creature, who is convinced of thy
right to him, and desires nothing in the world so much as to be
entirely thine.[59]

After the war, he moved back to Chebacco and resumed
the study of languages with his father, in preparation for
the ministry. After less than two years, he was licensed to
preach by the local ministerial association, in which his father, once an outcast, was now a senior and respected member. In October 1785, he was ordained in Stoneham, and
his proud father preached the sermon welcoming his oldest
son and namesake to the Christian ministry.[60] With the
ending of the war, the sons of John Cleaveland were all
placed respectably in the world, as were most of his daughters.

The structure of the Cleaveland houshold had undergone
a fundamental change. There still remained old John, his
second wife, Mary, and his unhappy daughter Elizabeth. As
in the earlier case of his first wife's orphaned niece, family

REVOLUTION

misfortune had brought into the household his grandson John (b. 1779), son of his late son Ebenezer, and Lois (b. *ca.* 1778), illegitimate daughter of his daughter Elizabeth. Elizabeth married and moved away in 1795, but she left her rough-hewn husband two years later and returned to her father's house, bringing with her a baby girl, Mary Cleaveland Channel (b. 1796). Because of the labor needs of the family farm, now lacking a son to manage it, a black boy called Titus was added, possibly the son of Mrs. Cleaveland's slave Violet, and a series of "boys," young men whom Cleaveland hired to live with him for a time and help him with the farm.[61] The size of the household remained remarkably stable, never fewer than seven nor more than ten, from the mid-1750s to Cleaveland's death in 1799, but the underlying structure changed greatly as growth and maturation took children out of the household and family circumstances and the labor needs of the farm brought others in.* Cleaveland confronted old age in the postwar world still carrying heavy domestic and pastoral responsibilities. He struggled vigorously, as always, to meet them, but changing times and his failing strength gradually increased his dependence on his sons.

IV. Fathers and Sons

In many ways, life in the village went on as it had before the war. Most families continued to support themselves by a mixture of agricultural and maritime pursuits. The greatest wartime demands on the village labor supply were made in the early years of the war, so that even before 1783 many village farms were back to full use. The end of the war removed the threat of the Royal Navy and English privateers, thereby reviving the maritime life of the North Shore. Fishing boats went out again without fear of interference, and

*See Table 13, Appendix.

merchants began to restore old trade routes and to construct new ones.

Although the 1780s were not a prosperous time, the village economy seemed to recover more quickly than that of Ipswich-town. While Ipswich slipped into long-term economic doldrums, Chebacco took part in the postwar commercial expansion through her growing shipbuilding industry. In this decade, the Story family's boat yard built, besides small "Chebacco" boats for local fishermen, thirteen vessels between twenty and ninety tons, which were sold to merchants from Gloucester.[62]

But Chebacco did not, and could not, return to the pre-war status quo. The rising generation, the children of John Cleaveland and his generation, had come of age during the long war for independence. They had borne the brunt of the fighting, while their fathers stayed at home to tend family farms. Military service introduced these young men to much more of the world than their fathers would ever know, and these experiences had an important effect on choices made by this generation as it went out into the world.

The familial mechanisms by which men and resources in the village were balanced continued to function. With varying degrees of family support, a certain number of young men in each generation had to seek their fortunes elsewhere so that those that remained would have a sufficiency. Those that left went as before to new farming towns inland or to the growing seaports nearby. Twice as many chose farming, which is probably a rough measure of the relative importance of the maritime and agricultural elements in the local economy.

Yet there were some important differences between the pre- and postwar generations. More than three fifths of the older generation had remained in the village, whereas about half of their sons did so. Not only did more sons leave in the younger generation, but they left at an earlier age. More than 60 percent of those that left were in their twenties or younger, while only 13 percent were forty or older. The figures for the older generation were 51 percent and 23 percent, respectively. Moreover, almost half of these postwar migrants were single, while only about a quarter of the older generation had migrated before marriage.[63]

The migrants continued to move toward the sea or the back country. The movement to seaport towns was now heavily concentrated in Gloucester. Chebacco was helping to build and man Gloucester's postwar fleet. New Hampshire continued to be the most important destination for rural migrants, who followed trade routes up the Merrimac Valley. The postwar penetration was, necessarily, much deeper. Dunbarton and Hopkinton attracted a large part of the prewar migration, whereas Enfield was the most popular postwar destination, and some moved as far as what is now Coos County in northernmost New Hampshire. Migration to Maine, once limited to the seacoast towns, now extended northward into Aroostook County. Other intrepid postwar migrants ventured into Vermont, upstate New York, and Ohio. A fair-sized group went so far as Canada, mostly into Ontario province.

The postwar migrants were younger and more venturesome, and were more apt to move off single and unencumbered. The experience of military service, which moved young men about the countryside and brought them into contact with a wider variety of people than they would see at home, weakened local loyalties. The members of the rising generation began adult life with a somewhat more cosmopolitan perspective than that of their elders, who were raised in a more sheltered and isolated rural world.

The different behavior and attitudes of the younger generation posed a challenge to Cleaveland as pastor of the community. He struggled to understand and to meet those challenges. With a vague sense that the parish boundaries no longer circumscribed his community, he added a category to his records entitled "deaths of relatives who died abroad or who lived out of this place."[64] At about the same time, he made a more serious attempt to confront the dispersion of his community. In 1782, he and the lay elders organized the entire village into ten "catechistical districts," thereby hoping "to promote reformation by a revival of the exercise of church-watch and discipline." This was deemed necessary since the pastor and elders were "aged" and "the people [are] living scattered and remote from one another." The districts were organized "for the purpose of catechising the children, instructing the youth and conferring with the heads of families together," and would be visited by the pastor at least once a year. The underlying principle of this elaborate scheme was "that not only such as have personally owned the convenant but all baptized are under the watch and discipline of the church."[65]

This attempt at greater inclusiveness by the church was necessary because the last great time of revival was twenty years past. Most villagers joined the church during times of revival, and the last one had occurred during the childhood of the rising generation. Although Cleaveland lived on for almost twenty years after the war, he could not stimulate another revival. The younger generation, including Cleaveland's children, excepting only the unfortunate Elizabeth, could not make a commitment to the church of their fathers. His scheme was an attempt to recapture the spiritual fervor he had known as a young pastor in Chebacco. It was not a successful attempt. He had helped his people to adapt and preserve their conservative religious and political beliefs in times of crisis in the past, but now increasing age made further change hard for him. The rising generation would find new leaders and spokesmen.

Cleaveland's later years were mostly occupied with pastoral and ecclesiastical duties. His children were settled, the war was over, and the desire to comment on political affairs seldom took hold of him. Political matters did not ordinarily come within Cleaveland's purview as a minister. Only when English policies were seen as a fundamental threat to the New England Way had Cleaveland engaged actively in politics, describing the conflict in the language of the covenant and placing it in the historical context of God's dealings with New England. His friend the Reverend Elijah Parish described him as "a careful observer of Providence, being in the habit of seeing God in every event. Every circumstance he viewed as a providence of God, constituting a necessary part of a great, a glorious whole."[66]

This habit of mind, which Cleaveland shared with his people, was the product of an education in rural New England. Cleaveland relied on this shared understanding in explaining to his people the necessity of revolution. But politics in the postwar world seldom called for explication from this cosmic perspective, so Cleaveland turned back to ecclesiastical affairs. He continued his vigorous defense of "the faith once delivered to the saints." Before the war he had taken the proto-Unitarian Jonathan Mayhew to task for his view of the atonement (*An Essay, to Defend some of the Most Important Principles in the Protestant Reformed System of Christianity* [1763]). For this effort on behalf of orthodox theology, Thomas Clap and Yale College awarded Cleaveland with his long-delayed degree. During the war he had attacked the universalist John Murray (*An Attempt to Nip in the Bud the Unscriptural Doctrine of Universal Salvation* [1776]). After the war he jumped into the middle of a long, rancorous dispute about baptism (*Infant-Baptism . . . As the Only Mode of Baptism . . .* [1784]).[67] His opponent was a bright young Baptist minister named Benjamin Foster, who was a graduate of Yale College and quite unlike the lay Baptist preachers Cleaveland had known in the 1740s. But the rigor of his orthodox theology, and his energy in its defense, were unaffected by the onset of old age.

He also took an active part in local ministerial affairs. He exchanged pulpits, preached at the quarterly fast held in Ipswich, and faithfully attended meetings of the ministerial association. His eulogist commented on the

particular and tender affection he had for his brethren in the ministry. With the most cordial hospitality he welcomed them to his dwelling. Most punctual in *all* his engagements, nothing but necessity could prevent his being with them at their stated meetings. And rarely did he retire from their society without giving a word of timely instruction, of pious advice, of paternal admonition.[68]

His professional commitment was of long standing. He had early chosen the role of established minister and had slowly won the respect of his ministerial colleagues. Now, as an elderly minister presiding over a reunited church, his standing was secure. This was in no small part because of his efforts in creating a bastion of orthodoxy on the North Shore, which was proof against Harvard's heresies. In his time, he welcomed Joseph Dana (Yale, 1760), Manasseh Cutler (Yale, 1765), Levi Frisbie (Dartmouth, 1772), and Gilbert Tennent Williams (Dartmouth, 1784) into various Ipswich parishes, as well as Daniel Hopkins (Yale, 1758), brother of Samuel, into Salem, Samuel Spring (Princeton, 1771) into Newburyport, and Elijah Parish (Dartmouth, 1785) into Byfield. As their collegiate training would suggest, they shared Cleaveland's "zeal for the *Old Doctrines* and the *New Measures.*"[69]

Old age and failing health gradually reduced all of his activities, ecclesiastical and otherwise. In 1774 and 1778, he was "seized by the apoplexy," from which he only slowly recovered. In 1781, in a letter to his son Parker, he apologized for postponing a visit, saying, "I am old and can't turn out as formerly." He later suffered from fevers, colds, kidney pains, and a running sore on one of his legs, the symptoms and treatment of which he described in graphic detail to his medical progeny. An illness in the winter of

1790 led his children to fear for his life. He increasingly came to rely on a chaise for traveling, and even with that told Parker not to expect him in the winter season, because "I remember the last winter's fatigue."[70]

His failing health at last led him, in October 1794, to draw up a will and plan for the provision of his complex household after his death. He was then seventy-two years old and responsible for his wife, one daughter, two grandchildren, and a young male slave. He provided for the continued support of his wife and daughter Elizabeth, and a dowry for his grandchild Lois. His grandson John, "as the only son and representative of my late son Ebenezer," was given his father's share of the estate and training in a trade. Titus, his slave, was to be given his freedom at age twenty-one as well as training in a trade. He made his three sons jointly executors of this last will and testament.[71]

Cleaveland came increasingly to rely on his sons in old age, though he still exerted himself on behalf of their professional advancement. After the war, he wrote Parker about an opportunity in New Hampshire and added, somewhat testily,

My advice is that you would not delay, for delays are dangerous in temporals as well as spirituals; if I remember right Hopkinton was lost, as to you, this way.[72]

He continued to look out for medical opportunities for Parker and Nehemiah and strove mightily to find a post for John, Jr., when he separated from his first congregation. But more and more, as the years passed, he turned to them for support. He frequently urged them "to write as often as you can, and to come and see us as soon as you can."

John, Jr. was able, on occasion, to ease his father's professional burden by preaching in his place, which he did often between 1794 and 1798 while seeking a permanent ministerial post. But his younger sons lived closer to him and consequently bore a greater part of the burden. They were becoming men of affairs in their communities as well as doctors. Both received appointments as justices of the peace in the mid-1780s, and Parker represented Rowley in the state constitutional convention of 1780.[73]

The old man took great comfort in the success of his sons; it was his reward for his great efforts on their behalf. He solicited their advice in their areas of expertise and increasingly recognized their greater competence in a world far different from that which he had known in his own young manhood. His sons embodied in their generation, as he had in his, the family spirit, comprised in equal parts of piety and enterprise, which had brought them from subsistence farming on the seventeenth-century frontier to their present professional competency. Like his ancestor Moses, he had grasped the opportunity of his day and time and made a fresh start for himself and his sons. Cleaveland helped his sons to make their way in the world as he had done, with a professional education rather than with land.

Parker and Nehemiah performed many services for him. They saw his publications through the press and helped to arrange his exchanges with neighboring ministers. They also helped to manage his farming business and financial affairs, as well as overseeing his wife's investments. With the pressure of providing for his sons and daughters now largely relieved, Cleaveland was able to clear off most of the remaining encumbrances on his estate. His resources, long stretched to their limits by his children's needs, now produced a surplus that Cleaveland invested in securing his estate and buying state bonds, the income of which would help to support his dependents after his death. But the strength to conduct these affairs was increasingly hard to find. In the mid-1790s, he turned the responsibility for his grandson John and the young slave Titus over to his son Nehemiah, who apprenticed them in the shoemaker's trade. He gave up the labor of the two boys, as well as the responsibility for them, because he was increasingly inclined to rent parts of his holdings rather than farm them himself.[74]

But for all their help and sympathy, the concerns of his sons were not his. Even John, Jr., though a minister like his father, took an interest in missionary work that was foreign to his father's day. Parker and Nehemiah, for their part, were lesser Federalist politicians actively interested in electoral politics. Nehemiah would eventually serve in the state senate, be appointed to the circuit court of common pleas, and help to organize one of the first turnpike corporations. The difference between father and sons is perhaps nowhere so clearly illustrated as in their observations on politics. His two younger sons were interested in the mechanics of politics, as Nehemiah's 1789 letter to Parker indicates.

I like your list of senators, *but still I am firmly for Dorne.* I should choose to exchange him for Bartlet, if I could but if not then for Pulling. . . . I believe I shall be able to do something for Bradbury. Isackson will not have a vote in this town and I hope he will not any where.[75]

The old man made passing comments on electoral politics but preferred the cosmic perspective. He always looked for the divine pattern in human affairs, and thus he saw the French Revolution as the "principal instrument" in the destruction of the Anti-Christ. He consulted the best authorities on Revelations and then wrote his son Nehemiah to say

that I am persuaded He will not suffer the combined powers of Europe to overthrow it; but that the more they [strive?] to uphold tyranny—the more it will tumble down about their ears, and that within two or three years from this time you may see Babylon sink as a mighty mill-stone cast into the midst of the sea.[76]

The old minister survived to preach a half-century sermon in March 1797. In his last years, he occupied his mind with genealogical records and millennial calculations, with his hopes for the future undimmed.[77] In his last letter, written April 11, 1799, to his son Nehemiah, he talked of his financial affairs, sent a message to Parker, and closed this way:

Christ is head over all things to his church, *and will shortly* bring Satan under her feet! Give my love to your families, Ma'am joins with me, from your affectionate father.[78]

John Cleaveland died suddenly eleven days later, on his seventy-seventh birthday, just eight months short of the new century. The world of John Cleaveland, the world he had known in his youth and young manhood, had passed on before him.

APPENDIX

APPENDIX

TABLE 1

Annual Rates of Population Growth

1695–1718	1718–1749	1749–1770
5.3%	2.6%	1.2%

SOURCE: See Table 4 for the tax lists on which the calculations are based, except for the 1695 lists, which are in the Ipswich Historical Society, Ipswich Public Library. For methods, see Chapter Three, note 6.

TABLE 2

Landless Taxpayers

In Expectation of Inheritance	37 (67%)
Received Inheritance, or Expecting None	12 (22%)
Passed on Land to Sons	2 (4%)
Widows	4 (7%)

SOURCE: For all tables, the economic reconstitution of 1771 taxpayers, unless otherwise noted. See Chapter Three, note 32.

TABLE 3

Taxpayers with Less than 35 Acres

Received Only Part of Inheritance	10 (23%)
Received Inheritance	26 (60%)
Passed on Part of Lands	2 (5%)
Widows	5 (12%)

APPENDIX

TABLE 4

Distribution of Taxable Wealth

Taxpayers	1718	1749	1770
top 20%	46%	50%	51%
"	27%	23%	24%
"	16%	14%	13%
"	8%	8%	7%
bottom "	3%	6%	5%

SOURCE: 1718: Chebacco Parish Papers, 1718–1800, Ipswich, MSS. Essex Institute. 1749 and 1770: Mass. Archives, XIII, 39–40, and CXXX, 160–165.

TABLE 5

Age at Inheritance

			Cumulative
Under 20	6	(14%)	(14%)
21–30	5	(12%)	(26%)
31–40	13	(31%)	(57%)
41–50	7	(17%)	(74%)
51–60	10	(24%)	(98%)
61–70	1	(2%)	(100%)
Unknown	7		

APPENDIX

TABLE 6

Disposition of Estate by Size

Acreage	Will and/or Deed	Posthumous Settlement
under 20	1 (1%)	11 (44%)
21–40	3 (4%)	0
41–60	7 (10%)	3 (12%)
61–80	8 (11%)	0
81–100	9 (13%)	2 (8%)
101–150	16 (23%)	6 (24%)
151–200	9 (13%)	1 (4%)
201–250	7 (10%)	1 (4%)
250 and above	10 (14%)	1 (4%)
Unknown	6	
Total	76 (70 known)	25

TABLE 7

Persistence by Birth Order

Birth Order	Persistence	Migration
1st	33 (89%)	4 (11%)
2nd	22 (69%)	10 (31%)
3rd or later	20 (53%)	18 (47%)

SOURCE: Demographic reconstitution of 1771 taxpayers, Chapter Three, note 32.

APPENDIX

TABLE 8

Children of John and Mary Cleaveland

Name	Birthdate	Source of Name
Mary	7-10-1748	mother
John	1-6-1750	father
Parker	10-14-1751	mother's father, d.1742
Ebenezer	3-19-1754	father's brother
Elizabeth	1-25-1757	probably mother's brother's wife, d.1754
Nehemiah	8-26-1760	mother's brother, d.1758
Abigail	12-28-1762	father's mother, d.1762
Lois	7-17-1767	father's sister, d. 1736
Eunice		?

SOURCE: Cleveland and Cleveland, *Genealogy of the Cleveland and Cleaveland Families,* I, 165–171.

TABLE 9

Percentage Legacies/Assessed Value of Estate

under 20%	23 (68%)
21–50%	9 (26%)
51% and above	2 (6%)

APPENDIX

TABLE 10

Percentage Debt/Assessed Value of Estate

under 20%	15 (54%)
21–50%	9 (32%)
51% and above	4 (14%)

TABLE 11

Number of Debts Owed by Estates

under 20	10 (36%)
21–40	13 (46%)
41 and above	5 (18%)

TABLE 12

Literacy in Chebacco

Year	Signature	Mark	Unknown
1675 Men	29 (76%)	9 (24%)	7
1675 Women	2 (25%)	6 (75%)	
1771 Men	124 (99%)	1 (1%)	37
1771 Women	77 (74%)	27 (26%)	

SOURCE: See Chapter Four, note 19.

APPENDIX

TABLE 13

Size of Cleaveland Household

	Parents	Children	Other Relatives	Servants	Slaves	Total
1750	2	2	—	—	—	4
1755	2	4	—	—	1	7
1760	2	6	1	1	—	10
1765	2	7	1	—	—	10
1770	2	6	—	—	1	9
1775	2	2	—	—	1	5
1780	2	3	2	1	1	9
1785	2	2	2	1	1	8
1790	2	1	2	1	1	7
1795	2	1	2	1	1	7
1799	2	1	3	1	1	8

SOURCE: Cleveland and Cleveland, *Genealogy of the Cleveland and Cleaveland Families*, and domestic correspondence in the Cleaveland Papers.

✦

Notes

CHAPTER ONE

1. Edmund J. Cleveland and Horace G. Cleveland, *The Genealogy of the Cleveland and Cleaveland Families* (Hartford, Conn., 1899), I, 24. (Hereafter, *Cleveland Genealogy.*)

2. Freeman: Horace G. Cleveland, *A Genealogy of Benjamin Cleveland* (Chicago, Ill., 1879), p. 5; Johnson: Edward Johnson, *Johnson's Wonder-working Providence 1628–1651*, ed. J. Franklin Jameson (New York, 1910), pp. 217–218. For the act making church membership requisite for freemanship, see *Records of the Governor and Company of the Massachusetts Bay in New England,* ed. Nathaniel B. Shurtleff (Boston, 1853), I, 87. (Hereafter *Mass. Records.*)

3. According to John Winthrop, *The History of New England from 1630 to 1649,* ed. James Savage (New York, 1972); reprint of Boston, 1852 ed. [2 vols. in one], II, 110.

4. Woburn's petition, in Joseph B. Felt, *The Ecclesiastical History of New England* (Boston, 1855), II, 98.

5. Felt, *Ecclesiastical History,* II, 304; *Cleveland Genealogy,* I, 30–31; *Mass. Records,* IV, Pt. 2, 73–74, 164–166; Paul R. Lucas, "Colony or Commonwealth: Mass. Bay, 1661–1666," *William and Mary Quarterly,* 24 (1967), 95–97 (hereafter *WMQ*).

6. See Robert G. Pope, *The Half-Way Covenant: Church Membership in Puritan New England* (Princeton, N.J., 1969), chaps. V–VI, and David D. Hall, *The Faithful Shepherd: A History of the New England Ministry in the Seventeenth Century* (Chapel Hill, N.C., 1972), chaps. IV–VI.

7. Thomas Hutchinson, *A History of the Colony and Province of Massachusetts-Bay,* ed. L. S. Mayo (Cambridge, Mass., 1936), I, 232; Pope, *Half-Way Covenant,* p. 53.

8. William G. McLoughlin, *New England Dissent, 1630–1833: The Baptists and the Separation of Church and State* (Cambridge, Mass., 1971),

I, 50, and chaps. III–IV; Nathan E. Wood, *The History of the First Baptist Church of Boston* (Philadelphia, Pa., 1899).

9. For the Woburn Baptists, see Samuel Sewall, *The History of Woburn* (Boston, 1868), pp. 152–164; Wood, *First Baptist Church*, pp. 75, 90, 100–108, 129–130; the list of Woburn Baptists was compiled from the Middlesex County Court Records, County Court House, Cambridge, Mass. See also E. Brooks Holifield, "On Toleration in Massachusetts," *Church History*, 38 (1969), 192.

10. Woburn Town Records, I, 15. They are kept in a vault in the clerk's office, City Hall, Woburn, Mass. For the town's founding, see Sewall, *Woburn*, pp. 7–30.

11. Sewall, *Woburn*, pp. 36–41.

12. Johnson, *Wonder-Working Providence*, p. 213.

13. Calculations based on lists of proprietors, Town Records, I, 43–44, 78.

14. Town Records, I, 24, 28, 38–40; *Cleveland Genealogy*, I, 27.

15. Based on lists of proprietors (see note 13) and "Genealogical Noticea," in Sewall, *Woburn*, pp. 591–657.

16. See, for example, Philip J. Greven, Jr., "Family Structure in Seventeenth-Century Andover, Massachusetts," *WMQ*, 23 (1966), 238–239.

17. Town Records, I, 81; Sewall, *Woburn*, pp. 40, 82–83.

18. *Cleveland Genealogy*, I, 32–50; Wilson Waters, *History of Chelmsford* (Lowell, Mass., 1917), pp. 44–45, 64–65, 93–94, 121, 134; there is no will extant for Moses, Sr. The fact that Aaron was the only son to remain in Woburn, and that he left an estate containing eighty-nine acres at his death in 1716, suggests that he inherited most of Moses, Sr.'s, land.

19. See Ellen D. Larned, *History of Windham County, Connecticut* (Worcester, Mass., 1874), I; Richard L. Bushman, *From Puritan to Yankee: Character and the Social Order, 1690–1765* (Cambridge, Mass., 1967), chap. VI.

20. Roy H. Akagi, *The Town Proprietors of the New England Colonies: A Study of Their Development, Organization, Activities and Controversies, 1620–1770* (Philadelphia, Pa., 1924), pp. 67–73; Kenneth A. Lockridge, *A New England Town: The First Hundred Years* (New York, 1970), p. 9; Edward S. Perzel, "Landholding in Ipswich," *Essex Institute Historical Collections*, 104 (1968), 325–327 (hereafter *EIHC*); George W. Chase, *The History of Haverhill* (Haverhill, Mass., 1861), p. 75; George D. Langdon, Jr., *Pilgrim Colony: A History of New Plymouth, 1620–1691* (New Haven, Conn., 1966), p. 53.

21. Bushman, *Puritan to Yankee*, p. 83; Douglas R. McManis, *Colonial New England: A Historical Geography* (New York, 1975), pp. 68–69, Table I.

22. For Fitch and the Winthrops, see Larned, *Windham County*, I, 5–6, 16–17, 105, 118; Bushman, *Puritan to Yankee*, pp. 84–96, 103; Richard S. Dunn, *Puritans and Yankees: The Winthrop Dynasty of New England 1630–1717* (Princeton, N.J., 1962), pp. 108, 110, 141, 295, 317, 330.

23. The John Cleaveland Papers, in the Essex Institute, Salem, Mass.,

II, 42 (hereafter JCP); this fragment, entitled "The Life of John Cleave-land," is undated. In the account of his family, he mentions the death of his grandfather Paine and his sister Lois (1736) but not his father's (1750). He talks of his education at Yale in the past tense. It was proba-bly composed between 1745 and 1750, perhaps inspired by his reading of Edwards's memoir of Brainerd (see Sept. 11, 1749, in "A Private Jour-nal. 1749," JCP, II, 50).

24. For the Cleaveland tenancy and related conflicts, see Massachusetts Historical Society, *Collections,* 5th ser., VIII, 499, 504–508, 511, 514–516, 517–522; Larned, *Windham County,* I, 107–108 (who confuses the sides); Bushman, *Puritan to Yankee,* p. 88.

25. Larned, *Windham County,* I, 108, 110; Bushman, *Puritan to Yankee,* pp. 87–88.

26. Canterbury Land Records, Connecticut State Library, Hartford, Conn. (microfilm), II [grantee], 35 (hereafter CLR); Larned, *Windham County,* I, 110.

27. Larned, *Windham County,* I, 110–111, 118–120.

28. Larned, *Windham County,* I, 114–116, 126–128; Dunn, *Puritans and Yankees,* pp. 328–330.

29. Larned, *Windham County,* I, 128, 143–149.

30. Larned, *Windham County,* I, 144.

31. CLR, I [grantee], 9, 11; the early Canterbury land records are very incomplete. The earliest records were made in 1704; the earliest transac-tions recorded were in 1699, although there was much dealing in land in the 1690s. There is a record of the two purchases that Josiah made in 1699/1700 of the same 100 acres (see text), and of another of 200 acres that he bought from the Tracys of Norwich, speculators who bought their land from Fitch, in 1707. Larned mentions (p. 110) a purchase that Josiah made from Richard Bushnell of land at Wanungatuck, "both sides of Tadneck Hill," *ca.* 1699, which I could not locate in either the Plain-field or the Canterbury land records. Josiah's 1709 inventory (#1209, New London probate district) lists the following:

"The hom farm together with the buildings orchards & fencing containing two hundred & twenty six acres:
£160
[partly the Bushnell/Owaneco purchase, which was in 1699/1700 'where said Cleaveland now liveth']

The two hundred acres at Pine Medow [the Tracy purchase]:
£ 40

The seventy six acres near Tadneck [the Bushnell purchase]:
£ 12

Total: 502 acres
£212"

32. "Property was very unequally distributed. Such settlers as were able to buy their land at the outset were soon in comfortable circumstances, but the mass of the people were poor and found it difficult to pay their

taxes." (Larned, *Windham County*, I, 262); for Massachusetts land trans-actions, see *Cleveland Genealogy*, I, 40; Edward F. Johnson, *Abstracts of Early Woburn Deeds Recorded at Middlesex County Registry, 1649–1700* (Woburn, Mass., 1895), pp. 57, 72.

33. Calculations based on Canterbury tax list of 1716, Connecticut State Library.

34. Larned, *Windham County*, I, 156–157.

35. Pope, *Half-Way Covenant*, pp. 20–21, 25–26, 53, 134–135, 187–188, 198, 200–201, 226–231; Langdon, *Pilgrim Colony*, pp. 132–133.

36. *Records of the Congregational Church in Canterbury, Connecticut, 1711–1844*, ed. Albert C. Bates (Hartford, Conn., 1932), "Confession of Faith," pp. 1–3, "Covenant," pp. 3–4, esp. articles 5–7. (Hereafter *Church Recs.*)

37. See Pope, *Half-Way Covenant*, pp. 268–269.

38. John Langdon Sibley (vols. I–III) and Clifford K. Shipton (vols. IV–XVII), *Sibley's Harvard Graduates*, 17 vols. (Cambridge and Boston, 1873–1975), VI, 389–390 (hereafter *Sibley's Harvard Graduates*); Larned, *Windham County*, I, 291.

39. Larned, *Windham County*, I, 60–61, 250–252, 263, 283, 291–292, 345–347, 372, 379–380; Bushman, *Puritan to Yankee*, pp. 151–156; Francis M. Caulkins, *History of Norwich, Connecticut* (Hartford, Conn., 1866), pp. 285–286, 318–319; Williston Walker, *The Creeds and Platforms of Congregationalism* (New York, 1893), p. 508; Clarence C. Goen, *Revivalism and Separatism in New England, 1740–1800* (New Haven, Conn., 1962), pp. 187–188.

40. *Cleveland Genealogy*, I; *Church Recs.*, pp. 39–47.

41. [John Cleaveland], *An Epicedium, or a Poetical Attempt on the Life & Death of Mr. Josiah Cleaveland, late of Canterbury* (Boston, 1753), p. 1.

42. Larned, *Windham County*, I, 110, 134, 137, 143, 145–148, 150, 154, 156–158, 293–294; *Church Recs.*, pp. 1, 6, 39; *Paine Family Records*, ed. H. D. Paine, 2 vols. (New York, 1883), II, 47–48. The Barnstable church, with Elisha as its representative, and Elisha himself endowed the Canterbury church with most of its communion silver. The Johnson and Cleaveland families of Woburn gave the rest (*Church Recs.*, p. 39).

43. Josiah Cleaveland's land transactions can be found in CLR, III–V; see also John Cleaveland, probate #1289, New London district, Conn. State Library, Hartford, Conn.; Josiah II was the executor.

44. Will, see abstract in *Cleveland Genealogy*, I, 81–82; contemporary copy of will and inventory in court record books (microfilm), pp. 136–138, 364–366, Connecticut State Library; inventory, probate #454, Plainfield district, Connecticut State Library.

45. [John Cleaveland], *An Epicedium*, p. 5.

46. JCP, II, 47.

CHAPTER TWO

1. [John Cleaveland], *An Epicedium,* p. 1.
2. JCP, II, 47.
3. See *Paine Family Records,* II, 12–17, 44–48, 54–61. For Solomon and Elisha Paine, esp. the latter, see Isaac Backus, *A History of New England,* 2nd ed. (Newton, Mass., 1871), II, 64–69, 72, 77, 80, 100–101, 114, 450, 518; Isaac Backus, *A Fish Caught in his own Net* (Boston, 1768), reprinted in *Isaac Backus on Church, State, and Calvinism: Pamphlets, 1754–1789,* ed. William G. McLoughlin (Cambridge, Mass., 1968), pp. 205–214; Larned, *Windham County,* I, 400–403, 440–444; Ellen D. Larned, *Historic Gleanings in Windham County* (Providence, R.I., 1899), pp. 15–51; *Paine Family Records,* II, 157–160, 161–162; Goen, *Revivalism and Separatism,* pp. 71–75, 115–123; for Elisha as attorney, see Connecticut Archives, State Library, Hartford, Conn.
4. JCP, II, 47.
5. JCP, II, 46–47; most young men were prepared for college by the local ministers (Richard Warch, *School of the Prophets: Yale College, 1701–1740* [New Haven, Conn., 1973], p. 189).
6. *Church Recs.,* p. 41; Larned, *Windham County,* I, 396–397; *Paine Family Records,* II, 157–163, 259–260; Goen, *Revivalism and Separatism,* p. 110, who mistakenly identifies brother Abraham, rather than his son, as the Separate preacher. For church membership, calculations are based on Canterbury *Church Recs.,* pp. 39–46.
7. Warch, *School,* p. 190.
8. *Boston Post-Boy,* Sept. 28, 1741; see also Samuel Johnson, *Samuel Johnson, President of King's College: His Career and Writings* (New York, 1929), I, 28, 106–107; Charles Chauncy, *Seasonable Thoughts on the State of Religion in New England* (Boston, 1742), pp. 98–99; Daniel Wadsworth, *Diary of Rev. Daniel Wadsworth, 1737–1747,* ed. George L. Walker (Hartford, Conn., 1894), p. 63; Jared Ingersoll, "An Historical Account of some Affairs Relating to the Church, especially in Connecticut," Library of Congress, Washington, D.C., p. 3; for a full account of the Great Awakening at Yale, see Ross W. Beales, Jr., "Cares for the Rising Generation: Youth and Religion in Colonial New England" (unpublished Ph.D. dissertation, University of California, Davis, 1971).
9. This was Edwards's famous defense of revivalism—*The Distinguishing Marks of a Work of the Spirit of God* (Boston, 1741). This sermon virtually ended Edwards's affiliation with Yale; see Clarence C. Goen's introduction to Jonathan Edwards, *The Great Awakening* (New Haven, Conn., 1972), pp. 52–60.
10. George Whitefield, *A Continuation of the Reverened Mr. Whitefield's Journal* (London, 1741), pp. 50–52, in Stephen Nissenbaum, ed., *The Great Awakening at Yale College* (Belmont, Calif., 1972), p. 23.
11. Gilbert Tennent to George Whitefield, April 25, 1741, in Nissenbaum, ed., *Yale College,* p. 27.
12. Franklin B. Dexter, ed., *The Documentary History of Yale University under the Original Charter of the Collegiate School of Connecticut, 1701–1745*

(New Haven, Conn., 1916), p. 351; Johnson, *Writings*, I, 102–103.

13. Samuel W. S. Dutton, *The History of the North Church in New Haven* (New Haven, Conn., 1842), p. 6; see also Mary H. Mitchell, *History of the United Church of New Haven* (New Haven, Conn., 1942), pp. 9–17, 215–234; Benjamin Trumbull, *A Complete History of Connecticut* (New Haven, Conn., 1797–1818), II, 340–350; Leonard Bacon, *Thirteen Historical Discourses, on the Completion of Two Hundred Years, from the Beginning of the First Church in New Haven* (New Haven, Conn., 1839), pp. 211–242.

14. The original of the diary is among the Cleaveland papers at the Essex Institute; there are copies in JCP, I, 57–74, and a photostat in the Yale Archives. The best published version, which I will cite by date and page, is in *EIHC*, 108 (1971), 143–172, ed. Ross W. Beales, Jr. For others, see Nissenbaum, ed., *Yale College*, pp. 146–163; Larned, *Windham County*, I, 397–398; George P. Fisher, *A Discourse Commemorative of the History of the Church of Christ in Yale College* (New Haven, Conn., 1858), pp. 59–67.

15. Norman M. Isham, "The First Yale College House," *Yale Alumni Weekly*, 26 (1916–1917), 114–120; Wadsworth's 1748 map of New Haven in Reuben A. Holden, *Yale, A Pictorial History* (New Haven, Conn., 1967), fig. 9; Franklin B. Dexter, *Biographical Sketches of the Graduates of Yale College with Annals of the College History* (New York, 1885–1912), I, 661; II, 10–11 (hereafter Dexter, *Yale Graduates*); Thomas Clap, *The Annals or History of Yale College* (New Haven, Conn., 1766), p. 54; according to surviving rooming plans, the college house ordinarily contained about fifty undergraduates, the tutors (three after 1743), and a resident graduate or two. The house contained twenty-eight rooms, on three floors, for the students, plus the kitchen, library, and hall. For the 1746 rooming plan, the earliest surviving, see Holden, *Yale*, fig. 7. For the others, see the Clap papers, Yale Archives, Sterling Library, Yale University, New Haven, Conn.

16. For Clap, see Louis L. Tucker, *Puritan Protagonist: President Thomas Clap of Yale College* (Chapel Hill, N.C., 1962); *Sibley's Harvard Graduates*, VII, 27–50.

17. For the "great apostacy," see Warch, *School*, pp. 100–117; Clap, *Annals*, pp. 31–55, 40–41.

18. Clap, *Annals*, pp. 40–43, 44–52; Tucker, *Puritan Protagonist*, pp. 39–42, 70–71; Thomas Clap, *A Catalogue of the Library of Yale College in New Haven* (New London, Conn., 1743); Dexter, *Yale Graduates*, II, 2–18.

19. Calculations based on Dexter, *Yale Graduates*, I–II; Ezra Stiles, *The Literary Diary of Ezra Stiles*, ed. F. B. Dexter (New York, 1901), II, 513.

20. See Warch, *School*, pp. 193–195, for an overview of the curriculum to 1740 and the changes under Clap, and see chaps. VIII–IX for a detailed description by subject.

21. JCP, II, 46.

22. Compiled from "Diary," pp. 147–165 (Jan. 15–Mar. 31).

23. Pemberton's *The Knowledge of Christ Recommended* (New London,

Conn., 1741), partially reprinted in Nissenbaum, ed., *Yale College,* pp. 28–36, quotations on pp. 32–33.

24. Jonathan Edwards, ed., *An Account of the Life of the Late Rev. Mr. David Brainerd* (Boston, 1749), in Nissenbaum, ed., *Yale College,* pp. 49, 51.

25. "Diary," pp. 149 (Jan. 20), 152 (Jan. 28), 156 (Feb. 18), 157 (Feb. 20).

26. "Diary," p. 148 (Jan. 18).

27. "Diary," p. 151 (Jan. 27).

28. "Diary," p. 153 (Feb. 1).

29. "Diary," pp. 153 (Jan. 31), 159 (Mar. 2), 154 (Feb. 8), 161 (Mar. 11); the Separates met in private homes until 1743. These men were all founders of the church (Dutton, *North Church,* p. 7).

30. Brainerd: Nissenbaum, ed., *Yale College,* p. 144; "Diary," pp. 157 (Feb. 23), 159 (Mar. 1).

31. "Diary," pp. 151 (Jan. 26), 159 (Mar. 2), 160 (Mar. 6), 160 (Mar. 8), 161 (Mar. 11).

32. Ingersoll, "An Historical Account," p. 15; Thomas Brainerd, *The Life of John Brainerd* (Philadelphia, Pa., 1865), chap. III; on the Tent, see Goen, *Revivalism and Separatism,* pp. 62–63, 69, 175; Edwin S. Gaustad, *The Great Awakening in New England* (New York, 1957), pp. 108, 137.

33. Clap to Dickinson, May 3, 1742; Thomas Clap to Solomon Williams, New Haven, June 8, 1742; *ibid.,* July 16, 1742, Gratz Collection, Historical Society of Pennsylvania, printed in Nissenbaum, ed., *Yale College,* pp. 169–170, 174–176; "A" to Eleazar Wheelock, New Haven, Mar. 28, 1743, #743228, Wheelock Papers (microfilm), Microtext Division, Lamont Library, Harvard University, Cambridge, Mass.; Bacon, *Historical Discourses,* pp. 220–221.

34. "Diary," pp. 164 (Mar. 28), 165 (Mar. 31).

35. [Charles Chauncy?], *The State of Religion in New England Since the Reverend Mr. George Whitefield's arrival there in a letter from a Gentleman in New-England to his Friend in Glasgow* (Glasgow, 1742), pp. 13–14.

36. The above and most of the information in this section is based on a computer analysis of the 626 Yale graduates in the classes of 1702 to 1750. Data from Dexter, *Yale Graduates,* I and II. Basing my analysis on the limited information in Dexter, *Yale Graduates,* on student backgrounds, I divided them into four groups: unknown—no information, local—local officeholder, provincial—provincial officeholder, ministerial —minister; on placing and students' backgrounds, see Warch, *School,* pp. 252, 256–257, and Clifford K. Shipton, "Ye Mystery of Ye Ages Solved, or, How Placing Worked at Colonial Harvard & Yale," *Harvard Alumni Bulletin,* 57 (1954–1955), 258–263.

Warch estimates the basic cost of a Yale education in the late 1730s at a little more than 100 pounds (Warch, *School,* pp. 151–153). Extrapolating from Cleaveland's one quarter bill ("Diary," p. 159 [Mar. 2]) and the charges mentioned by Warch, his three years at Yale cost his family about 125 pounds.

37. Also, the more rural countries and districts that sent men to Yale

had a disproportionate percentage of ministers among their graduates. Forty-eight percent of Yale graduates whose occupation is known became ministers, but fifty-seven percent of the graduates from western Massachusetts, 64 percent from Windham County, 71 percent from Litchfield County, and 77 percent from central Massachusetts became ministers.

38. Dexter, ed., *Documentary History*, pp. 365–366.

39. Edwards, ed., *Brainerd*, in Nissenbaum, ed., *Yale College*, p. 38; Samuel Hopkins, *Sketches of the Life of the Late Rev. Samuel Hopkins, D.D.*, ed. Stephen West (Hartford, Conn., 1805), pp. 23–27; JCP, II, 46–47.

40. Edwards, ed., *Brainerd*, in Nissenbaum, ed., *Yale College*, p. 38.

41. Congregational/Presbyterian ministers only.

42. Quotation from Robert Crowell, *History of the Town of Essex* (Essex, Mass., 1868), p. 246. See Conrad Wright, *The Beginnings of Unitarianism in America* (Boston, 1955), pp. 252–259, esp. charts on distribution of Harvard and Yale graduates in New England in 1775 and 1804; Sydney E. Ahlstrom, "The Saybrook Platform: A 250th anniversary retrospect," *Bulletin of the Congregational Library*, 11 (1959–1960), 5–10, 31–45; Alpheus C. Hodges, "Yale Graduates in Western Massachusetts," *Papers of the New Haven Colony Historical Society*, 4 (1888), 253–298.

43. [Chauncy?], *The State of Religion*, p. 14.

44. See Clap to Dickinson, May 3, 1742, in Nissenbaum, ed., *Yale College*, p. 117.

45. *Ibid.*; the New Light Fairfield East Association, which ordained David Brainerd, among others, was the cause of Clap's fears (Goen, *Revivalism and Separatism*, pp. 77n, 87n, 111).

46. "Walcott Papers," Connecticut Historical Society, *Collections*, XVI, 455–458, reprinted in Nissenbaum, ed., *Yale College*, pp. 132–134, quotation on p. 134.

47. Dexter, ed., *Documentary History*, pp. 356–358.

48. *The Public Records of the Colony of Connecticut*, ed. C. J. Hoadly (Hartford, Conn., 1850–1890), VIII, 454–457 (hereafter *Conn. Records*); it was at this session that Isaac Stiles preached his vehemently anti-New Light *A Prospect of the City of Jerusalem* (New London, Conn., 1742).

49. *Conn. Records*, VIII, 500–502.

50. *Conn. Records*, VIII, 521–522, 509–510.

51. Goen, *Revivalism and Separatism*, pp. 24–26, 59–62; Eleazar Wheelock to Thomas Clap, Lebanon, Sept. 1743, #742900.1, Wheelock Papers.

52. Clap to Williams, June 8, 1742, in Nissenbaum, ed., *Yale College*, pp. 169–170.

53. Ingersoll, "An Historical Account," p. 12.

54. See notes 30–32.

55. William Allen, "Memoir of Rev. Eleazar Wheelock, D.D., Founder and First President of Dartmouth," *American Quarterly Register*, 10 (1837), 16–17; Eleazar Wheelock to Sarah Wheelock, New Haven, June 28, 1742, #742378, Wheelock Papers.

56. Clap to Wheelock, Nov. 17, 1743, in Nissenbaum, ed., *Yale*

College, pp. 204–205. Cleaveland's poem is dated Oct. 15, 1743, and is in JCP, III, 22–23, and printed in Thomas H. Billings, "The Great Awakening," *EIHC*, 65 (1929), 90. The reference for the student expelled can be found in Ingersoll, "An Historical Account," p. 17.

57. Larned, *Windham County*, I, 297.

58. The best account of the Canterbury Separates, with many of the relevant documents, is Larned, *Windham County*, I, 396–427, 437–444; see also the 3 vols. of the Canterbury Separate papers, Connecticut Historical Society, Hartford, Conn.; Goen, *Revivalism and Separatism*, pp. 70–75, 115–123, 149–150, 164–167.

59. Elisha Paine, quoted in *A Letter from the Associated Ministers of the County of Windham* (Boston, 1745), p. 8, quoted in Goen, *Revivalism and Separatism*, p. 120. Several churches expressed their dissent by avowing the Cambridge Platform (Goen, *Revivalism and Separatism*, pp. 148–150).

60. Larned, *Windham County*, I, 404–411, esp. the examination of Adams, pp. 405–406.

61. Larned, *Windham County*, I, 412–417, 423–425.

62. *Ibid.*, I, 415–416; *Cleveland Genealogy*, I, 65–66; Backus, *A History*, II, 68–70.

63. The most detailed account is John Cleaveland, "A Just Narrative of the Proceedings," JCP, III, 5–14, first printed in Nissenbaum, ed., *Yale College*, pp. 232–244; see also Thomas Clap, *The Judgement of the Rector and Tutors of Yale College* (New London, Conn., 1745), partially reprinted in *ibid.*, pp. 224–231; Trumbull, *Complete History*, II, 178–183; Backus, *A History*, II, 70–72; Solomon Paine, *A Short View of Differences* (Newport, R.I., 1752), pp. 15–20; Tucker, *Puritan Protagonist*, pp. 138–141; Larned, *Windham County*, I, 419–422, 427; Dexter, ed., *Documentary History*, pp. 368–372.

64. Clap, *The Judgement*, in Nissenbaum, ed., *Yale College*, p. 227.

65. Cleaveland, "A Just Narrative," in Nissenbaum, ed., *Yale College*, p. 236.

66. *Ibid.*, pp. 236–237.

67. *Ibid.*, pp. 239–240.

68. *Ibid.*, pp. 241–243.

69. *Ibid.*, pp. 243–244; in the next year Clap forced Cooke from the Board. Tucker, *Puritan Protagonist*, pp. 135–136.

70. *Ibid.*, pp. 244.

71. Thomas Clap, "Some observations relating to the government of the college," Yale Archives, p. 13; see also Clap, *Annals*, pp. 85–86.

72. Eleazar Wheelock to John Cleaveland, Lebanon, Mar. 9, 1745, JCP, .III, 26–27, printed in Nissenbaum, ed., *Yale College*, pp. 245–246; Josiah Cleaveland, memorial to General Assembly, Connecticut Archives, Colleges and Schools, 280a–280d, printed in *ibid.*, pp. 246–250; Dexter, ed., *Documentary History*, p. 366.

73. Larned, *Windham County*, I, 440; Cleaveland, "A Just Narrative," in Nissenbaum, ed., *Yale College*, p. 243; *Sibley's Harvard Graduates*, VIII, 616–627.

74. There is no record of the call. He began a journal while ministering to that church, on Feb. 9, 1746 (see JCP, I, 95–103). His mother's younger sister, Hannah Watts, and Philemon Robbins's brother were members of that congregation (*Paine Family Records,* I, 48; JCP, I, 97).

75. Hamilton A. Hill, *History of the Old South Church* (Boston, 1890), I, 538; for the history of the Separate church in Boston, see Hill, *Old South Church,* I, 538–546, 570, 585–597; Goen, *Revivalism and Separatism,* p. 97; Andrew Croswell, *A Narrative of the Founding and Settling of the New-Gathered Congregational Church in Boston* (Boston, 1749); [Ephraim Clark?], *A Narrative, Containing an Account of the Founding and Settling [of] the New Gathered Congregational Church of Christ in Boston* (Boston, 1751); Thomas Prince, "Some Account of the Late Revival of Religion in Boston," *Christian History,* 2 (1745), 408, 411–412; *Sibley's Harvard Graduates,* VIII, 397; "Report of a Council for Ordaining Rev. Ephraim Clark, Sept. 28, 1748," JCP, III, 142–144.

76. Hill, *Old South Church,* I, 539–540. Compare the first half of Thomas Prince, "Some Account," written 1743–1744, with the second, written in 1745.

77. Benjamin Colman, *One Chosen of God* (Boston, 1746), quoted in Hill, *Old South Church,* I, 570.

78. John Cleaveland to Philemon Robbins, Nov. 12, 1745, JCP, III, 19–21. Cleaveland is paraphrasing from Amos 7:10–17. Amos's confrontation with Amaziah was the "climactic moment" in the book, according to Norman K. Gottwald, *A Light to the Nations* (New York, 1959), p. 283. Gottwald goes on to say that "Amaziah and Amos, sharply set against one another in mutual distrust and antipathy, are the classic examples of the age-long tension between priest and prophet." Cleaveland, who like Robbins and other New Lights prided himself on his command of the Bible, was using Amos to convey a precise image of his understanding of his situation.

79. John Cleaveland to Philemon Robbins, Nov. 12, 1745, JCP, III, 19–21; "Boston Journal," March 26, 1746, JCP, I, 100.

80. For Isaiah, see Gottwald, *A Light to the Nations,* pp. 308–326, esp. pp. 321–323.

81. "Boston Journal," Feb. 10, 1746, JCP, I, 96; John Cleaveland to Philemon Robbins, Mar. 14, 1746, JCP, III, 33–35. Family visit: Mar. 6–8, 1746; end of Mar.: Mar. 25, 1746, "Boston Journal," JCP, I, 98, 100.

82. John Cleaveland to Boston Separates, n.d. [draft copy, fall 1746], JCP, III, 78.

83. John Cleaveland to Boston Separates, n.d. [draft copy, fall 1746], JCP, III, 80–81.

84. The phrase is from a letter to John Cleaveland in Chebacco from a Boston parishioner, Samuel Frothingham, eager for his return. He wrote, "God knows what will be the end of the present strife in this littell blessed cluster of that precious vine." Dec. 9, 1746, JCP, III, 43–44.

85. James Eveleth and Francis Choate to John Cleaveland, Jan. 27, 1746, JCP, I, 104–105; "Boston Journal," Feb. 17–22, 1746, JCP, I,

97; see also Theophilus Pickering to John Cleaveland, Feb. 18, 1746, JCP, I, 109–110.

86. Feb. [last week], 1746, JCP, III, 256–259.

87. George Whitefield, *Journals* (London, 1960), p. 465. Richard H. Ekman, "Conversion East of Boston," unpublished honors thesis, Harvard College, 1966, Harvard Archives, Cambridge, Mass.

88. Information about the Rogers family from William Haller, *The Rise of Puritanism* (New York, 1938; reprint, ed. 1957), pp. 35–48; *Sibley's Harvard Graduates*, I, 166–171; III, 273–276; V, 580–583; VI, 556–560; VII, 554–560; *The Dictionary of National Biography*, ed. Leslie Stephen and Sydney Lee (Oxford, 1921–1922), XVII, 117–118, 119, 129–130, 135–136, 137–138.

89. *Sibley's Harvard Graduates*, VI, 331–336; Harrison Ellery and Charles P. Bowditch, *The Pickering Genealogy* (Cambridge, Mass., 1897), I, 75–80; Edward P. Crowell, "Historical Discourse," in *Two Centuries of Church History* (Salem, Mass., 1884), pp. 53–64; see also his journal in the Pickering House, Salem, Mass.

90. William Giddinge, et al., to Daniel Rogers, Chamberlain MSS F.1.44, Boston Public Library, Boston, Mass.

91. Theophilus Pickering, *The Rev. Mr. Pickering's Letters to the Rev. N. Rogers and Mr. D. Rogers of Ipswich* (Boston, 1742), p. 7.

92. *Ibid.*, p. 10.

93. Theophilus Pickering, "Proposal," Jan. 10, 1743, JCP, I, 75–76.

94. [John Cleaveland, et al.], *A Plain Narrative of the Proceedings Which caused the Separation* (Boston, 1747), p. 5; *The Pretended Plain Narrative Convicted of Fraud & Partiality; A Letter from the Second Church in Ipswich, to Their Separated Brethren* (Boston, 1748), p. 12.

95. Edward P. Crowell, "Historical Discourse," p. 61; List of Grievances, Mar. 12, 1744, "Parish Records, 1745–1814," pp. 2–3. Town of Essex MSS., Box 10, Essex Institute, Salem, Mass.

96. [John Cleaveland, et al.], *A Plain Narrative*, pp. 6–7.

97. *Ibid.*, p. 10.

98. Salary: "Town [Parish] Meeting Records of Chebacco, 1725–1775," pp. 67–68, Town of Essex MSS., Box 9, Essex Institute. Parish Trustee: same, pp. 67–77; Tax List, 1749, divided into old and new church adherents, Mass. Archives, XIII, 39–40.

99. [John Cleaveland, et al.], *A Plain Narrative*, pp. 11–12; *The Pretended Plain Narrative Convicted*, pp. 18–21; Theophilus Pickering, *Mr. Pickering's Letter to Mr. Whitefield* (Boston, 1745), quoted in Crowell, "Historical Discourse," p. 59.

100. Meeting of Chebacco Separates, Jan. 13, 1746, JCP, III, 32; Covenant of Separation, Jan. 20, 1746, "Parish Records, 1745–1814," p. 5; James Eveleth and Francis Choate to John Cleaveland, Jan. 27, 1746, JCP, I, 104–105; see notes 20–21; Meeting Records, Jan. 15, 1746, JCP, III, 36.

101. Church Meeting Notes, May 30, 1746, JCP, III, 45–46; James Eveleth, et al., July 28, 1746, JCP, I, 111–112; Recommendation for Ebenezer Cleaveland, preacher, from the Chebacco Church, Mar. 26,

1750, "Parish Records, 1745-1814," p. 257; Records of a Council, May 20, 1746, JCP, III, 41-42.

102. The lists I have used for these and the following calculations are William Giddinge, et al., to Daniel Rogers, Feb. 3, 1742, Chamberlain MSS., F.1.144, Boston Public Library; Pickering's "Proposal," Jan. 10, 1743, JCP, I, 75-76; List of Grievances, Mar. 12, 1744, "Parish Records, 1745-1814," pp. 2-3; Covenant of Separation, Jan. 20, 1746, "Parish Records, 1745-1814," p. 5; List of the Male Members of the Second Church, Apr. 10, 1746, "Misc. Records and Correspondence, 1705-1815"; signers of *A Plain Narrative*, Sept. 15, 1747, p. 16; 1749 Tax List, divided into new and old church adherents, Mass. Archives, XIII, 39-40.

103. (Boston, 1747).

104. (Boston, 1747), p. 3.

105. [John Cleaveland, et al.], *A Plain Narrative*, pp. 3-4.

106. (Boston, 1748), pp. 5-6.

107. For reunion negotiations, see JCP, I, 77, 150-152; III, 114-117; the documents for the debate over parish status can be found in Mass. Archives, XII, 492-501, 504-505, 554-555, 620-625, 645-647; XIII, 30-48, 138-147, 203-208, 269-270, 272, 335-341. For a summary, see Abner C. Goodell's note in *The Acts and Resolves, Public and Private, of the Province of the Massachusetts Bay*, ed. Abner C. Goodell (Boston, 1869-1922), V, 533-537. See also "Parish Records, 1745-1814" [New Church], pp. 30-52; "Town [Parish] Meeting Records, 1725-1775" [Old Church], pp. 70-100; and the suits by Timothy Pickering, on behalf of his brother Theophilus, against the parish, and Samuel Low, whose property was taken by distraint, against the parish tax collector, in the Court of General Sessions Records, Essex County Court House, Salem, Mass.

108. See Church Articles of Faith and Discipline, "Parish Records, 1745-1814," pp. 9-12, reprinted in *Two Centuries of Church History*, pp. 202-204.

109. For doctrine, see "Principles and Fundamentals of John Cleaveland's Faith," JCP, I, 133-136, and John Cleaveland to Jonathan Parsons, Sept. 28, 1749, JCP, III, 144-147. For preaching, see Daniel Dana to William B. Sprague, Mar. 28, 1856, printed in William B. Sprague, *Annals of the American Pulpit* (New York, 1857-1865), I, 460-461; and Goen, *Revivalism and Separatism*, pp. 174-185, on New Light preaching in general.

110. *An Historical Narrative and Declaration* (Providence, R.I., 1781), p. 36, quoted in Goen, *Revivalism and Separatism*, p. 157. See also James P. Walsh, "The Conservative Nature of Conn. Separatism," *Bulletin of the Conn. Historical Society*, 31-35 (1966-1970), 9-17.

CHAPTER THREE

1. "The Life of John Cleaveland," JCP, II, 47; chap. III, note 83.
2. See Nina Fletcher Little, "John Cogswell's Grant and Some of the

Houses Thereon, 1636–1839," *EIHC*, 76 (1940), 152–173, esp. the map on p. 161.

3. For the origins of Chebacco parish, since 1819 the town of Essex, see the various works of Robert Crowell, who was minister in Chebacco from 1815 to 1855. See his *A Sketch of the History of the Second Parish in Ipswich* (Andover, Mass., 1815); *History of the Town of Essex, from 1634 to 1700* (Boston, 1853); *History of the Town of Essex from 1634 to 1868* (Essex, Mass., 1868). The last work incorporates the earlier ones and was completed by his son, Robert Payson Crowell, a professor of classics at Amherst. The eighteenth- and nineteenth-century sections abandoned Rev. Crowell's "visits" to the homes of early settlers, complete with fabricated "conversations," in favor of more conventional local history. See also Edward S. Perzel, "The First Generation in Colonial Ipswich, Mass." (unpublished Ph.D. dissertation, Rutgers, 1967), pp. 22–25; Joseph B. Felt, *History of Ipswich, Essex, and Hamilton* (Cambridge, Mass., 1834), pp. 257–258; *Records and Files of the Quarterly Courts of Essex County, Mass.* (Salem, Mass., 1919), VII, 245; "Records of Chebacco Parish, 1676–1726," Essex Institute; "Ipswich Commoners Records, 1720–1788," original with town clerk, microfilm copy at the Ipswich Public Library (reel 13) and the Massachusetts Historical Society (reel 149). See also Thomas F. Waters, *Ipswich in the Massachusetts Bay Colony* (Ipswich, Mass., 1905–1917), I, 71–73. For the population of Ipswich generally, see Susan L. Norton, "Population Growth in Colonial America: A Study of Ipswich, Mass.," *Population Studies*, 25 (1971), 433–451.

The population estimates are based on a 1683 militia list (see Crowell, *Essex*, p. 110), 1695 tax lists (Ipswich Historical Society), 1718 tax lists ("Chebacco Parish Papers, 1718–1800," Ipswich MSS., Essex Institute), and a 1749 tax list (Mass. Archives, XIII, pp. 39–40). I used a multiplier of five to derive the estimates from the lists. See Philip J. Greven, Jr., *Four Generations: Population, Land, and Family in Colonial Andover, Mass.* (Ithaca, N.Y., 1970), pp. 104–105, and note 13 below. The estimates are 1683: 256; 1695: 330; 1718: 610; 1749: 750; 1770: 975.

4. Amicus Patriae [John Wise], *A Word of Comfort to a Melancholy Country*, in *Colonial Currency Reprints*, ed. A. M. Davis (Boston, 1911), II, 189.

5. I used the land transactions of the 1771 taxpayers to establish a land-price series, 1720–1775. I averaged the prices by decade and adjusted them annually to account for the soaring inflation of 1720–1749. I adjusted the prices in these years to 75 percent of the value of sterling, which prevailed in Massachusetts currency from 1750–1775, after resumption. For the rate of inflation, see Roger Weis, "Colonial Monetary Standard of Massachusetts," *Economic History Review*, 2nd ser., 27 (1974), 586–587.

6. 1695–1718: 5.3; 1718–1749: 2.6, based on the number of taxpayers. For the method of calculation, see Roderick Floud, *An Introduction to Quantitative Methods for Historians* (Princeton, N.J., 1975), pp. 90–93. For the relationship of population growth to migration, see

Duane E. Ball, "Dynamics of Population and Wealth in Eighteenth-Century Chester County, Pennsylvania," *Journal of Interdisciplinary History,* 6 (1975–1976), 622–623.

7. Abijah P. Marvin, *History of the Town of Winchendon* (Winchendon, Mass., 1868), pp. 30–56; Augustus A. Gould and Frederic Kidder, *The History of New Ipswich* (Boston, 1852), pp. 22–28. For the settlement of central Massachusetts, see John F. Sly, "Geographical Expansion and the Town System," in *Commonwealth History of Massachusetts,* ed. A. B. Hart (New York, 1928), II, 102–113.

8. See esp. James G. Lydon, "North Shore Trade in the Early Eighteenth Century," *American Neptune,* 28 (1968), 261–274.

9. A. P. Usher, "Colonial Business and Transportation," in *Commonwealth History* II, 386, with 1765 population-density figures recalculated and corrected. The population-density figures for the towns of Essex County were calculated by converting the acreage figures from Henry Colman, *Report on the Agriculture of Mass.: County of Essex* (Boston, 1838), pp. 136–138, into square miles and dividing them by the 1765 census figures, from Evarts B. Greene and Virginia D. Harrington, *American Population Before the Federal Census of 1790* (New York, 1932), pp. 21–25. Population density, people per square mile, in 1765 ranged, in the seaport towns, from Beverly's 153 to Salem's 789 and Newburyport's 3431. Most of the old farming towns ranged between 40 and 100, with Ipswich and Chebacco at about 60.

10. W. J. Latimer and M. O. Lanphear, *Soil Survey of Essex County, Mass.* (Washington, D.C., 1925), pp. 1–3, 5, 8, and attached map of soil types in each area; pp. 11–55 describe the agricultural potential of each soil type on the map.

11. For this point I am indebted to Robert A. Gross, "The Problem of Agricultural Crisis in Eighteenth-Century New England: Concord, Massachusetts, as a Test Case" (unpublished paper presented at the American Historical Association Convention, Dec. 29, 1975), pp. 5–6. See also Usher, "Colonial Business and Transportation," pp. 391–394, and Max G. Schumacher, *The Northern Farmer and His Markets During the Late Colonial Period* (New York, 1975), pp. 22–24, for similar observations. Based on the improved-land list in the 1771 valuation, the Chebacco figures are as follows:

	Tillage	English & Upland Mowing	Fresh Meadow	Salt Marsh	Pasture
Acres	361.5	353	144.75	1478	2605.5
Percent	7.3%	7.1%	2.9%	29.9%	52.7%

12. Based on 1785 valuation, 6296 acres, or 60 percent of the whole Chebacco acreage, was woodland, unimporved, or unimprovable. The quality of Chebacco's unimproved land might be inferred from Concord's experience. Concord had 60 percent unimproved land in 1749, and 40 percent in 1785, as marginal lands were brought into production. See

Gross, "The Problem of Agricultural Crisis," pp. 14–15. It may also be that Chebacco turned to the sea—fishing, trade, boat building—rather than to their unpromising land to supplement their strained resources. For hay exports, see John Hayward, *A Gazetteer of Massachusetts* (Boston, 1849), p. 147.

13. Based on fifteen widows' provisions found in wills, see note 32, and a "List of Necessaries" made up for Rev. Porter, the Old Light minister, in 1749, in "Town Meeting Records of Chebacco 1725–1775," p. 82. For methods and similar results, see James T. Lemon, "Household Consumption in Eighteenth-Century America," *Agricultural History,* 41 (1967), 59–70, and Robert A. Gross, *The Minutemen and Their World* (New York, 1976), pp. 213–214. Lemon's assumption of a family of five better fit the average household size in Essex County (based on the 1765 census), especially in the seacoast towns. He assumes a widow's, or wife's, share to be one, a husband's one and a half, an eldest son's one and a half, and the younger children's a half each, thereby providing the basis for extrapolation from the widow's provision to the needs of a family of five. This comports well with the household composition in my reconstructed census (based on the 1771 valuation). Average household size in Chebacco was about 4.8; for the rest of the Essex County seacoast towns (in 1765) it ranged between 4.6 and 5.4.

The average holding in improved land in Chebacco in 1771 is a little less than fifty acres. That is, three and a half acres of tillage, twenty of mowing land (English upland and fresh meadow one fourth and salt marsh three fourths), and twenty-six acres of pasture. The average here has been calculated for farmers, that is, those with both land and livestock, and not for taxpayers. I wanted an average size for farms in the village, not land per capita.

14. John Cleaveland to Parker Cleaveland, Nov. 13, 1772, JCP, II, 64–65.

15. Cogswell: Ephraim O. Jameson, *The Cogswells in America* (Boston, 1884), p. 109; Probate No. 5835; for Nehemiah, see *Cogswell,* p. 166; the genealogist put him in the wrong family. Choate: Ephraim O. Jameson, *The Choates in America* (Boston, 1896), pp. 25–26; Probate No. 5383. Groton: see note 51.

16. Burnham: 1771 valuation; the account book is in the Essex Institute. Emmerton: see 1771 valuation, and Joseph A. Emmerton, *Materials Toward a Genealogy of the Emmerton Family* (Salem, Mass., 1881), pp. 31–33, esp. quote from Chebacco Church Records on p. 32; Probate No. 9040.

17. Only adult livestock were taxable, that is, horses and mares above three years of age, oxen above four, cows and heifers above three, goats and sheep above one, swine above one. So the actual number of livestock would be larger according to the number of colts, calves, lambs, and piglets, although probably not distributed differently.

18. Ipswich figures from 1771 valuation; Concord for the same year from Gross, "The Problem of Agricultural Crisis," p. 16. Sheepholding in Concord fell 45 percent between 1749 and 1771; see p. 15. Decline in

Massachusetts: Usher, "Colonial Business and Transportation," pp. 392–393. Decline in exports: Schumacher, *The Northern Farmer*, p. 157; the figure actually refers to sheep and hogs, but since the number of hogs in the three eastern counties of Massachusetts was only 4 percent of the number of sheep in 1767 (Usher, p. 392), and since pork could be and was salted for export (Schumacher, p. 162), I assume that the figure refers mostly to sheep. The per capita number of sheep for Essex County in 1767 was .61 (Usher, p. 392), and for Chebacco in 1771 it was 1.3. On the problems with mutton, see Percy W. Bidwell and John I. Falconer, *History of Agriculture in the Northern United States, 1620–1860* (Washington, D.C., 1925), p. 110. Sheep-raising in Ipswich began in the seventeenth century, but in 1702 the commons were divided into several large sheep pastures for the town's nine flocks, two of which were in Chebacco. See Waters, *Ipswich*, I, 65, 71–73. See also L. G. Connor, "A Brief History of the Sheep Industry in the United States," *Annual Report of the Am. Hist. Assoc.* (Washington, D.C., 1921), pp. 93–97.

19. Sheep: widows' provisions for sheep range between four and twelve. Lemon, "Household Consumption," p. 69, suggests about eight sheep for a family of five. Hay: English mowing produced .56 tons per acre, fresh meadow .695, and salt marsh .74; salt hay comprised about 1100 tons out of a total production of 1400 (Chebacco, 1771 valuation). See, for Massachusetts in 1801 by county and kind of hay, Bidwell and Falconer, *History of Agriculture*, p. 105, and for Concord 1749 and 1771, Gross, "The Problem of Agricultural Crisis," p. 18; see Amos E. Jewett, "The Tidal Marshes of Rowley and Vicinity with an Account of Old-Time Methods of Marshing," *EIHC*, 85 (1949), 272–291.

20. The total tonnage was 233. This figure most probably represents a fleet of ten to twelve "Chebacco" boats, small twenty-ton fishing boats, which supposedly originated in the parish. (Howard I. Chapelle, *The History of American Sailing Ships* [New York, 1935], p. 252.) These were about half of the fleet Crowell claimed was here in 1770 (*History of Essex*, p. 194); the rest may have been owned by shipowners in Gloucester and Marblehead. These boats were manned by two men and a boy, thus offering supplementary employment for some seventy-five boys and men for the "spring fare," before planting, and the "fall fare," after harvest, to the Grand Banks. The fish were brought back and dried at "fish flakes" on Hog Island, Warehouse Island, Thompson Island, and Clay Point. See especially the papers and accounts of Joshua Burnham (three boxes at the Essex Institute), who sailed Gloucester-owned boats out of Chebacco from 1763 to 1791. For the participation of young men, see the Diary of George Norton (Essex Institute) and the Diary of David Choate (Jameson, *Choate*, pp. 109–112, original at the Essex Institute). See also Joseph Emmerton (note 16), and Waters, *Ipswich*, II, 600. See also Percy W. Bidwell, *Rural Economy in New England at the Beginning of the Nineteenth Century* (New Haven, Conn., 1916), pp. 291–292, "The Relation of the Maritime Industries to Agriculture."

21. All enterprises are listed on 1771 valuation. Burnham, *Burnham*, pp. 309–310, 312, 314–315, 320–321; Waters, *Ipswich*, I, 78; see also Deed of Gift from John Burnham to son Thomas, Vol. 8, p. 110. Deed

of Gift from Thomas to son Nathan, Vol. 92, p. 32, and Probate No. 4178.

22. Felt, *Ipswich, Essex and Hamilton,* p. 95, says that it was first granted to William Story, father of Seth, in 1671. The 1715 ownership is recorded in a Deed of Gift from Joseph Eveleth to his son James (Vol. 27, p. 196) conveying half of his share of the sawmill owned jointly with Seth Story. James Eveleth was given the rest in 1734 (Vol. 89, p. 246). Seth Story died in 1732 and passed his share to his sons Seth and Zechariah (Probate No. 26799). For the first Story, see Perzel, "The First Generation," p. 364, and Emma Story White, "Descendants of William Story" (MSS., New England Historic Genealogical Society [hereafter N.E.H.G.S.]), pp. 1–4. The other Story sawmill is listed on the 1771 valuation. I don't know when it began operation.

23. Burnham, *Burnham,* pp. 312, 315–316; John Burnham, Probate No. 4115 and Deed of Division between Jonathan and David Burnham, Vol. 25, p. 12; Jacob's share was in the control of his son Solomon although ownership did not pass until his death in 1773 (see 1771 valuation and Probate No. 4103). In 1771 Jacob was eighty-nine years old, Jonathan eighty-six, and David eighty-three.

24. Brewery: Crowell, *Essex,* pp. 119–121, and Samuel Low, Probate No. 17233. Tavern: Crowell, *Essex,* p. 106; Rust, *Rust,* pp. 31–37, 54–55, 86–87; Nathaniel Rust, Jr., Probate No. 24467; Joseph Rust (d.1735), Probate No. 24460; Joseph Rust (d.1771), Probate No. 24461. Tannery: Perkins, *Perkins,* pp. 63–64; Deeds, Vol. 84, p. 270, and Vol. 97, p. 327; Jameson, *Choate,* pp. 25–26, 57.

25. On the nature of rural enterprise, see Bidwell, *Rural Economy,* pp. 251–276.

26. Jameson, *Choate,* pp. 37–39.

27. Based on analysis of self-designated occupations in the land transactions of the 1771 taxpayers. See also Bidwell, *Rural Economy,* pp. 260–262, 291–292.

28. The only exception to the pattern of nonresident land ownership, omitted from these calculations, was the fifty-six-acre Wainwright farm. It was owned by the widow Wainwright, who lived in Boston and was Rev. John Wise's granddaughter, and rented, between 1754 and 1771 at least, to David Low, Sr. See *Sibley's Harvard Graduates,* XI, 174.

29. See note 78 below, and deeds in Vol. 117, p. 113; Vol. 134, p. 74; Vol. 117, p. 114. The number of land transactions for the men in Cleaveland's generation comes from the economic reconstitution of the 1771 taxpayers; see note 5 and note 32 below.

30. Deeds: Vol. 104, p. 79; Vol. 117, p. 128; Vol. 43, p. 46; Vol. 63, p. 111; Vol. 47, p. 125; Vol. 39, p. 270; Vol. 43, p. 222; Vol. 47, p. 125; Vol. 47, p. 152; Vol. 46, p. 34; Vol. 46, p. 44; Vol. 55, p. 40; Vol. 66, p. 36; Vol. 66, p. 42; Vol. 67, p. 275; Vol. 41, p. 275; Vol. 70, p. 209; Vol. 80, p. 31; Vol. 85, p. 96; Vol. 93, p. 70; Vol. 101, p. 216. See also Nathaniel Goodhue, Probate No. 1119. William Goodhue was landless in 1771; see Arlin I. Ginsburg, "Ipswich, Mass., during the American Revolution, 1763–1791" (unpublished Ph.D. dissertation, University of California, Riverside, 1972), p. 67.

31. More than 80 percent of the 1771 taxpayers inherited 50 percent or more of the largest number of acres they ever held during their lifetimes; more than 60 percent inherited 90 percent or more of their lands. Fully 50 percent of the taxpayers inherited all the lands they would ever own, and almost half of those suffered a net loss of land during their lifetime. Even these high figures do not tell the whole story, since most of the land purchased was unimproved wood or marsh land. The far more valuable homestead land—including house, barn, tillage, and pasturage—was inherited in all but two cases. These figures and those for the land transactions were derived from the economic reconstitution of the 1771 taxpayers; see note 32 below. For family values, see James A. Henretta, "Families and Farms: *Mentalité* in Pre-Industrial America," *WMQ,* 25 (1978), 3–32.

32. The civil record of births in Ipswich is very incomplete, especially regarding the outlying parishes. The Chebacco Parish baptismal record does not begin until 1725. These figures are derived from the baptismal records from 1725 to 1740, after which time disturbances in the parish render them suspect. All the families involved were reconstituted and the children traced in the *Vital Records* and relevant genealogies. To get a maximum estimate of child mortality I assumed all the unknowns to have died. For methods, see Daniel Scott Smith, "Population, Family and Society in Hingham, Mass., 1635–1880" (unpublished Ph.D. dissertation, University of California, Berkeley, 1973), pp. 26–32. See also Smith's "The Demographic History of Colonial New England," in *The American Family in Social-Historical Perspective,* ed. Michael Gordon (New York, 1973), p. 403.

The phrase "Cleaveland's generation" refers to the birth cohort of 1710–1729 of men on the 1771 valuation. It also includes their brothers even if they were not born between these two dates. This is a compromise between birth cohort and biological generation. I hope thereby to avoid the pitfalls of including only men of the same biological generation of descent from the founders with widespread birth dates and life experiences, on the one hand, and arbitrarily dividing sons of the same father, on the other. The latter is particularly important because of the crucial role of inheritance. Ideally, his generation would include every child born between those dates in the village, but the baptismal records do not survive for most of this period. My reliance on the 1771 list undoubtedly causes me to understate the amount of migration.

Most of the data on which this chapter is based come from a demographic reconstitution of taxpayers' families on the 1749 tax list and the 1771 valuation. The reconstitution was based on the published *Vital Records,* published and unpublished genealogies at the New England Historic Genealogical Society, town histories, probate records, and deeds. Douglas Jones of Tufts University helped me to design the reconstitution forms. The 1771 list includes a detailed listing of taxable property, real and personal. The 1749 list is in the Mass. Archives, XIII, 39–40, and the 1771 in CXXXIII, 71–74. The latter is also available in microfilm (reel A-70) in the Microtext Division, Lamont Library, Harvard College.

The 1771 list of property served also as the basis for an economic reconstitution. To trace the transfer of property, I abstracted all the available probate information for the taxpayers on that list and for their fathers. I also abstracted all the available land transactions for the 1771 taxpayers. These are available in the Essex County Registry of Probate and Registry of Deeds, in Salem, Mass. Since the 1771 valuation did not include unimproved land, I supplemented it with the 1785 valuation, which does. For that document, see Mass. State Library, under "Ipswich."

Some of the demographic data were analyzed by means of FORTRAN programs written by John Larson of M.I.T.

33. John Cleaveland to Mary Dodge, Apr. 6, 1747; Mar. 5, 1747, JCP, III, 84–86, 71–73.

34. Mary Dodge to Ezekiel Dodge, Feb. 12, 1747, JCP, III, 91–93. Mary's father and Ezekiel's father were brothers. See Joseph T. Dodge, *Dodge,* pp. 42–43. Olive Johnson to John Cleaveland, Sept. 18, 1747, JCP, I, 113–114; Alfred Johnson, *History and Genealogy* [Johnson family] (Boston, 1914), pp. 74–79.

35. John Cleaveland to Mary Cleaveland, Jr., May 17, 1769, JCP, II, 55–56. Marital choice may always have been a mixture of affection and more practical considerations; see Alan MacFarlane, *The Family Life of Ralph Josselin* (Cambridge, Eng., 1970), pp. 94–96. A theoretical discussion of the interaction of these factors can be found in William J. Goode, *The Family* (Englewood Cliffs, N.J., 1964), pp. 31–43. On marital bargaining, see also Greven, *Four Generations,* pp. 74–76, 78–82; Gross, *Minutemen,* pp. 99–101; Smith, "Hingham," pp. 167–170.

36. Zechariah Story (1741–1831), "Diary," unpaginated, Essex Institute, Salem, Mass.

37. Father's wealth rank from 1749 tax list; see Daniel Scott Smith, "Parental Power and Marriage Patterns," *Journal of Marriage and the Family,* 25 (1973), 419–428, and Gross, *Minutemen,* pp. 210–211.

38. John Cleaveland to Josiah Cleaveland, Sept. 9, 1748, JCP, III, 139–142; for land transactions, see Stephen Boardman to Nehemiah Dodge, Vol. 92, p. 60; same to Francis Choate, Vol. 100, p. 97; same to Robert Choate, et al., Vol. 95, p. 43, in the Registry of Deeds, Essex County Courthouse, Salem, Mass. The deeds say thirty-eight acres.

39. For the birth cohorts 1710–1719 and 1720–1729, the average male age at marriage is 25–26, for women about four years lower. See Smith, "Hingham," pp. 55, 236.

40. See Greven, *Four Generations,* pp. 10, 82–83, 131.

41. Based on 1749 reconstitution. For Burnham, see Thomas Burnham, Probate No. 4178, and Roderick H. Burnham, *The Burnham Family* (Hartford, Conn., 1869), p. 321. For Goodhue, see John Goodhue, Probate No. 11174, and Jonathan E. Goodhue, *History and Genealogy of the Goodhue Family* (Rochester, N.Y., 1891), p. 29.

42. On coresidence, see Philip J. Greven, Jr., "The Average Size of Families and Households in the Province of Massachusetts in 1764 and in the United States in 1790: An Overview," in *Household and Family in Past Time,* ed. Peter Laslett and Richard Wall (Cambridge, Eng., 1972), pp. 545–560. Note, however, that since those families without houses must

live in another family's house, and assuming no more than two families to a house, the percentage of coresident families is double his percentage. On housing, see David H. Flaherty, *Privacy in Colonial New England* (Charlottesville, Va., 1972), pp. 35–40. For the Cleaveland house, see Chebacco [Rufus Choate], "Some Old Houses of Essex," *Essex Echo,* Dec. 10, 1909.

43. In Andover:

	Persisted	Migrated
2nd Gen.	78.3%	21.7%
3rd Gen.	61.0%	39.0%
4th Gen.	43.7%	56.3%

Greven, *Four Generations,* p. 212. See, however, the review by Maris Vinovskis, in *Historical Methods Newsletter,* 4 (1971), 141–148.

44. The pre-1690 acts relating to inheritance can be found in William H. Whitmore, ed., *The Colonial Laws of Massachusetts* (Boston, 1890), pp. 32–33, 42, 50–51, 96, 157–158. See also *The Charters and General Laws of the Colony and Province of Massachusetts Bay* (Boston, 1814) for "Acts Respecting Wills and the Distribution of Intestate Estates" (1641–1685), pp. 203–208, "An Act Respecting Dowers, Etc." (1641), pp. 99–100, and "An Act for the Settlement and Distribution of the Estates of Intestates," pp. 230–232. For a discussion of inheritance law, see Thomas E. Atkinson, "The Development of the Massachusetts Probate System," *Michigan Law Review,* 42 (1943), 425–452; George L. Haskins, "The Beginnings of Partible Inheritance in the American Colonies," *Yale Law Journal,* 51 (1942), 1280–1315; Richard B. Morris, *Studies in the History of American Law* (New York, 1930), pp. 74–81, 92–103, 111–125.

45. Morris, *Studies in the History of American Law,* pp. 135–173. See also M. Robert Cobbledick, "The Property Rights of Women in Puritan New England," in *Studies in the Science of Society,* ed. G. P. Murdock (New Haven, Conn., 1937).

46. Information on transmission of property from deeds and probate information for 1771 taxpayers and their fathers, based on an analysis of 109 estates probated or passed by deed between 1692–1790. See note 32.

47. Gidding, Probate No. 10826, and Minot S. Giddings, *The Giddings Family* (Hartford, Conn., 1882), pp. 25–26. Cogswell, Probate No. 5837, and Jameson, *Cogswell,* p. 40.

48. Mary Dodge [Cleaveland], "Diary," Dec. 28, 1742, JCP, I, 49; Dodge, *Dodge,* pp. 26, 43, 78–79.

49. Alternative forms of substitute heirship are discussed in Jack Goody, "Strategies of Heirship," *Comparative Studies in Society and History,* 15 (1973), 3–20. Choate: Jameson, *Choate,* pp. 37, 40, 41. Proctor: Probate No. 22824. Dodge: Dodge, *Dodge,* p. 125.

For naming patterns, see Daniel Scott Smith, "Child-Naming Patterns and Family Structure Change: Hingham, Mass., 1640–1880," unpublished paper, Clark University Conference on the Family and Social Structure, Apr. 27–29, 1972, and Alice S. Rossi, "Naming Children in

Middle-Class Families," *American Sociological Review*, 30 (1965), 499–513.

50. Wade: Probate No. 28634. Grover: Probate No. 11962. Cogswell: Jameson, *Cogswell*, p. 51; Probate No. 5825; Father's bonds of guardianship in Probate No. 11071. Wheeler: Probate No. 29432.

51. See Deed of Gift, Vol. 131, p. 205; Samuel Cogswell's family is not in the genealogy, perhaps because only one daughter survived him; so, see *Vital Records* for his marriage and children. For nephews, see Jameson, *Cogswell*, pp. 51, 109, 227–228. Groton, the artisan, was left no land (see Thomas Groton, Probate No. 11942) and had none on the 1771 valuation, but on the 1785 valuation he had fifty-eight acres.

52. See note 45. These paragraphs on women and land are based on both the law and observed behavior in the transmission of property. See also Daniel Scott Smith, "Inheritance and the Position and Orientation of Colonial Women," unpublished paper, Second Berkshire Conference, Cambridge, Mass., Oct. 27, 1974.

53. Mary Cleaveland to John Cleaveland, July 26, 1758, JCP, I, 198–200.

54. See note 46.

55. Low: Probate No. 17185; Cogswell: Probate No. 5844; see also note 14. Gidding: Gidding, *Gidding*, p. 23; "Chebacco Parish Records, 1676–1726"; Probate No. 10871. For a similar economic minimum in farm size, see Greven, *Four Generations*, p. 224.

56. Cogswell: Jameson, *Cogswell*, pp. 40, 80–84; Probate No. 5871. Eveleth: Jonathan B. Butcher, *Eveleth Genealogy* (bound typescript, 1973, N.E.H.G.S.), pp. 34–37, 52–56; Probate No. 9168.

57. For the law, see note 44. Burnham: Deeds, Vol. 125, p. 111; Vol. 86, p. 250; Vol. 138, p. 69; Vol. 100, p. 22; see also Thomas Burnham, Probate No. 4178. Butler: Probate No. 4337. Foster: Probate No. 9898.

58. See "Parish Records 1745–1814," p. 275. See also Daniel Scott Smith and Michael S. Hindus, "Premarital Pregnancy in America, 1640–1971: An Overview and Interpretation," *Journal of Interdisciplinary History*, 5 (1974–1975), 537–570.

59. Abigail Paine Cleaveland to John Cleaveland, Mar. 14, 1750, JCP, I, 170–174.

60. For Ebenezer Cleaveland, see chapter II.

61. Mary Cleaveland, "Journal," JCP, I, 42–54.

62. "Journal," Apr. 8, 1750, JCP, I, 44.

63. "Journal," Oct. 14, 1751; Jan. 25, 1757; Dec. 28, 1762, JCP, I, 45, 46, 50.

64. See note 32.

65. Pompe: see John's father's will in Cleveland and Cleveland, *The Genealogy of the Cleveland and Cleaveland Families*, I, 81–82; the original is missing from the probate collection at the Connecticut State Library. Bear: for her birth date, see the Manchester *Vital Records;* for her residence in the household, see Mary Cleaveland to John Cleaveland, June 12, 1758, JCP, I, 188–190, and July 2, 1758, JCP, I, 195–197; for her

conversion, see the conversion relations in JCP, I, 363–405. Dodge: Dodge, *Dodge*, p. 79; Probate No. 7937.

66. Mary's dowry was worth 700 pounds in the inflated currency of 1742, or 186 pounds, 13 shillings, 4 pence in the currency of 1758. For the rate of inflation, and the relationship of Massachusetts currency to sterling, see Rogers Weis, "Colonial Monetary Standard of Massachusetts," *Economic History Review*, 2nd ser., 27 (1974), 577–592.

67. The context of my observations on slavery in Massachusetts I owe to conversations with Janet Campbell, whose unpublished honors thesis, "Slavery in Colonial Boston," is available in the Harvard Archives. See also Richard Hofstadter, *America at 1750: A Social Portrait* (New York, 1971), pp. 102–104.

68. See Robert V. Wells, *The Population of the British Colonies in America Before 1776* (Princeton, N.J., 1975), pp. 87–88, and Smith, "Hingham," pp. 279–281.

69. Coresidence figures for widows are based on the mention of widows in wills, deeds, or probate settlements and the description of their right to house space by the fathers of men in John Cleaveland's generation. See also Alexander Keyssar, "Widowhood in Eighteenth-Century Massachusetts: A Problem in the History of the Family," *Perspectives in American History*, 8 (1974), 83–119.

70. Cogswell, Probate No. 5825; see also Jacob Perkins, Probate No. 21326. About 14 percent left detailed lists of widow's provisions; mentions of household space were much more common.

71. John Burnham, Probate No. 4117.

72. *Ibid.*; see also Burnham, *Burnham*, p. 190, and the Hopkinton *Vital Records* for the birth of children to Jeremiah and Nehemiah.

73. Legacies, debts, and the number of debts are all from the estates that passed to the men of John Cleaveland's generation. The legal priority of debts over legacies was recognized by the legal formula used in most wills leaving property to heirs only after payment of "my just debts." The payment of debts is recorded in the "administration" of the estate, supervised by the judge of probate, and secured by bonds. See note 44. The average number of debts and the chracter of indebtedness in Chebacco are quite like those found in Kent, Conn. See Charles S. Grant, *Democracy in the Connecticut Frontier Town of Kent* (New York, 1961), pp. 66–69.

74. These four sets of account books are at the Essex Institute. I examined each one for the years 1760 and 1770, and for the length of accounts with individuals. For eighteenth-century business practice and credit arrangements, see William T. Baxter, *The House of Hancock* (Cambridge, Mass., 1945), pp. 11–38, and "Accounting in Colonial America," in *Studies in the History of Accounting*, eds. A. C. Littleton and B. S. Yamey (Homewood, Ill., 1956). See also Michael Merrill, "Cash Is Good to Eat: Self-Suficiency and Exchange in the Rural Economy of the United States," *Radical History Review*, 3 (1976), 42–66.

75. Low: Probate No. 17188. Cogswell: Probate No. 5844.

76. See note 3; Rev. Robert Crowell, minister in Chebacco after 1815, in his *History of Essex* (1868), p. 247.

77. John Cleaveland to Josiah Cleaveland, Sept. 9, 1748, JCP, III, 139–142.

78. The Cleaveland farm was purchased in 1748 in three land transactions (see deeds in Vol. 92, p. 62; Vol. 100, p. 97; Vol. 43, p. 95) for 3600 pounds in the inflated currency called Old Tenor (O.T.), or 433 pounds in the currency in use after 1750 called New Tenor (N.T.). One share (1200 pounds O.T., or 144 pounds 6 shillings 8 pence N.T.) was purchased by Nehemiah Dodge, Mary Cleaveland's brother; one share (1200 pounds O.T.) was purchased by Elder Francis Choate, Mary Cleaveland's uncle; and the final share by a Choate uncle and two Choate cousins (800 pounds O.T.) and five other supporters (400 pounds O.T.). About 90 percent of the price was met by Mary Cleaveland's family. According to Robert Crowell, local historian and minister in Chebacco from 1815 to 1855, the farm "became his, as from time to time he paid the original value, without rent or interest" (Crowell, *Essex,* p. 247). In the mid-1750s Cleaveland's parish tried to raise money to buy his farm from the proprietors, apparently unsuccessfully, since Cleaveland continued to pay individual proprietors (see "Parish Records, 1745–1814," pp. 8–13, 18). The repayment was quite lengthy and complex.
Share one:
Nehemiah Dodge, as executor of his father Parker's estate (d. 1742, Probate No. 7941), owed his sister Mary 700 pounds O.T. in installments over twelve years. About 300 pounds O.T. (or 80 pounds N.T. if O.T. is of 1742) was owing in 1748, when the farm was purchased. On a 1762 account sheet (JCP, IV, 71–72) Cleaveland made the notation "Liet^n Dodge to Ma'am his sister—£59.8.3." This sum plus the 80 pounds owed by Nehemiah to Mary equals 139 pounds 8 shillings 3 pence N.T., which is quite close to the 144 pounds 6 shillings 8 pence N.T. value of a one-third share in the farm. Cleaveland's 1794 will (JCP, I, 271–274) mentions a deed, not recorded otherwise, from Nehemiah to Mary of his share in the farm. That Nehemiah's share included the inheritance, a dowry in fact, owed to Mary is supported by Cleaveland's intention to "lay out the little that I am to have by my wife to help buy this farm" (John Cleaveland to father Josiah, Sept. 9, 1748, JCP, III, 139–142). Since Nehemiah's share is not mentioned in his will or inventory (Probate No. 7937), I assume he transferred it to Mary before his death in 1758.
Share two:
An undated account sheet (JCP, II, 27–28) records the fact that Cleaveland had paid 13 pounds 6 shillings 8 pence to Elder Francis Choate. At the time of Choate's death in 1777 (Probate No. 5339) only 40 pounds was still owing, meaning that about 104 pounds had been paid. Choate left the 40-pound share to his son Abraham of Wiscasset, Me. In 1799 Abraham sold it to his nephew Job of Pownalboro, Me. (Vol. 165, p. 123). I do not know what Job did with it, but six months later Job's

brother David bought the whole farm from Cleaveland's heirs (Vol. 167, p. 60).

Share three:
The last share was divided among eight people and became even more dispersed by sale and inheritance. The 1762 account sheet records payment of 44 pounds 15 shillings 7 pence; the undated account sheet (before 1777, see share two) records payment of another 65 pounds. In 1800, Cleaveland's heirs purchased a right in the estate from Ebenezer Choate, a son of one of the original proprietors, and then sold the whole estate, so that presumably that was the last right in the estate outstanding (Vol. 167, p. 59).

In summary, in 1748 Cleaveland owned by right of his wife about 80 pounds N.T. in the estate (total 433 pounds N.T.), or 18 percent; by 1762 he owned about 190 pounds, or 44 percent; by 1777 he owned about 358 pounds, or 83 percent.

79. John Cleaveland to Josiah Cleaveland, Sept. 9, 1748, JCP, III, 139–142.

80. These tables reflect the relative progress of surviving 1749 taxpayers on the 1770 tax list. It is an aggregate measure of the transferral of property. For methods, see Smith, "Hingham," pp. 107–120.

1749 Taxpayers on 1770 Tax List

Quintile	1st	2nd	3rd	4th	5th	Total
Migrated	1	3	1	5	5	15
Died	17	8	6	4	5	40
Moved up	—	8	9	7	6	30
Moved down	2	3	6	1	—	12
Same	9	5	4	1	—	19
Unknown	1	3	5	12	16	37

1749 to 1770

Age Group	Upwardly Mobile	%	Stable	%	Downwardly Mobile	%
30 and under	11	41%	4	22%	1	7%
31 to 40	10	37%	2	11%	2	14%
41 and over	6	22%	12	66%	11	79%
Avg. Age	37		46		53	

The age is, of course, that of the taxpayer at the time of the earlier list. Sixty-seven percent of those who moved up from 1749 to 1770 were under thirty-five in 1749; and 79 percent of those who moved down were over forty-five in 1749. The second table reflects the position of surviving 1749 taxpayers among all 1770 taxpayers, not just among themselves. See Gross, *Minutemen*, pp. 207–209, 234–235. For inheritance, see note 31. See also John J. Waters, "Patrimony, Succession, and Social Stability: Guilford, Conn., in the Eighteenth Century," *Perspectives in American History,* 10 (1976), 131–160.

CHAPTER FOUR

1. Data from 1771 reconstitution. For Story and Burnham families, see chap. III, notes 21–23.

2. See the photographs in *Essex in Pictures* (Essex, Mass., 1969), and Hugh Morrison, *Early American Architecture* (Oxford, Eng., 1952), pp. 95–98, 473. Nina Fletcher Little, the current owner of the house, discusses it in detail in her article "John Cogswell's Grant and Some of the Houses Thereon, 1636–1839," *EIHC*, 76 (1940), esp. 163–171 and illustrations opposite pp. 152 and 164. For Cogswell, see Jameson, *Cogswell*, pp. 35–37. For the Foster-Hutchinson house, see Abbott Lowell Cummings, "The Foster-Hutchinson House," *Old Time New England*, 54 (1963–1964), 59–76.

3. See chap. III, and Percy W. Bidwell and John I. Falconer, *History of Agriculture in the Northern United States, 1620–1860* (Washington, D.C., 1925), pp. 84–87.

4. See, for example, *Ancient Ballads Traditionally Sung in New England,* ed. Helen H. Flanders (Philadelphia, Pa., 1960–1965), I–IV, which are correlated with F. J. Child's listing of ancient English and Scottish folk songs and ballads. See also Samuel A. Drake, *A Book of New England Legends and Folk Lore* (Boston, 1902), and Benjamin A. Botkin, ed., *A Treasury of New England Folklore* (New York, 1965, rev. ed.). Many of these stories, even in the romanticized versions of the nineteenth century that survive, bear witness to an earlier system of belief that recognized the power of the supernatural in everyday life.

5. For the premodern understanding of the operation of the natural world that makes such beliefs possible, see Keith Thomas, *Religion and the Decline of Magic* (New York, 1971), pp. 3–21; see also Paul Boyer and Stephen Nissenbaum, *Salem Possessed* (Cambridge, Mass., 1974), pp. 9–21, and the "remarkable providences" tradition in Puritan history and biography (Cecilia Tichi, "Spiritual Biography and the 'Lords Remembrancers,' " *WMQ*, 28 (1971), 64–85, and Kenneth B. Murdock, "Clio in the Wilderness: History and Biography in Puritan New England," *Church History*, 24 (1955), 221–238) for evidence of New England beliefs in malevolent and providential interventions in human affairs. For Ipswich examples, see Richard M. Dorson, *Jonathan Draws the Long Bow* (Cambridge, Mass., 1946), pp. 61 (quotation from *N. E. Journal*), 160; Waters, *Ipswich,* II, 116. The phrase is the title of Cotton Mather's defense of the witchcraft proceedings, *The Wonders of the Invisible World* (Boston, 1692).

6. "Records of Chebacco Parish, 1676–1726," Mar. 10, 1702; Crowell, *Essex,* p. 106; Waters, *Ipswich,* II, 276; Alfred D. Rust, *Rust Family* (Waco, Texas, 1891), p. 32.

7. *Records of the Governor and Company of the Massachusetts Bay,* ed. Nathanial B. Shurtleff (Boston, 1853), II, 203.

8. Waters, *Ipswich,* I, 146–149; II, 277–284; Robert Middlekauf, *Ancients and Axioms* (New Haven, Conn., 1963), pp. 16–17; Richard W. Hale, ed., "Ipswich Grammar School Documents," Colonial Society of

Mass., *Transactions*, 35 (1942–1946), 287–297; Felt, *History of Ipswich, Essex, and Hamilton*, p. 83.

9. "Records of Chebacco Parish, 1676–1726," Mar. 10, 1702; Waters, *Ipswich*, II, 281–282; "Chebacco Parish Records, 1725–1775," pp. 15, 50–53, 61–62.

10. Waters, *Ipswich*, II, 284–285; Crowell, *Essex*, pp. 155–156, 174–175, 183.

11. Ipswich schoolmasters listed in Waters, *Ipswich*, II, 274–292. For Chebacco schoolmasters, see Crowell, *Essex*, pp. 106, 110–112, 148, 174–175, 183. See Bernard Bailyn, *Education in the Forming of American Society* (New York, 1960), pp. 95–98, on colonial teachers, and Walter H. Small, *Early New England Schools* (Boston, 1914), pp. 107–114, on local schoolmasters of writing and reading schools.

12. Calculated from Robert F. Seybolt, *The Public Schools of Colonial Boston 1635–1775* (Cambridge, Mass., 1935), pp. 12–27; for the grammar-school curriculum, see Middlekauf, *Ancients and Axioms*, chaps. V–VI.

13. "Records of Chebacco Parish, 1676–1726," Mar. 10, 1702; "Chebacco Parish Records 1725–1775," p. 51.

14. *The New England Primer*, ed. Paul L. Ford (New York, 1897), esp. pp. 29–31. See also Michael Zuckerman, *Peaceable Kingdoms* (New York, 1970), pp. 72–83.

15 *Primer*, ed. Ford, 32–37; see Plate I opposite title page; for the Rogers family, see chap. II, note 94.

16. *Primer*, ed. Ford, pp. 37–41.

17. From town records cited in Small, *Early New England Schools*, pp. 193–200. The average age was 5.8 to 11.6.

18. The "Accompt of children sent to school in the year 1760" can be found on the first page of Joseph Perkins's ledger, 1756–1763, in the Essex Institute. I presume that this is the total school population, since the second district school was not opened until the next year (Crowell, *Essex*, p. 183). I calculated the number of taxpayers (householders) for 1760 from the growth rate observed between the lists of 1749 and 1770, multiplied that by five to get the total population, took the percentage under sixteen from that listed for all of Ipswich in 1765, and then divided the number in school by that number. The number of Bostonians under sixteen is from the 1765 census; the number in schools from the chart in Seybolt, *Public Schools*, p. 64. For the 1765 census with breakdown by age and sex, see the copy in the Tucker Family MSS., Vol. I, Essex Institute.

19. The seventeenth-century Chebacco residents come from two petitions to the Assembly for parish status on April 16, 1678 (Mass. Archives, X, 121) and on May 29, 1679 (Mass. Archives, X, 132). The names were then checked against surviving wills and deeds in the Essex County Courthouse, as well as in the published *Records and Files of the Quarterly Courts of Essex County Massachusetts* (Salem, Mass., 1911–1975), I–III. The literacy of the 1771 taxpayers and their wives was done as part of the reconstitution and is based on wills, deeds, and the occasional sur-

vival of letters, journals, or financial records. The deeds are only copies, but they indicate marks when used. Deeds are signed only by the seller; his wife signs because of her dower rights. For an assessment of literacy based on a sample of wills alone from various New England counties, and somewhat lower than mine, see Kenneth A. Lockridge, *Literacy in Colonial New England* (New York, 1974). See also Bailyn, *Education,* pp. 78–84; Felt, *Ipswich,* pp. 87–90; Lawrence A. Cremin, *American Education: The Colonial Experience, 1607–1783* (New York, 1970), pp. 524–526, 548–549. For comparable English data on education and literacy, see Margaret Spufford, *Contrasting Communities: English Villages in the Sixteenth and Seventeenth Centuries* (Cambridge, Eng., 1974), pp. 171–218.

20. For lists of Chebacco college graduates, see Crowell, *Essex,* p. 475, and Felt, *Ipswich,* pp. 93–94. I checked these lists against the indexes in the volumes of *Sibley's Harvard Graduates.*

21. Based on the estates of the 1771 taxpayers and their fathers, in the Essex County Registry of Probate. See John Andrews, Probate No. 650; Thomas Choate, No. 5383; Humphrey Choate, No. 5343; Francis Choate, No. 5339; John Cleaveland, No. 5617 and original in JCP, III, 287–289; Jonathan Cogswell, Jr., No. 5847; William Grover, No. 11962; John Foster, No. 9898; Daniel Gidding, No. 10826; William Goodhue, No. 11210; John Goodhue, No. 11174; Daniel Low, No. 17183; Joseph Marshall, No. 17808; David Marshall, No. 17796; Isaac Perkins, No. 21318; Stephen Story, No. 26801; John Wise, No. 30189.

References to Books by Type
in Chebacco Wills and Inventories

Religious	Legal	Classical & Belles Lettres	Nautical	"Sundry Books"
10	4	1	1	3

22. Harriet S. Tapley, *Salem Imprints, 1768–1825* (Salem, Mass., 1927), pp. 3, 7; Isaiah Thomas, *The History of Printing in America,* ed. Marcus McCorison (New York, 1970), pp. 177, 274–275; Conrad Wright, *The Beginnings of Unitarianism in America* (Boston, 1955); for a sketch of the Anglo-American world, see Michael Kraus, *The Atlantic Civilization: Eighteenth-Century Origins* (Ithaca, N.Y., 1949).

23. Based on a survey of *Sibley's Harvard Graduates* from the classes of 1690 to 1764 to ascertain the location and occupation (minister or non-minister) of those surviving the census year of 1765.

Living Harvard College Graduates, 1765

County	Ministers	Nonministers	Total
Essex	48 (30%)	110 (70%)	158
Middlesex	39 (29%)	96 (71%)	135
Plymouth	25 (39%)	39 (61%)	64
Suffolk (w/o Boston)	24 (29%)	59 (71%)	83
Boston	22 (19%)	140 (81%)	162

County	*Per Capita, 1765* *Graduates to* *Whites*	*Graduates to White* *Males over 16*
Essex	1 to 271	1 to 61
Middlesex	1 to 243	1 to 61
Plymouth	1 to 353	1 to 83
Suffolk (w/o Boston)	1 to 250	1 to 69
Boston	1 to 91	1 to 18

24. On Cleaveland's education, see chap. II, parts I and II.

25. Crowell, *Essex,* pp. 84, 171.

26. Morrison, *Early American Architecture,* p. 79.

27. For the liturgy, see Alf E. Jacobson, "Evolution of Worship in Congregational New England," *Bulletin of the Congregational Library,* 14 (May 1963), 3–7; 15 (Oct. 1963), 6–10. See also Crowell, *Essex,* p. 253.

28. Prayer: Larzer Ziff, *Puritanism in America* (New York, 1973), pp. 122–124. Mather: Cotton Mather, *Ratio Disciplinae* (Boston, 1726), p. 42.

29. Letter by Reverend Daniel Dana, son of Cleaveland's friend Reverend Joseph, pastor of Ipswich's South Church (1765–1827), in a letter to William B. Sprague, reprinted in Sprague's sketch of Cleaveland in his *Annals of the American Pulpit* (New York, 1857), I, 458–461.

30. John Cleaveland to Josiah Cleaveland, Sept. 9, 1748, JCP, III, 139–142.

31. John Cleaveland to Parker Cleaveland, Mar. 23, 1780, JCP, II, 146–148.

32. The sermons consist usually of four small, tightly written pages and include the text in the right-hand corner and the dates and places preached in the left-hand corner of the first page. There are three collections of his sermons: in Vol. IV of the John Cleaveland papers and another collection given by Mary Neale Cleaveland, at the Essex Institute, and one at the Sterling Library, Yale University, intermixed with his sons's. His preaching schedule in Chebacco can be seen in his "A Private Journal 1749," JCP, II, 49–52.

Two sermons on Psalm 66:18, first given in April 1753, are numbered 621 and 622. Two sermons on Galatians 6:14, first given in Nov. 1778, are numbered 2014 and 2015. From this I calculate a rate of about seventy new sermons per year. If the numbering begins with his first post in Boston in 1745, then he wrote sermons at the following rates:

1745 to 1753	622 sermons	78 per year
1745 to 1778	2015 sermons	58 per year
1753 to 1778	1393 sermons	56 per year

This exactly matched the average of Reverend William Lawrence of Lincoln, Mass., between 1748 and 1780; see Edward G. Porter, *A Sermon*

Commemorative of One Hundred and Fifty Years of the First Church in Lincoln, Mass. (Cambridge, Mass., 1899), p. 9.

33. From information on sermons as to dates and places of preaching, see note above.

34. The physical description is from Dana's letter, see note 29; the weight of Cleaveland and his family in Nov. 1769 and Oct. 1773 is in JCP, 11, 35–36. Cleaveland weighed 207 in 1769 and 230 in 1773. See *The Diary of William Bentley, D.D.* (Gloucester, Mass., 1962), I, 123, 160–161, 213, 230–231, on John Cleaveland and New Lights. For a more positive view, see *Life, Journals and Correspondence of Rev. Manasseh Cutler, LL.D.*, ed. W. P. and J. P. Cutler (Cincinnati, Ohio, 1888), II, 136, 149.

35. From Dana's letter, see note 29.

36. The sermon is in the Mary Neale Cleaveland Collection, Essex Institute, see note 32. Poole's *Commentary*, standard reference text for Puritan preachers, says that "the sense [of the text] is, the vengeance of God is very near to be revealed, men must repent now or never" and that "it letteth us know, that it is not unproper, nor dissonant to the style of John Baptist, and Christ, and others the most eminent first gospel preachers, to press repentance, faith, and holiness of life, from arguments of terror." See Matthew Poole, *A Commentary on the Holy Bible* (London, 1962; first published 1683–1685), III, 15. For Puritan sermon style, see Arthur W. Plumstead, ed., *The Wall and the Garden* (Minneapolis, Minn., 1968), pp. 31–37. The last quotation from the sermon is from Matt. 7:20, in which Cleaveland has changed the "ye" of the original to "we."

37. On Cleaveland in Boston, see chap. II.

38. The first sermon is in the Mary Neale Cleaveland Collection and the second in JCP, IV, 48–50. See Solomon Stoddard, *A Guide to Christ* (Boston, 1714), p. 2.

39. 363 people joined a church in Chebacco between 1726 and 1775; of those 229 (63 percent) joined in the revival years of 1727–1728, 1742–1743, 1763–1764. The membership statistics are from "Church Records, 1725–1869" [Old Church], and "Parish Records, 1745–1814" [New Church], Essex Institute.

40. John Cleaveland, *A Short and Plain Narrative of the Late Work of God's Spirit at Chebacco in Ipswich* (Boston, 1767), pp. 5, 16.

41. Cleaveland, *Short and Plain*, p. 14.

42. Relation of Daniel Low, JCP, I, 374–375; "Life of John Cleaveland," JCP, II, 42.

43. Relation of Martha Andrews, JCP, I, 366.

44. Relation of Benjamin Marshall, JCP, I, 370–371. The text Marshall cites is Deut. 32:35, which is the text of Edwards's famous "Sinners in the Hands of an Angry God" (see Jonathan Edwards, *Representative Selections*, eds. C. H. Faust and T. H. Johnson [New York, 1962, rev. ed.], pp. 155–172).

45. On the structure of the provincial government, see Marcus W. Jer-

negan, "The Province Charter (1689–1715)," and F. W. Grinnell,
"Bench and Bar in Colony and Province (1630–1776)," *Commonwealth
History of Massachusetts* (New York, 1928), II, 1–28, 156–191; Emory
Washburn, *Sketches of the Judicial History of Massachusetts* (Boston, 1840),
pp. 151–187; *The Legal Papers of John Adams,* ed. L. Kinvin Wroth and
Hiller Zobel (Cambridge, Mass., 1965), I, xxxviii–xliv; Archibald
Hanna, "New England Military Institutions, 1693–1750" (unpublished
Ph. D. thesis, Yale, 1950).

46. See Robert Zemsky, *Merchants, Farmers, and River Gods* (Boston,
1971), pp. 62–63, 157–159, 251–252, on the "back-benchers" in the
Assembly.

47. See chap. III. For the connection between property and liberty, see
Bernard Bailyn, *The Ideological Origins of the American Revolution* (Cambridge, Mass., 1967), pp. 233–235.

48. Lists of parish officeholders from "Town Meeting Records of Chebacco 1725–1775" and "Church Records 1752–1878," Essex Institute.

49. Cogswell: Jameson, *Cogswell,* pp. 35–37; *Sibley's Harvard Graduates,* V, 403–406, 495–498; Probate No. 5844; Waters, *Ipswich,* II,
36–40, 54–60, 92–93, 100, 151. Choate: Jameson, *Choate,* pp. 37–39;
Crowell, *Essex,* p. 219.

50. From the list of soldiers in the French and Indian War in Waters,
Ipswich, II, 775–782, supplemented by data from the reconstitution.

51. Crafts's journal and letters can be found in James M. Crafts and
William F. Crafts, *The Crafts Family* (Northampton, Mass., 1893), pp.
659–671, and in *EIHC,* 6 (1864), 181–194, and Gidding's journal in
EIHC, 48 (1912), 293–304, and his letter to John Cleaveland in JCP,
III, 133–135. The originals of all these are in the Essex Institute. See also
"Military Records Relating to Chebacco Parish, Ipswich, Now the Town
of Essex, 1744–1748," *EIHC,* 49 (1913), 95–96. There is a good, brief
account of the Louisbourg expedition in Howard H. Peckham, *The Colonial Wars 1689–1769* (Chicago, Ill., 1964), pp. 97–106, 117–118. See
also Nathan O. Hatch, *The Sacred Cause of Liberty: Republican Thought and
the Millennium in Revolutionary New England* (New Haven, Conn., 1977),
chap. I.

52. Crafts, *Crafts Family,* pp. 664, 659, 663.

53. Gidding, "Journal," pp. 300, 302.

54. *Ibid.,* pp. 302, 301, 303.

55. See Peckham, *Colonial Wars,* pp. 156–172, and the map on p. 130
in Ray Allen Billington, *Westward Expansion* (New York, 1949). Cleaveland's letter of appointment from Gov. Pownall, is in JCP, I, 187. See also
"The Journal of Dr. Caleb Rea," *EIHC,* 18 (1881), 81–120, 177–205.

56. John Cleaveland to Mary Cleaveland, Aug. 22, 1759, JCP, III,
194–195; John Cleaveland to Mary Cleaveland, Sept. 3, 1758, JCP, III,
170–172; "Journal of Rev. John Cleaveland," *Bulletin of the Fort Ticonderoga Museum,* 10 (1957–1962), 192–236, quote on p. 203. The original of the journal is in the Fort Ticonderoga Museum Library.

57. "Journal," pp. 200–201; field officers: John Cleaveland to Mary
Cleaveland, July 25, 1758, JCP, III, 162–165.

58. "Journal," pp. 210, 204; Mary Cleaveland to John Cleaveland, Aug. 21, 1758, JCP, I, 201–203; Mary Cleaveland to John Cleaveland, Aug. 4, 1758, JCP, I, 204–207; Mary Cleaveland to John Cleaveland, July 26, 1758, JCP, I, 198–200. Increase Mather's sermon was called *Ichabod, or, A Discourse Shewing What Cause There Is to Fear That the Glory of the Lord Is Departing from New England* (Boston, 1702). Perry Miller, in *The New England Mind: From Colony to Province* (Boston, 1953), p. 247, called it "a jeremiad-to-end-all-jeremiads." See Miller's discussion of the genre in the above, pp. 27–39. For Ichabod, see 1 Sam. 4:19–22.

59. Mary Cleaveland to John Cleaveland, Aug. 21, 1758, JCP, I, 201–203.

60. A good, brief summary of postwar British policy can be found in Edmund S. Morgan, *The Birth of the Republic, 1763–1789* (Chicago, Ill., 1956), pp. 4–77.

61. Ipswich's reactions to British policy are discussed in detail in Arlin I. Ginsburg, "Ipswich, Massachusetts During the American Revolution, 1763–1791" (unpublished Ph.D. dissertation, University of California, Riverside, 1972), chap. III. The quotation is from the town's instructions to its representative, printed in the *Boston Gazette*, Nov. 4, 1765.

62. Cleaveland, "Journal," p. 222; John Cleaveland, *A Short and Plain Narrative* (Boston, 1767), p. 64.

63. There is a full account of the *Gazette* in Tapley, *Salem Imprints*, pp. 5–35. See also Thomas, *History of Printing*, pp. 177, 274–275; Arthur M. Schlesinger, Sr., *Prelude to Independence* (New York, 1971), pp. 93–94, 135–136, 152, and Stephen Botein, " 'Meer Mechanics' and an Open Press," *Perspectives in American History*, 9 (1975), esp. pp. 152–156.

Hall's Press, 1768–1775

	1768	1769	1770	1771	1772	1773	1774	1775
Religious	3	4	8	5	4	5	2	2
Political	1	1	—	—	—	2	10	16
Scientific	—	—	—	—	1	2	2	—
Sensational	—	—	1	—	4	4	1	—
Almanacs	1	1	1	1	1	—	—	1
Primers	—	—	—	—	1	1	—	1

Based on Tapley, pp. 303–323, including broadsides.

64. Tapley, *Salem Imprints*, pp. 17–18.

65. Essays: Schlesinger, *Prelude to Independence*, p. 136n; the first essay (Oct. 25, 1768), was written under the name "North America" (original in JCP, IV, 169–170), and the seventh as "Vox Vociferantis in Eremo," which I assume from subject and style is his. There are fragments and drafts of the Johannes essays in his Papers, which identify him as the author. Alice M. Baldwin (*The New England Clergy and the American Revolution* [Durham, N.C., 1928], p. 114) assumes that his identity was generally known. He also wrote in this period on ecclesiastical affairs as "A Lover of Impartiality" (JCP, I, 234–237) and, I think, "Pacificus," in

which he gives a history of the Chebacco church division and reunion (*Essex Gazette,* Nov. 8, 1774). Mather: Cotton Mather, *Johannes in Eremo* (Boston, 1695), reprinted in his *Magnalia Christi Americana* (London, 1702), pp. 8–68. Wheelock: Leon B. Richardson, *History of Dartmouth College* (Hanover, N.H., 1932), I, 132. Cleaveland: *Essex Gazette,* Jan. 1, 1771, and May 31, 1774.

66. *Essex Gazette,* Oct. 25, 1768; for Wise, see *Sibley's Harvard Graduates,* II, 428–444.

67. *Essex Gazette,* Jan. 1, 1771; Mar. 19, 1771 (politicical union . . .).

68. [John Cleaveland, et al.], *A Plain Narrative,* pp. 3–4.

69. Cleaveland, *A Short and Plain Narrative,* p. 64.

70. *Essex Gazette,* Apr. 14, 1772.

71. See Goen, *Revivalism and Separatism,* pp. 300–327.

72. *Essex Gazette,* May 31, 1774. For a similar response to crisis, see the parish's declaration of a fast day for the relief of a drought (Crowell, *Essex,* pp. 169–170).

73. *Essex Gazette,* July 6, 1775; Apr. 18, 1775.

74. The quotation is from Waters, *Ipswich,* II, 358, but can also be found in E. P. Crowell, "Historical Discourse," p. 92, and Crowell, *Essex,* p. 208. The latter, who was a successor of Cleaveland's in the Chebacco church from 1815 to 1855, wrote that the statement about Cleaveland had been "remarked to the author by aged people, forty years ago."

CHAPTER FIVE

1. The charter is reprinted in Crowell, *Essex,* pp. 203–204.

2. See Allen French, *The First Year of the American Revolution* (Boston, 1934), chap. IV.

3. Waters, *Ipswich,* II, 318–319.

4. Waters, *Ipswich,* II, 319–322, quotation on p. 320.

5. "Johannes in Eremo," *Essex Gazette,* Apr. 18, 1775.

6. The following statistics on military service are based on the reconstitution of the 1771 valuation of taxpayers' families. I checked a list of all those between the ages of sixteen and fifty in 1775 against the seventeen volumes of *Massachusetts Soldiers and Sailors of the Revolutionary War* (Boston, 1896–1908). For similar levels of participation, see John Shy, "Hearts and Minds in the American Revolution: The Case of 'Long Bill' Scott and Peterborough, N.H.," in *A People Numerous and Armed* (Oxford, Eng., 1976), pp. 163–179. See also Crowell, *Essex,* pp. 201–234. On Little, see Frank A. Gardner, "Colonel Moses Little's Regiment," *Massachusetts Magazine,* 9 (1916), 18–44. On the Chebacco soldiers, see Crowell, *Essex,* p. 206. There are photostats of Little's orderly book in the MHS.

7. For Hodgkins, see Herbert T. Wade and Robert A. Lively, *This*

Glorious Cause: The Adventures of Two Company Officers in Washington's Army (Princeton, N.J., 1958), esp. chap. VI.

8. For Calef and Stickney, see Waters, *Ipswich,* II, 306–310, 334–336. For Porter, see the 1771 valuation and *Sibley's Harvard Graduates,* XV, 473–475.

9. On the village economy before the war, see chap. III, part I.

10. The journal is partially reprinted in Jameson, *Choate,* p. 109. The original is at the Essex Institute.

11. There is a "Table of Depreciation" in Joseph B. Felt, *An Historical Account of Massachusetts Currency* (Boston, 1839), p. 186; see also pp. 162–200, and Oscar and Mary F. Handlin, "Revolutionary Economic Policy in Mass.," *WMQ,* IV (1947), 3–26.

12. See chap. III, part III.

13. Crowell, *Essex,* p. 225, changed to past tense.

14. John Cleaveland to the Second Parish in Ipswich, Nov. 30, 1779, JCP, II, 135–136.

15. For an account of her death, see John Cleaveland to Eleazar Wheelock, July 4, 1768, Wheelock Papers, No. 768404.

16. Mary Cleaveland's will, Mar. 23, 1768, JCP, II, 56–57.

17. John Cleaveland to Mary Cleaveland, Jr., May 17, 1769, JCP, II, 55–56; John Cleaveland to Eleazar Wheelock, July 4, 1768, Wheelock Papers, No. 768404.

18. See Harrison Ellery and Charles Pickering Bowditch, *The Pickering Genealogy* (Cambridge, Mass., 1897), I, 80, 86–87, 167–171.

19. *Sibley's Harvard Graduates,* XV, 448–473; James D. Phillips, *Salem in the Eighteenth Century* (Boston, 1937), pp. 265–268.

20. Mary Neale Foster's financial affairs are rather difficult to untangle. See her father's probate record (Joseph Neale, Probate No. 19181), her guardianship papers (Timothy Pickering, No. 19168), and her uncle Theophilus's will (No. 21820). Various deeds record the division of her father's house with her sister and the settling of an annuity on their mother (Vol. 99, pp. 233–234; Vol. 100, p. 150; Vol. 106, p. 113; Vol. 116, p. 246). Her first husband's probate record lists the 29 pounds 13 shillings 6 pence worth of property she received and the value of the slave Violet (John Foster, No. 9904). The sale of her properties and the mortgage she retained on one are recorded (Vol. 126, p. 31; Vol. 125, p. 254). Her investments are listed in John Cleaveland's 1794 will (JCP, I, 271–274). The houses she inherited are still standing at 358 and 345 Essex Street, Salem, Mass.

21. Cleaveland's salary from 1754 to 1775 can be found in the Records of the Sixth Parish, a volume titled "Church Records, 1752–1878"; from 1776 to 1799 in "Accounts of Chebacco Parish 1776–1825." Both volumes are among the Essex, Mass., Church Records on deposit at the Essex Institute.

22. The Cleaveland Papers include a copy of the account from Choate's ledgers, which served John Cleaveland as a receipt, JCP, III, 363–364. For Mansfield's work on John Cleaveland's farm, see John Cleaveland's

journal concerning his laborers, JCP, IV, 420–428. These credit transactions are best explained by Baxter, *The House of Hancock,* chap. II, pp. 11–38.

23. See "A Discharge from All Debts by Sundry Inhabitants of 6th Parish, March 8, 1770," JCP, III, 373–374.

24. The description is from the deeds (Vol. 92, p. 60; Vol. 95, p. 43; Vol. 100, p. 97). The house was built by Cogswell, probably about the time of his marriage (see Nina Fletcher Little, "John Cogswell's Grant," *EIHC,* 76 [1940], 162–163). Cleaveland's children sold it to David Choate in 1800 (Vol. 167, p. 59), who tore it down in 1803 and raised another on the same spot (see "Chebacco," *Essex Echo,* Dec. 10, 1909). See also chap. III, part IV.

25. See deeds in Vol. 117, p. 133; Vol. 117, p. 114; Vol. 140, p. 212.

26. For the farm, see chap. III, note 78. Cleaveland served two terms in the provincial militia in 1758–1759, from mid-March to late October 1758 and from early July to mid-October 1759, a little more than thirteen months, at 10 pounds 15 pence per month. A voucher from the first expedition (Mass. Archives, XCVI, 538) indicates that he expended only a little more than 15 percent of his pay while on duty. Assuming the same rate for the second expedition, he cleared about 110 pounds for his military service.

27. John Cleaveland to Josiah Cleaveland, Sept. 9, 1748, JCP, III, 139–142.

28. John Cleaveland to "All My Children Together," Sept. 3, 1759, JCP, I, 214–216, for quotations in this and paragraph below.

29. For their dowry, see John Cleaveland's 1797 will in JCP, III, 287–289, or Probate No. 5617.

30. John Cleaveland to Mary Cleaveland, Jr., May 17, 1769, JCP, II, 55–56.

31. For Isaac Proctor, see Probate No. 22847 and his conversion relation ("Isaac Proctor's Relation Taken From His Mouth") in JCP, I, 363.

32. For Jonathan Cogswell, see Probate No. 5846 and Jameson, *Cogswell,* pp. 81–82.

33. Mary Cleaveland Proctor's husband Jonathan inherited, at his father's death in 1799, a 120-acre farm in Hopkinton, N.H., which they had moved to in about 1789. Abigail Cleaveland Cogswell's husband Joseph inherited, at his father's death in 1812, a farm in Londonderry, N.H., which they had moved to in 1794.

34. There is no direct evidence of the illegitimate birth in the Parish Records or in the Cleaveland correspondence. The Cleaveland family genealogy does not mention the child, and the Pillsbury family genealogy, her future husband's family, calls her a daughter of John, Jr., who had no children and later adopted two girls [*Cleveland Genealogy,* I, 354–355, 358; David B. Pillsbury and Emily Getchell, *The Pillsbury Family* (Everett, Mass., 1898), pp. 75–76; John Cleaveland, Jr., Probate No. 4047, Norfolk Co. Court House, Dedham, Mass.]. In John Cleaveland's 1794 will (JCP, I, 271–274), he calls her "my grandaughter Lois Cleaveland who has lived in my family from birth." His grandson John was

"the only son and representative of my late son Ebenezer"; John, Jr., had no children; Parker had but one male child before 1797; and Nehemiah, his first in 1793. The latter three were fully capable of caring for such children as they had. Elizabeth's late (age thirty-eight) and déclassé (see text) marriage, plus the hint in Bentley's diary (William Bentley, *The Diary of William Bentley, D.D.* [Salem, Mass., 1905], I, 123), and the lack of alternatives to account for this grandchild, strongly suggest illegitimacy. The girl was under eighteen in 1794, but turned eighteen before her grandfather's second will in 1797 (JCP, III, 287–289). In the second will neither she nor the Commonwealth of Massachusetts security, worth $159.65, which she was to receive at age eighteen, was mentioned. After John Cleaveland's death, she apparently went with the rest of John Cleaveland's family to live with her uncle Nehemiah in Topsfield. She was married in Topsfield in 1802 to Moses Pillsbury, then of Danvers, Mass. Their first child, John Cleaveland Pillsbury, was born in Ipswich. Then they moved in 1803 to Londonderry, N.H., where her aunt Abigail Cleaveland Cogswell lived. Moses Pillsbury later had a long (from 1818 to 1840) and distinguished career as a warden of state prisons in New Hampshire and Connecticut.

35. John Cleaveland to Parker Cleaveland, Dec. 25, 1769, JCP, II, 53–55. For acknowledgments of a breach of the seventh commandment with wife before marriage, see "Parish Records 1745–1814," p. 275.

36. JCP, I, 264–266.

37. John Cleaveland to Elizabeth Cleaveland, JCP, II, 257–258.

38. John Cleaveland to Elizabeth Cleaveland, JCP, I, 279–281.

39. John Cleaveland to Eleazer Wheelock, Wheelock Papers, No. 768465.2.

40. John Cleaveland, "Diary in the year 1776," Nov. 28, 1776, p. 15, Library of Congress (copy).

41. John Cleaveland to Parker Cleaveland, Dec. 25, 1769, JCP, II, 53–55.

42. John Cleaveland to Parker Cleaveland, n.d. (c.1769), JCP, II, 263–264.

43. John Cleaveland to Parker Cleaveland, Nov. 13, 1772, JCP, II, 64–65.

44. John Cleaveland to Parker Cleaveland, Apr. 5, 1773, JCP, II, 68–69.

45. John Cleaveland, Jr., to Parker Cleaveland, Apr. 5, 1773, JCP, II, 66–67.

46. John Cleaveland, Jr., to John Cleaveland, Dec. 29, 1773, JCP, II, 69–71.

47. John Cleaveland to Aaron Cleaveland, Nov. 2, 1775, JCP, II, 77–79.

48. John Cleaveland, Jr., to Parker Cleaveland, Nov. 9, 1779, JCP, II, 133–134.

49. John Cleaveland to Parker Cleaveland, July 11, 1774, JCP, II, 74–75 [Moultenborough]; same, Feb. 16, 1774, JCP, I, 213–214 [Ipswich].

50. John Cleaveland to Parker Cleaveland, June 1, 1775, JCP, II, 76–77.

51. John Cleaveland to P. D. Sargent, Dec. 14, 1775, JCP, II, 86–87.

52. John Cleaveland to Edmund Phinney, Dec. 15, 1775, JCP, II, 87–90.

53. Cleveland and Cleveland, *Cleveland Genealogy*, I, 357–358.

54. John Cleaveland, Jr., to Parker Cleaveland, Apr. 10, 1778, JCP, II, 125–127.

55. John Cleaveland to Parker Cleaveland, Mar. 28, 1778, JCP, II, 120–122.

56. Ebenezer's fatal adventures are recounted in John Cleaveland's letter to his son Parker (Mar. 23, 1780, JCP, II, 146–148), who heard it from his son Nehemiah, who had talked to a Captain Odle, a passenger on the *Eustis*.

57. See note 56. The note is mentioned in John Cleaveland's 1797 will, JCP, III, 287–289.

58. There is a biographical sketch of Nehemiah by his son in Nehemiah Cleaveland [Jr.], *An Address, Delivered at Topsfield in Massachusetts, August 28, 1850: The Two Hundredth Anniversary of the Incorporation of the Town* (New York, 1851), pp. xviii–xx. See also John Cleaveland's letters to Nehemiah in the army (July 12, 1780, JCP, III, 349–350; Sept. 8, 1780, JCP, III, 350–353).

59. There are extracts from his diary in "Memoirs of the Rev. John Cleaveland, Late Pastor of the North Church in Wrentham," *The Panoplist, and Missionary Magazine*, 11 (1816), 49–55; the quotation is on p. 50. The diary is no longer extant.

60. John Cleaveland, *Gospel-Ministers Must Be Wise, Faithful and Exemplary, In Order, To Be Pure From the Blood Of All Men. A Sermon Preached at the Ordination of the Rev. John Cleaveland, Jun. , . . . in Stoneham, Oct. 19, 1785* (Newburyport, Mass., 1785). For his career, see Mortimer Blake, *A Centurial History of the Mendon Association* (Boston, 1853), pp. 142–144; *History of Middlesex Co., Mass.*, ed. D. Hamilton Hurd (Philadelphia, Pa., 1888), II, 481–482; Nathanael Emmons, *A Discourse Delivered at the Funeral of the Rev. John Cleaveland, A.M.* (Dedham, Mass., 1815).

61. Titus: see John Cleaveland's 1794 will (JCP, I, 271–274); "Boys": see John Cleaveland's letters to Parker (Mar. 29, 1778, JCP, II, 118–119; June 17, 1778, JCP, II, 129–132; Mar. 18, 1785, JCP, II, 159–160) and to Nehemiah (Apr. 4, 1794, JCP, III, 318–319) and his almanac diary, entries under June 9, 1794, and Nov. 24, 1794, at the Essex Institute. See also his journal concerning his laborers, *ca.* 1780–1783 (JCP, IV, 420–428).

62. On Ipswich after the war, see Waters, *Ipswich*, II, 361–385, 398–402, and Ginsburg, "Ipswich, Mass. in the American Revolution," pp. 191–236.

On Chebacco shipbuilding, see Papers of Lewis Story, I, "List of Essex, Mass. Built Vessels, 1780–1939," Peabody Museum, Salem, Mass.

63. The statistics on migration are based on the reconstitution of tax-

payers' families, from the 1771 valuation. Information about migration was derived from genealogies, local histories, and vital statistics of New England towns available in the New England Historic Genealogical Society. Older generation is defined as birth cohort before 1749, younger generation as the 1750–1779 birth cohort. See chap. III, note 32.

64. See "Parish Records 1745–1814," back of the volume, "Deaths of Relatives Abroad [sic] or Who Lived Out of This Place."

65. See "Ipswich, Mass.: Chebacco Parish Papers, 1718–1800," for catechistical districts, in the Essex Institute.

66. Elijah Parish, *A Sermon Occasioned by the Death of Rev. John Cleaveland* (Newburyport, Mass., 1799), quoted in Crowell, *Essex,* p. 251. See chap. IV, part II.

67. *Ibid.* The places of publication were Boston, Salem, and Salem. For his degree, see Tucker, *Puritan Protagonist,* p. 141.

68. *Ibid.*

69. Crowell, *Essex,* p. 246. See, for local ministers, Wright, *The Beginnings of Unitarianism in America,* pp. 256–259, and biographical appendix for Hopkins, Spring, and Parish; and Waters, *Ipswich,* II, for Dana (477–481), and Frisbie (442–444); and Felt, *History of Ipswich, Essex, and Hamilton,* for Cutler (pp. 294–300), and Williams (pp. 253–254).

70. John Cleaveland to Parker Cleaveland (Apr. 10, 1774, JCP, II, 125–127; Jan. 29, 1778, JCP, II, 112–114; Feb. 9, 1778, JCP, II, 110–111; Feb. 16, 1778, JCP, II, 107–109; Nov. 27, 1781, JCP, II, 150); John Cleaveland, Jr., to Parker Cleaveland (June 12, 1790, JCP, II, 173–174); and John Cleaveland to Parker Cleaveland (Mar. 24, 1792, JCP, II, 201–202).

71. 1794 will, JCP, I, 271–274.

72. John Cleaveland to Parker Cleaveland, Oct. 1, 1781, JCP, II, 149–150; John Cleaveland to Parker Cleaveland, Mar. 24, 1792, JCP, II, 201–202.

73. For John, Jr.'s, career, see notes 59 and 60; on his preaching, see, for example, John Cleaveland to Nehemiah Cleaveland, Aug. 3, 1796, JCP, III, 308–309. For Nehemiah's career, see note 58. For Parker's career, see Thomas Gage, *The History of Rowley* (Boston, 1840), pp. 260–271, and Russell L. Jackson, *Physicians of Essex County* (Salem, Mass., 1948), p. 29.

74. For the bonds, see the 1794 (JCP, I, 271–274) and 1797 (JCP, III, 287–289) wills. When his sons sold the estate in 1800, there was only one share outstanding; see Vol. 167, pp. 59–60, Deeds, Essex County Court House, Salem, Mass. For his sons' aid, see correspondence of the 1790s generally, in JCP, II, 171–219, 232–235; III, 286–331.

75. Nehemiah Cleaveland to Parker Cleaveland, Apr. 4, 1789, JCP, II, 169–170.

76. John Cleaveland to Parker Cleaveland, Mar. 24, 1792, JCP, II, 201–202.

77. For the half-century lecture, see JCP, II, 226–231. For his genealogical research, see JCP, II, 26, 39–40. For the millennial speculations,

see note 76 and John Cleaveland to Nehemiah Cleaveland, Nov. 16, 1798, JCP, III, 290–292.

78. John Cleaveland to Nehemiah Cleaveland, Apr. 11, 1799, JCP, III, 298–300.

Bibliographical Essay

MANUSCRIPTS

The bulk of John Cleaveland's papers are at the Essex Institute in Salem, Massachusetts. They were donated, in 1874 [*EIHC*, 12 (1874), 87], by his grandson, Nehemiah Cleaveland, along with his war chest and buck-handled sword. The latter, unfortunately, cannot be located by the institute staff. The Cleaveland family had arranged the papers in four leather-backed volumes. In 1974, at my request, the staff of the institute dismantled the four volumes and, attempting to preserve the original order, microfilmed them. The institute has retained the negative and I have the positive copy. For easier reference, my copy of the three reels is numbered by frame. The numbering is by volume, not by reel. Reel one contains volume I; reel two, volume II; and reel three, volumes III and IV. Since a grant from a fund established by Frederick Merk paid for the microfilming, this copy will eventually go to the Microtext Division in Lamont Library.

The first volume of John Cleaveland's papers contains three of his journals (Yale 1742, Boston 1746, Chebacco 1749), two by his wife, as well as correspondence with his family in Connecticut, and with his wife while he was on military duty (Crown Point, 1758). The most important part of volume two is a long series of letters (1769–1798) from John Cleaveland to his son Parker. Volume three consists of correspondence and other materials relating to his experiences in New Haven, Boston, and Chebacco in the 1740s, letters to his wife while he was on military duty (Louisbourg, 1759), and a series of letters to his son Nehemiah (1780–1799). Volume four contains mostly sermons. There

BIBLIOGRAPHICAL ESSAY

are, of course, other family and professional letters, drafts and copies of publications, financial records, and other materials scattered about the four volumes, but these are the more important parts of the papers.

The story of the papers between John's death in 1799 and their arrival at the Essex Institute in 1874 is quite complex. In the 1780s, John and his son Parker began work on a genealogy of the Cleaveland family [see JCP, II, 26, 39–40.] After the old man's death, these genealogical interests, as well as respect for their father's memory, led Parker and Nehemiah to collect and preserve their father's letters to them [see JCP, I, 36–37]. The primary responsibility for gathering, preserving, and organizing them belongs, though, to three nineteenth-century gentlemen—the Reverend Elisha Lord Cleaveland, his brother, Nehemiah Cleaveland, and their brother-in-law, the Reverend Oliver A. Taylor. The Cleaveland brothers and Taylor's wife were children of John Cleaveland's youngest son, Nehemiah. The papers contain annotations by all three men, and volume three has copies of some twenty letters written in answer to Taylor's inquiries about Cleaveland [JCP, I, 297–362]. The papers seem to have mostly resided at first with E. L. Cleaveland, who was minister of a church in New Haven. George Bancroft consulted them there when composing the tenth volume of his *History* [see pages 300 and 303], which was published in 1852. Taylor, however, apparently had some in his custody, perhaps by right of his wife. His researches into John Cleaveland's life extended over many years and included trips to Canterbury, Connecticut. Taylor was a minister in Manchester, Massachusetts, which bordered on Cleaveland's old parish. When he died in 1851, he passed on his holdings to his brother-in-law, E. L. Cleaveland [see Timothy A. Taylor's *Memoir* (1854) of his brother, esp. pp. 385–426, 534].

Elisha Lord Cleaveland was working on a "memoir" of his grandfather as early as 1861 [see the entry for March 5, 1861, in his diary, Sterling Library, Yale University]. In August 1863 he made a research trip to Salem and Chebacco. He had copies made of some of the "Johannes in Eremo" letters and visited old people in Chebacco who had known his grandfather. The memoir that he was writing is not, however, among his papers at Yale University.

When Elisha died in 1866, the papers passed to his brother Nehemiah Cleaveland, who was a schoolteacher and the historian of Bowdoin College. He was headmaster at various times of Governor Dummer Academy and a girls' high school in Brooklyn,

New York. In 1842, he had made some preliminary researches into the Cleaveland genealogy, which he turned over to his brother-in-law Taylor [*Cleveland Genealogy*, I, 866]. Now the whole collection of papers and notes came to him, and he devoted his declining years to them. He may have been the one who organized the papers into the four bound volumes before turning them over to the Essex Institute in 1874. The only published work to emerge from the efforts of the three men was Nehemiah's edition of his grandfather's journal from the siege of Fort Ticonderoga in 1758, which was published in the *EIHC* in 1874.

Not all the papers, however, made it to the Essex Institute. The 1758 journal apparently remained with Nehemiah. When Francis Parkman consulted the journal in the 1880s, for his *Montcalm and Wolfe* (Boston, 1884), it was held by Abby E. Cleaveland, Nehemiah's daughter [see vol. II, 76–77, 89, 115–117, 120, 127]. It surfaced again in 1959, when it was purchased by one Armand Erpf, Esq., who gave it to the Fort Ticonderoga Museum. Another journal, recording Cleaveland's chaplain's duties on an expedition to New York in 1776, was copied in 1843 by Henry Stevens, presumably for Peter Force, and that copy is now among the Peter Force MSS. in the Library of Congress, along with Stevens's copies of the 1758 journal and some letters written from Ticonderoga by Cleaveland to his wife. All were then in the hands of Elisha Lord Cleaveland, but only the letters made it to the Essex Institute. The original of the 1776 journal is now lost. In 1915, Mary Neale Cleaveland, a granddaughter of Nehemiah, donated forty-five of Cleaveland's manuscript sermons to the Essex Institute and possibly an almanac diary for 1793 as well. In 1959, Ruth Cleaveland Monroe, presumably a descendant of Elisha Lord Cleaveland's, donated a collection of his papers to the Sterling Library at Yale. Among them I found fifty-two manuscript sermons by John Cleaveland, mostly from the 1790s.

There are probably more Cleaveland papers than I have been able to locate. In 1844, for example, Nehemiah Cleaveland observed that Reverend John Cleaveland, Jr.'s, share of his father's books and papers was in the hands of the Harris family, into which Reverend John, Jr.'s, widow had married. Nehemiah made a note expressing his intention to "apply to the Harris children," but there is no evidence of his having done so successfully.

There are also Cleaveland papers in other collections. There are about twenty Cleaveland items, letters from John or his brother Ebenezer, among the Eleazar Wheelock papers in the Dartmouth archives. Dartmouth has published *A Guide to the Microfilm Edi-*

tion of the Papers of Eleazar Wheelock (Hanover, N.H., 1971). Both *Guide* and microfilm are available in the Microtext Division of Lamont Library, thanks to Nathaniel Bunker, the Charles Warren bibliographer. Three volumes of Canterbury Separate papers at the Connecticut Historical Society in Hartford also have useful Cleaveland material. This is the fullest collection of material relating to a Separate church, and it contains several letters and petitions by John Cleaveland's brothers, sisters, and other relatives.

The Chebacco parish and church records are an important adjunct to the Cleaveland papers and are also at the Essex Institute. Among the more important are the "Parish Records, 1745–1814," which includes "Copies of documents relative to separation 1744–1746," plus some church-meeting records, vital records, and a few letters. There are vital records and church admissions in "Church records, 1725–1869." His salary can be found in the parish meeting records, titled "Church records, 1752–1878," and in "Accounts of Chebacco parish, 1776–1825." The record books, which contain records of all sorts from the Old Light church and parish, the New Light church and parish, and the reunited church well into the nineteenth century, are very confusing. There is a fairly accurate description of them in Harold Field Worthley's *An Inventory of the Records of Particular (Congregational) Churches of Massachusetts Gathered 1620–1805* (Cambridge, Mass., 1970), pp. 210–213. The best guide can be found at the Essex Institute, in a manuscript catalog of town papers. This includes both bound volumes of official records and collections of stray papers in folders and envelopes. For relevant material, see items numbers 1, 6, 7, 9, and 10 in the Essex papers, and items numbers 5, 6, 7, 15, and 16 in the Ipswich papers. The thesis upon which this book is based contains a bibliography and somewhat fuller annotation. It is available in the Harvard University Archives.

Index

Calef, John, 140
Calvinist doctrines, 44, 56,
104, 109, 119
Cambridge Platform, 53, 55
Saybrook Platform vs., 12,
36
Canada:
in French and Indian Wars,
123–28
postwar migrations to, 165
Quebec Act and, 129
Canada expedition (1690), 61
Canterbury, Conn., 9–11
antirevivalists in, 36–37
Cleaveland holdings in, 11
Canterbury (Conn.) church:
orthodoxy of, 11–12
revivalist positions in, 20,
36–37
Canterbury Separates, 41
capital, land investment and,
70
Channel, Mary Cleveland, 163
Channel family, 153, 163
Chauncy, Charles, 28
Chebacco boats, 141, 164
Chebacco parish (Ipswich,
Mass.): assembly of,
122–23
British encroachment feared
in, 132, 136
church reunification in, 55–
57
commercial development in,
61–63, 66–68
coresidence of householders
and heirs in, 73–74
cultural conservatism of, 95,
96–98, 104
debtor-creditor relationships
in, 91–93, 142–43, 146–
47

description and history of,
58–59, 96
economic structure of, 58–
70, 92–93
family system in economy of,
58–70, 92–93, 94, 164
in French and Indian Wars,
123–28
imperial policies as strain in,
128–35
inflation in, 142–43
inheritance patterns in, see
inheritance
John Cleaveland's ministry
in, 51–57, 58, 104–19
judicial system in, 119, 122,
123
jurisdictions in, 119–20
land holdings in, 59, 60,
63–65, 68–70, 81, 175
landless in, 63–64, 175
land transactions in, 68–69,
72–73
land use in, 62, 66, 97
leadership in, 120–21
literacy in, 102, 179
maritime occupations in, 61,
66, 141–42, 164
meetinghouse of, 105
military enlistments from,
138–40
officeholders in, 120–22
old vs. new church partisans,
socio-economic factors
and, 51–53
Old vs. New Lights
(Pickering vs. Rogers)
feud in, 47–55
open lands sought by, 60–
61
political life in, 119–23
poor in, 65

INDEX

INDEX

INDEX

INDEX

INDEX

INDEX

Woburn, Mass., 1, 5, 11
  freeman status in, 2
  land grants by, 5–7
Woburn (Mass.) church, 2, 3, 5
women:
  domestic role of, 149
  education of, 101, 102
  land ownership and, 75, 78, 79
  unmarried, 88, 149, 150
  see also inheritance; marriage
Wonder-Working Providence of Sions Saviour in New England (Johnson), 2
Woodstock (Conn.) church, 12
Woodward, John, 12
world view, New England:
  colonial autonomy and, 129–35
  conservatism of, 95
  culture transmission and, 95–104
  God's covenant and, 95, 119, 125–26, 128, 133–34, 164
  military actions and, 123–28
  political crisis of 1760s in, 95
  political environment and, 119–23
  worship style and, 104–19
Worthington, John, 24

Yale College, 1, 15, 16, 17, 20–42, 104, 167
  accommodation with re-
  vivalists attempted at, 27–28
  age at entrance to, 29
  commencement ceremonies at (1741), 20–21, 22
  costs at, 29
  curriculum at, 24
  description of, 23, 24
  expulsions from, 32, 34, 35, 40
  farmer's sons at, 28–31
  as later center of evangelical-style ministry, 31
  ministerial licensing and, 35, 40
  ministers' sons at, 29–31
  ministry students as majority at, 25, 29
  orthodoxy at, 23
  percentage of New vs. Old Lights graduated from, 31
  repression of revivalists at, 31–42
  revivalist movement and, 17, 20–31
  Separatists at, 27, 28, 32, 34, 38
  1745 charter of, 24
younger sons, 5, 15–16, 69, 83–84
  departure from paternal holdings of, 7, 16, 84, 164–65, 177
  legatees' obligations to, 90–91
Youngs, David, 34